IMAGES
of America

SOUTH DAVIS COUNTY

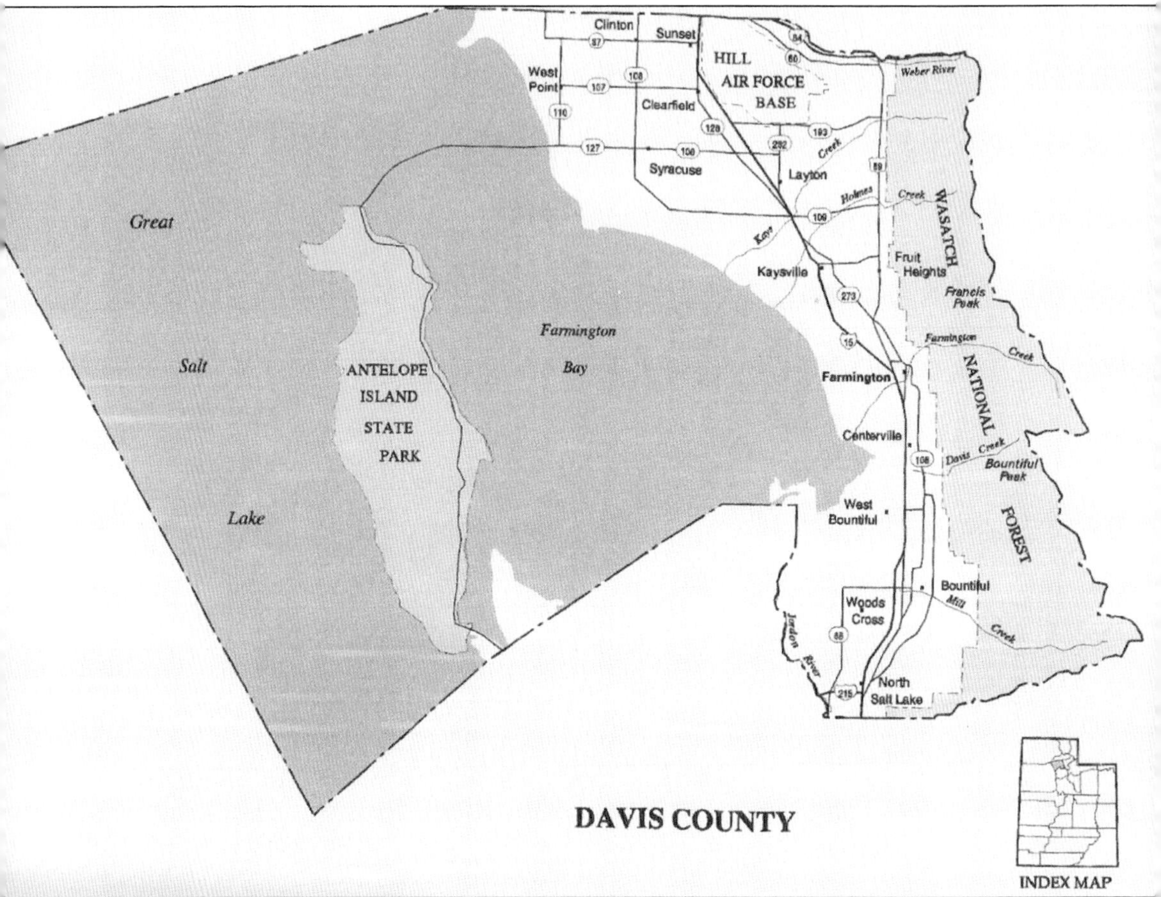

Starting just north of Salt Lake City, South Davis County comprises the region along the lakeside, extending 21 miles north. The county is defined on the east by the ridge of the Wasatch Mountains and on the west by the Great Salt Lake, and it includes Antelope Island. This region of foothills and lakeshore is populated with 142,234 people, according to the latest census. Bountiful, Centerville, Farmington, and Kaysville are the four largest commercial centers. Other towns in the area include North Salt Lake, Woods Cross, West Bountiful, and Fruit Heights. The Great Salt Lake is very briny and used for salt production. Tiny brine shrimp, the only thing living in the salty waters, grow profusely in the lake. The area along the lake is low and floods at times, so it is used mostly for grazing cattle and horses. Proceeding east to the raised areas, one finds fertile farmland and orchards. However, with the growing population, the farmland is rapidly being converted to residential use, with a significant business corridor along Highway 89. With the addition of Interstate 15, the area is readily accessible to Salt Lake City, Ogden, and the entire Wasatch Front. (Courtesy authors' collection.)

On the Cover: A romp in the cool, freshwater pool at Lagoon Resort is just the answer to the dry summer heat of Utah. Family and friends join in the fun of diving, swimming, and playing on the waterslides. This Farmington amusement park opened in 1896. The majestic Wasatch Mountains stand as a backdrop. (Courtesy Utah State Historical Society.)

IMAGES
of America

SOUTH DAVIS COUNTY

Royce Allen and Gary Willden

ARCADIA
PUBLISHING

ISBN 978-1-4671-3163-6

Published by Arcadia Publishing
Charleston, South Carolina

Printed in the United States of America

Library of Congress Control Number: 2013952053

For all general information, please contact Arcadia Publishing:
Telephone 843-853-2070
Fax 843-853-0044
E-mail sales@arcadiapublishing.com
For customer service and orders:
Toll-Free 1-888-313-2665

Visit us on the Internet at www.arcadiapublishing.com

To the early hearty pioneers who came to our area and made the "desert blossom like a rose," and to those who worked to preserve our heritage and build our communities, we express our lasting appreciation.

Contents

Acknowledgments

The authors are grateful to the following museums and individuals who provided photographs and helped in the preparation of this volume: the Bountiful Utah History Museum, Farmington Historical Museum, Centerville City Records at Whitaker Museum, Kaysville City Historical Records, North Salt Lake City, Thomas Tolman, Kathleen Dalrymple, John Hollingshead Jr., Roxanne Giles, Mark Giles, Ron Randall, Nola Tingey Hatch, Marilyn Giles, Beverly Nowak, Randy Jenkins, Lloyd Carr, Steve Porter, Lagoon Management, and Cherry Hill Management. Many others offered suggestions or directed us to photographs and historical records. The accounts published by Glen Leonard, Leslie T. Foy, B.H. Roberts, and the Daughters of Utah Pioneers (DUP) in *East of Antelope Island* contain excellent histories about the area and were a great guide to the authors. We acknowledge the tremendous task of the early settlers of the Church of Jesus Christ of Latter-day Saints (Mormons), who made the arduous trek to the Rocky Mountains. They carved out these communities from the dry, high-mountain desert by diverting the streams, developing farms, building cabins, cutting out roads, and establishing early commerce.

A century and a half later, the area is thriving. Many descendants of those early settlers still live in the area. The hearty pioneer spirit is still manifest in the residents of South Davis County. We also appreciate the editorial and positive support of Alyssa Jones, our editor at Arcadia Publishing. She worked with us to facilitate the formatting and submission of materials, which made the task much easier for the authors. Finally, to our wives, Mardette Allen and Joan Willden, we thank you for your support, patience, and listening ears when we were trying to sort out the various stories and facts.

Unless otherwise indicated, photographs were taken by, or belong to, the authors.

INTRODUCTION

Concerned that livestock would damage their new crops, the first Mormon settlers to the Salt Lake Valley formed community herds and sent them north to graze in 1847. They found rich soil with excellent grass and browse between the mountains on the east and the lakeshore to the west. Multiple freshwater streams flowed year-round from the mountains to the lake. Perrigrine Sessions, John Perry, and others drove 300 head of stock five miles north of Warm Springs to the mouth of North Canyon. Thomas Grover brought a herd, mostly cattle and horses, to the lakeside a few miles farther north. Hector Haight located another herd beyond that on North Cottonwood Creek. Camps and cabins were built over the winter by the herders. In the spring, they brought their families. Along with other settlers, they built cabins and developed farms along the streams.

The little clumps of farms and cabins soon took on the names of the settlers. Sessions' settlement, founded on Barton Creek, became Bountiful. Grover built a cabin and cultivated a small farm, but moved on at the end of the first summer. He sold his cabin to Aaron Cherry, who, along with the Deuel families and others, came north to settle Centerville. The North Cottonwood settlement became Farmington and was later selected as the county seat. Settlers soon moved beyond Farmington to a camp along Sandy Creek and formed the town of Kaysville, named after the first bishop of the Mormon ward. The collective region was named Davis County after Capt. Daniel C. Davis, an officer in the Mormon Battalion. Davis later commanded local forces to protect Utah and was promoted to the rank of colonel. Well respected by the local residents, Davis was killed while returning to the east. The name honors his memory.

The trail north from Salt Lake City quickly became a major road. It provided access to the Salt Lake markets. The small farm villages produced meat, vegetables, melons, fruit, and grain crops. Sawmills, a brick operation in Bountiful, a molasses mill in Centerville, and a tannery in Farmington were early businesses supplying local markets and shipping into Salt Lake City. Home industries supplied firewood, eggs, cheese, butter, vegetables, and homespun apparel. As settlements grew in Cache County, and farther north into Idaho, the Blooming Grove Inn in Farmington hosted numerous travelers. Built by Hector Haight and his wife, Julia, it became a popular stopover. Hot food, campsites, bathing facilities, and rooms were available, along with accommodations for horses.

Shoshone and Paiute Indians, who in previous years had formed winter camps or come to hunt and harvest fish from the streams, soon moved on. For a few years, they traded with the new settlers, but, as the towns grew, the Indians moved farther north and were eventually located to reservations.

The Gold Rush of 1849 brought hundreds of travelers through the area en route to California. The eager travelers bought supplies from the local settlers, increasing prices as much as tenfold. Household goods, tools, and farm implements could be purchased for a fraction of their value from the miners who wanted to lighten their load. The narrow strip of land between the Wasatch Mountain Range on the east and the lake on the west focused the northbound traffic through

Davis County. The pioneer migration by wagons and handcarts continued for another 15 years, bringing more settlers.

As the gold played out along the Pacific coast, prospectors turned their attention to the Rocky Mountains. Dozens of mineral claims were filed, many without significant proof. The mountains above South Davis County are scarred where rock outcroppings were blasted away, and unexplained excavations are now being reclaimed by wild grass and shrubs. Notable excavations are the A.L. Buckland mine above Centerville, the Patsy Morley mine near Farmington, and a natural gas discovery along the lakeshore, which all produced commercially for a short period. Unlike the rich silver discoveries east of the Salt Lake Valley, however, the mining efforts in South Davis County quickly played out.

Small trading posts and stores were established in each community. A courthouse was erected in Farmington as the seat of government. Soon after arriving, Mormon settlers built churches in each community, which usually doubled as schools. These early churches were also the centers of recreation, where dances, weddings, and harvest celebrations were held. Summer activities were conducted outside in shady places, such as the popular Haight's grove near Kaysville. Theater groups, bands, and variety shows performed in the churches and in new community buildings that were being constructed. In the 1880s, baseball and outdoor sports also became popular. Ball fields and competitive leagues were organized, attracting many spectators. A popular weekend or evening activity was a trip to cheer on the local team.

The lake attracted swimmers and boaters, and the Lake Side recreation facility was built in south Farmington, offering commercial facilities. Eden Park was developed in Bountiful on a three-acre plot adjacent to Barton Creek. In 1878, Ephraim Garn and George Chase of Centerville organized the Lake Shore Recreation facility, located west of Centerville, featuring swimming, dancing, boat trips, picnics, and even a bicycle track. It was a popular site, attracting patrons from across the region. A spur of the Utah Central Railroad was built to provide access. The park featured a 300-foot pier leading into the lake, with 74 bathing compartments complete with a shower/bath of fresh cold water. The Lake Park Bathing Resort, built west of Farmington in 1886, was an even larger venture. Eventually, the Black Rock Resort (later Saltair) expanded on the south shores, offering hotels and major entertainment. With stiff competition and receding water depths in the lake, an effort was led by Simon Bamberger, a Lake Park investor, to create a new freshwater facility on higher ground near Farmington. Draining the ponds and digging a large lake to accommodate swimming and boating, the Bamberger group moved much of the Lake Park resources to this new freshwater operation. The resort, called Lagoon, opened in July 1896, finding immediate success. Pools, a shooting gallery, a fun house, and more welcomed the eager guests. Even the first moving pictures were featured there in 1896. A racetrack was added nearby, which attracted horse owners until the track was destroyed by wind in 1919. Although it was revived for a short period, Utah laws changed, making the business unviable.

The first large building was the adobe courthouse, built in Farmington in 1855. It measured 35 feet by 45 feet and was two stories high. Other significant early buildings were constructed by the Mormon Church. In the old rock church in Farmington, completed in 1864, was the genesis of the Mormon children's program called Primary. This program now exists worldwide. Other significant buildings belonging to the Mormon Church also remain as landmarks, including the modern temple on the east bench of Bountiful; the tabernacle built from adobe bricks and logs located on Main Street in Bountiful; and the old church on 200 East in Centerville.

The area's growth remained limited for many years by the lack of available water. Although streams were diverted higher on the bench to allow irrigation in the foothills, there was still insufficient water for expansion. In 1884, a canal company was organized to bring water from the Weber River to Davis County. Nearly 20 miles of canal were completed, providing water to the north county area, but reaching only to Kaysville in South Davis County.

As more people built homes and created farms, the ranchers were forced to graze their cattle and sheep farther up into the mountains, an additional 5,000 feet above the settlements. There, they found green feed in the upper elevations, even late in the summer. Large sections of land were claimed by the ranchers, and herds of sheep and cattle were grazed from the foothills to the summits. With the depletion of the grass, shrubs, and vegetation in the mountains, the soil became compacted. Sheep ranchers often burned the underbrush to protect the wool from being snagged. As a result, winter snowmelt and spring rains could no longer be absorbed by the soil. In the 1920s and 1930s, this resulted in serious erosion and devastating floods from the canyons onto the villages below. Lives were lost, along with homes, farms, and outbuildings, all buried beneath tons of mud and debris.

Following the floods, the US Forest Service reclaimed the mountains and purchased the land from the ranchers. Further grazing in the mountains was banned. Then, working with the settlements, the federal government initiated conservation programs. With the labor of the Civilian Conservation Corps (CCC), established under Pres. Franklin Roosevelt, the upper canyons were terraced with over 660 miles of trenches. Spaced 25 feet apart, they were dug, mostly with hand labor, about 10 feet deep, following the contours of the mountainsides. A series of small stop dams were built in the bottoms of the ditches to hold the water, allowing it to disperse into the soil. Trees, shrubs, and new vegetation were planted, and beavers were reintroduced to help control the runoff. In the open draws, wire-wrapped rock dams were constructed in the upper canyons to hold the water, allowing it to sink into the soil. Snow Telemetry Monitoring Stations (SNOTEL) were built in the tops of the mountains, and stream monitors were built in the foothills. These systems still operate, transmitting periodic data to the Forest Service and the Bureau of Reclamation. They monitor the water stored in the upper canyons and the flow of the streams. This provides early warning of flood danger to the communities below. At the mouth of the canyons, debris basins have been constructed to slow down any future floods and give the residents ample time to escape.

South Davis County is also known for periodic high winds. Caused by various weather conditions, the air inversion over the mountains creates a downward flow toward the valley. As it is channeled down the canyons, the wind increases in velocity. Usually lasting only one or two days, the winds can reach sustained speeds of 90 miles per hour, with gusts exceeding 120 miles per hour. High-profile trucks and trains do not risk transiting the valley at those times, for fear of being overturned. Damage to fences, roofs, outbuildings, and road signs are common occurrences. In a recent storm, hundreds of trees, especially high-density evergreens such as blue spruce, were uprooted and laid on their sides. But the community is resilient and quick to join forces to help neighbors recover.

Growth remained limited by water until 1956, when a six-foot-diameter aqueduct was completed to bring water, diverted from the Weber River, as far south as Bountiful. The water is used for both drinking and irrigation. A series of holding reservoirs built along the foothills are filled daily, allowing pressurized irrigation for the lawns and gardens below. With ample water, the communities resumed growth. New housing was constructed farther up into the foothills, offering beautiful views of the lake. Businesses and service companies followed, and each community has grown with new vitality.

The transcontinental railroad was completed in 1869. In anticipation of this event, the Mormon leader, Brigham Young, organized the Utah Central Railroad, which connected Salt Lake City with the transcontinental railroad in Ogden. This provided daily rail service through South Davis County. Locally produced goods could now be delivered to markets just hours after harvest. The Great Salt Lake & Hot Springs Railway was organized in 1890 to provide passenger service north to Ogden. After failing financially, it was eventually purchased by Simon Bamberger, who converted it to run on electricity. With comfortable coaches, it provided local service to the small towns along the Wasatch Front with two express runs from Salt Lake to Ogden. During the one-hour trip, the train traveled at an average speed of 36.8 miles per hour. The Utah Light & Traction Company (ULTC) provided trolley passenger service from Holladay to Centerville. The Bamberger lines connected into the trolley system, and passengers could travel from anywhere in Salt Lake City to Ogden in comfort. With the end of World War II, the automotive industry prospered and rail dependency diminished. The Bamberger train service ended in 1958.

Paved highways were being built through Utah by 1927. Trucks now delivered goods to market, and passenger transport was by automobile and bus. Interstate 15 was built through South Davis County in 1974. As the population continued to expand, a light-rail system, Front Runner, was completed in 2008, with 25 runs per week from Ogden to Provo. Communication services were originally provided by overland freight companies hauling mail. This changed to the Pony Express, telegraph service, and then early stagecoaches. Now, mail service is provided by air transport and door-to-door delivery. Beginning with single, shared telephones, often hung on centrally located poles, modern communications systems, including a fiber-optic backbone for Internet service, are now provided.

Antelope Island, part of South Davis County, is the largest island in the Great Salt Lake. It forms the western shore of the lake as seen from the Wasatch Front. The early Mormon settlers formed a ranch there and began moving cattle and horses to the island in 1848. A ranch house and facilities were built at the site of a freshwater spring by Fielding Garr. Antelope Island was the site of a rich copper discovery in the late 1880s. Copper ore to 26 percent grade was mined on the island, and over 50 miners were working the operation. The most promising vein quickly played out, however, and the mine closed soon after. Although the island had seen some homesteading and limited development, it was acquired by the State of Utah and established as Antelope Island State Park in 1969. Buffalo were reintroduced to the island in 1893 and are now a major attraction to visitors.

Other small villages were formed around families or groups of pioneer settlers who farmed together or had other ties. Some of these sites have also grown into substantial communities. However, the three remote Mormon grazing areas of 1847 are still the main commercial centers of South Davis County. The area has produced state governors, congressmen, inventors, artists, professional sports figures, authors, and more. But the pioneer spirit can still be felt as the foundation of each town.

One

Carving Out Homes on the Lakeshore

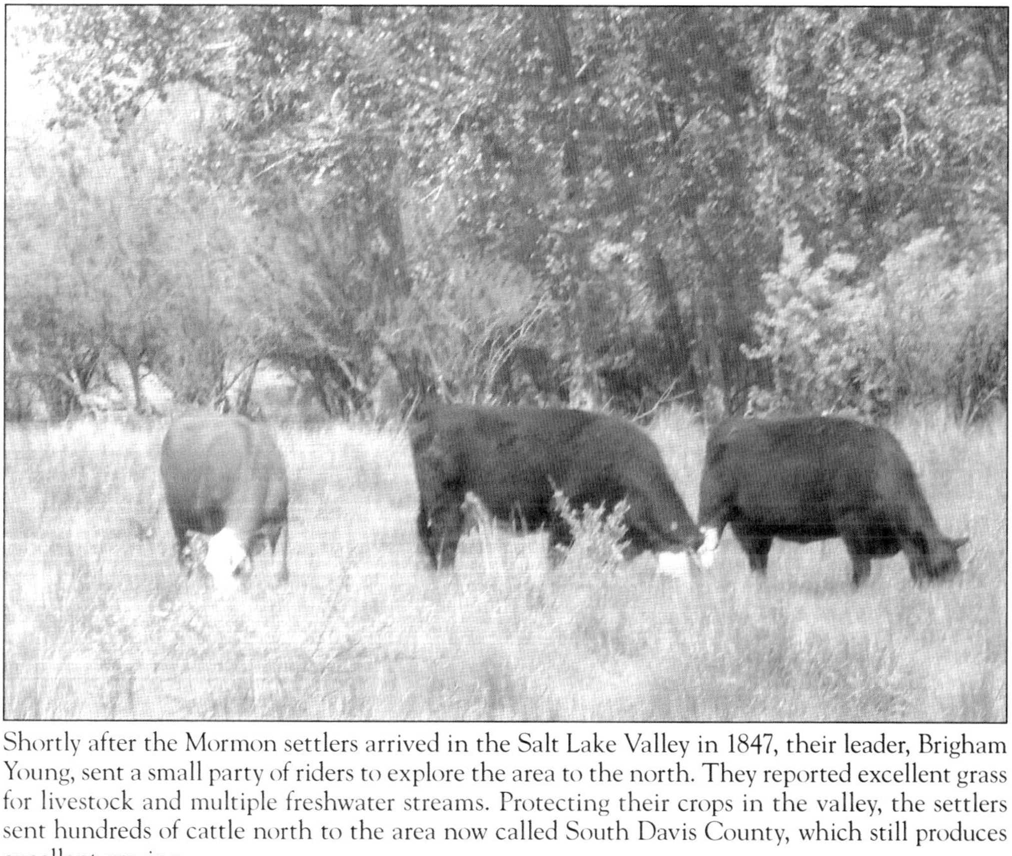

Shortly after the Mormon settlers arrived in the Salt Lake Valley in 1847, their leader, Brigham Young, sent a small party of riders to explore the area to the north. They reported excellent grass for livestock and multiple freshwater streams. Protecting their crops in the valley, the settlers sent hundreds of cattle north to the area now called South Davis County, which still produces excellent grazing.

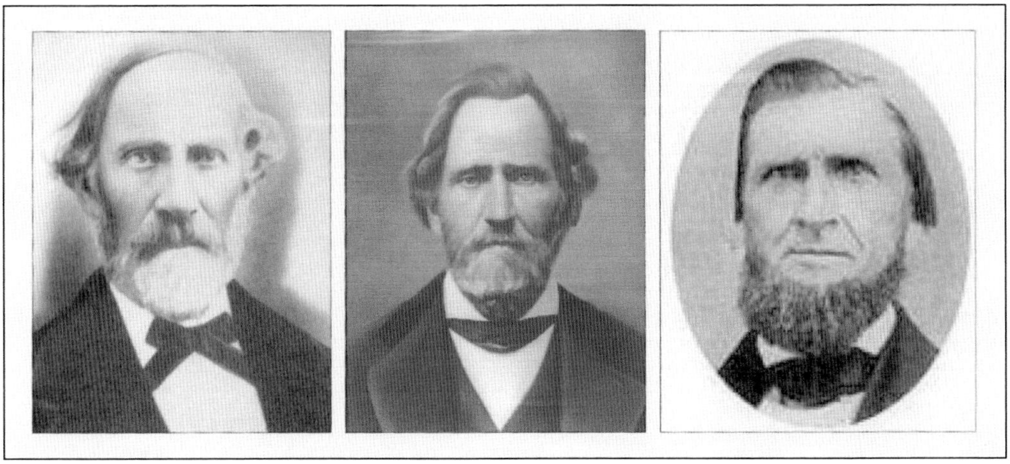

In the fall of 1847, pioneer settlers sent their cattle north to graze along the lakeshore. Perrigrine Sessions (left), Thomas Grover (center), and Hector Haight (right) stayed with the cattle, formed winter camps, built cabins, and planted crops the next spring. Each camp, located a few miles apart, spawned a new settlement—now Bountiful, Centerville, and Farmington. Later, the Farmington settlement extended north to form Kaysville. (Courtesy Farmington Historical Museum and Bountiful History Museum.)

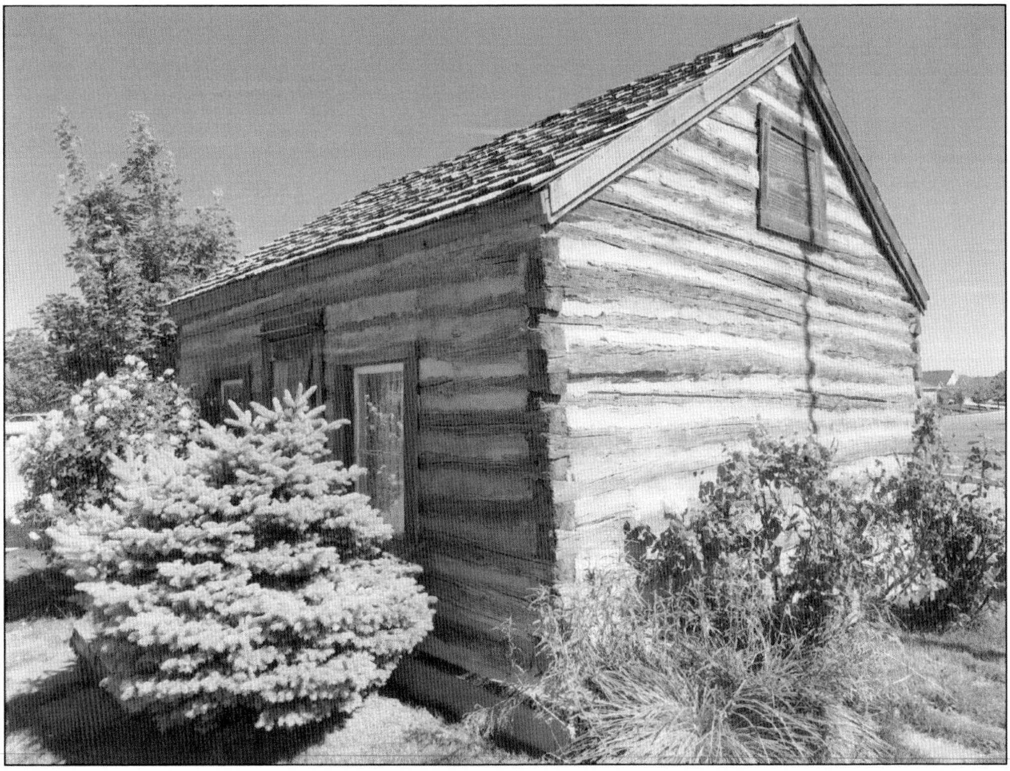

This cabin was built in Farmington in the 1850s, shortly after the first Mormon settlers arrived. Like many of the old cabins, it was sold to clear the land for other uses. This one was moved to Syracuse, Utah, and reassembled on a 160-acre farm owned by William and Emily Wilcox. They raised a family of 10 children in it, eight boys and two girls.

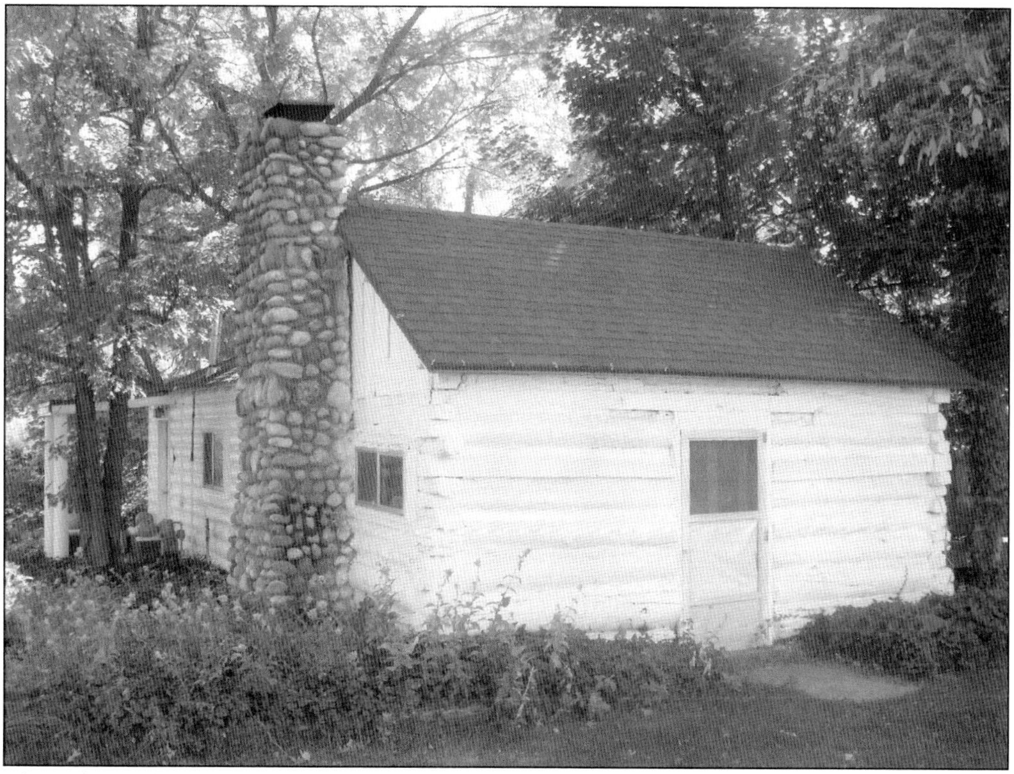

This cabin is the oldest remaining building in Centerville City. Built by Thomas and Rosetta Thurston in 1849, and originally located a mile farther north, it was sold to Brigham Young in 1853. Isaac Chase purchased the property in 1859 and then moved the cabin to its current site at 975 North Main Street in Centerville. There, Chase's son George and his wife, Josephine, raised nine children.

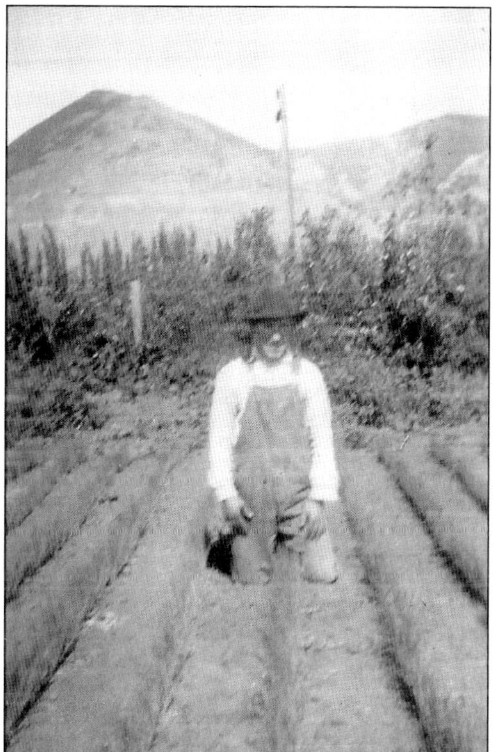

Oliver Dalrymple, shown here thinning onions around 1922, was typical of the farmers raising large gardens and selling the excess to markets in Salt Lake City or at the local cooperative store. Typical produce included squash, tomatoes, onions, beets, melons, and fruit such as apricots, cherries, and peaches. Each home was self-sustaining. (Courtesy Kathleen Dalrymple.)

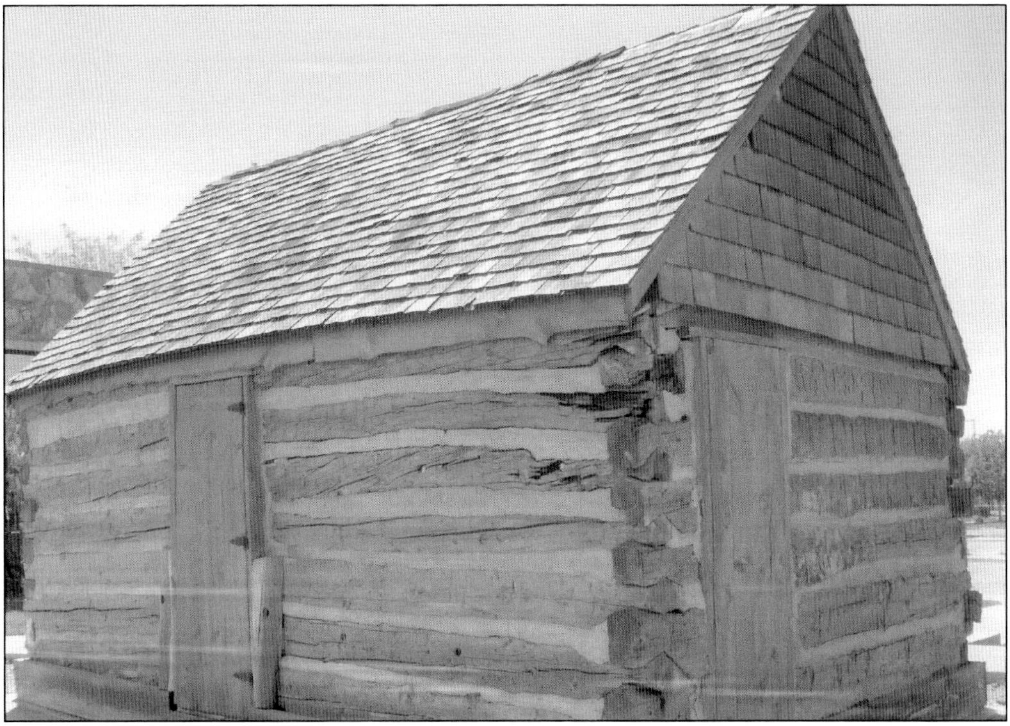

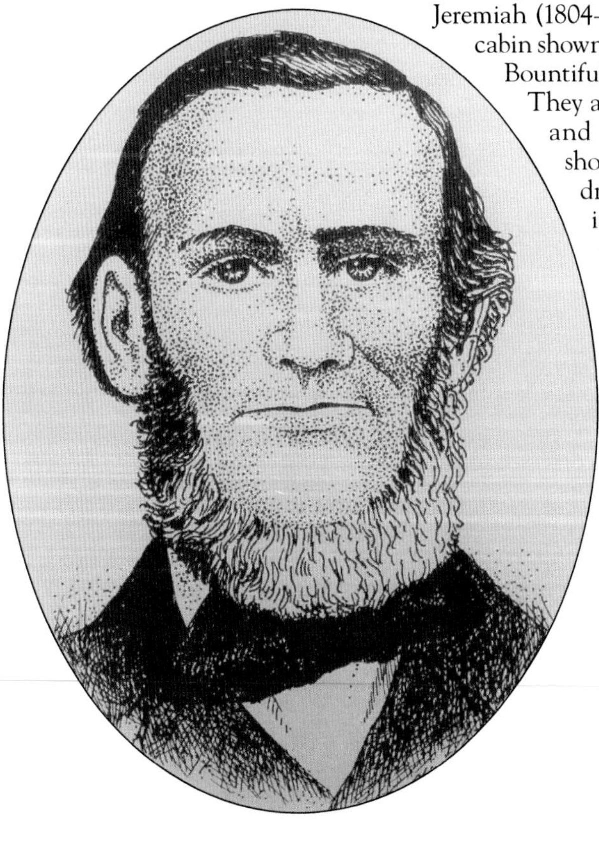

Jeremiah (1804–1868) and Samantha Willey built the cabin shown above in 1854 at 495 East 500 South in Bountiful, eventually raising two children in it. They acquired land on 400 East in Bountiful and built a larger, rock home in 1868, shortly before Jeremiah (left) accidentally drowned at age 63. His family remained in the house until the 1930s, when it was purchased by Grant Neath. Using the main cabin as a bedroom, Neath built around it. When the property was donated to South Davis Hospital, the structure was torn down, exposing the original cabin behind lath and plaster. Encased in a time capsule for the past half-century, the cabin has been preserved as a historical artifact, located next to the Bountiful City building. (Left, courtesy Bountiful History Museum.)

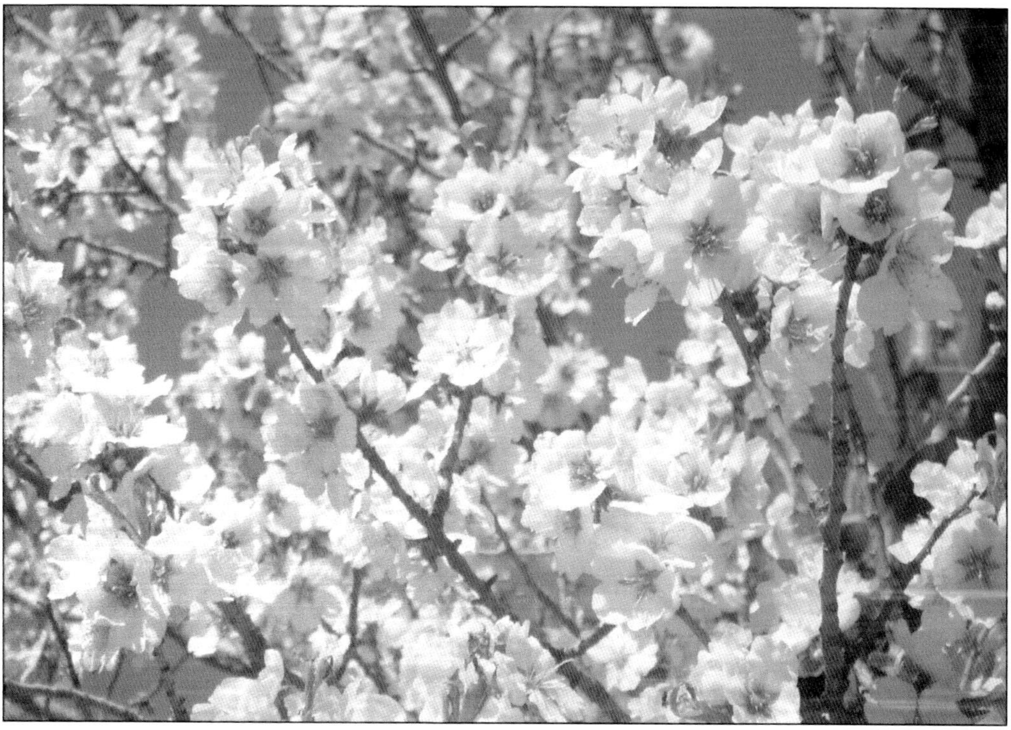

From the early 1850s, gardens and orchards began to mature, and spring blossoms, such as the almond blooms shown above, could be seen across the valley. The settlers organized their livestock into community herds under a bonded herdsman. Owners checked their cattle in and out, paying a small, preset fee for the number of animals the owner entrusted to the herdsman. Only the gardens of the settlers and a few corrals were fenced, using posts cut from the canyons and tied up with rope or rawhide. A section of such old pioneer fencing is shown at right. It was not until 1857 that the first barbed wire became available. Until then, grazing areas were designated and claimed by geographic features, such as a valley, a meadow, a mountain, or alongside a stream. Once claimed, everyone respected those boundaries.

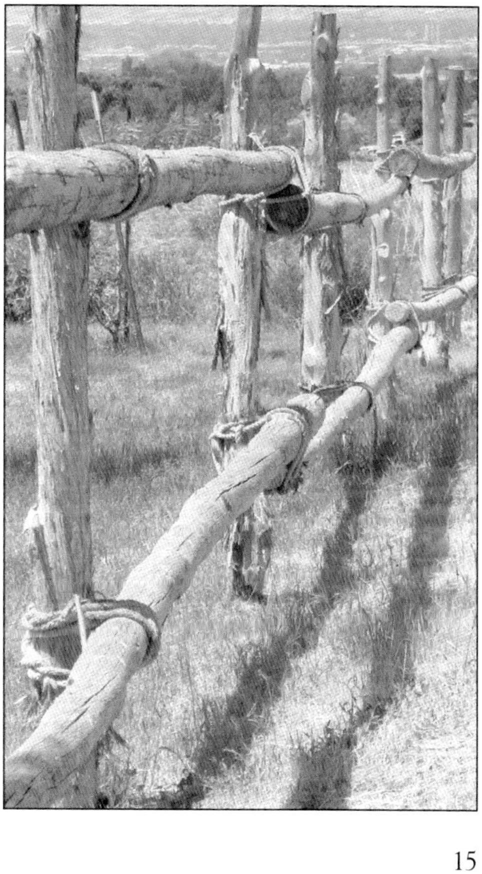

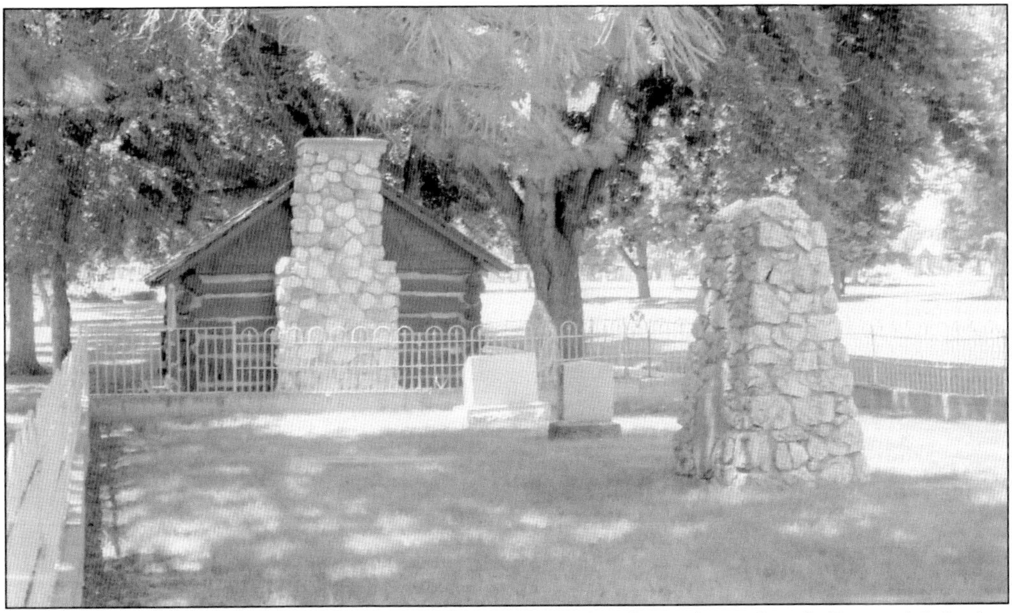

In 1848, Eric C.M. Hogan, a Norwegian immigrant and early settler to South Bountiful, built a cabin for his wife, Ingeborg. His third wife, Hannah Neilson, moved in with Ingeborg, who cared for her five children while Hannah worked as a carpet weaver. A ladder in the corner of the cabin led to a living space in the attic. The cabin presently stands at 720 West 1500 South.

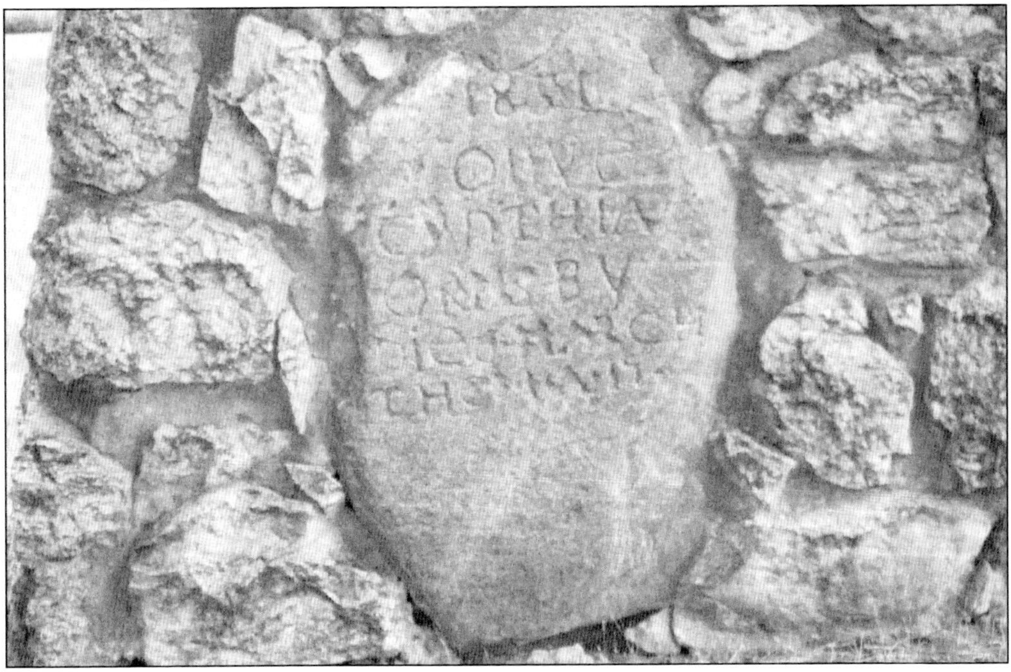

The pioneer cemetery at 720 West 1500 South in Bountiful was used only from 1849 to 1856, due to subterranean water levels. It is a unique cemetery, as it contains the remains of pioneer immigrants and California prospectors, as well as an old Indian grave. The carved stone marker shown here indicates the grave of a traveler who died en route to California. It is now embedded in the site monument.

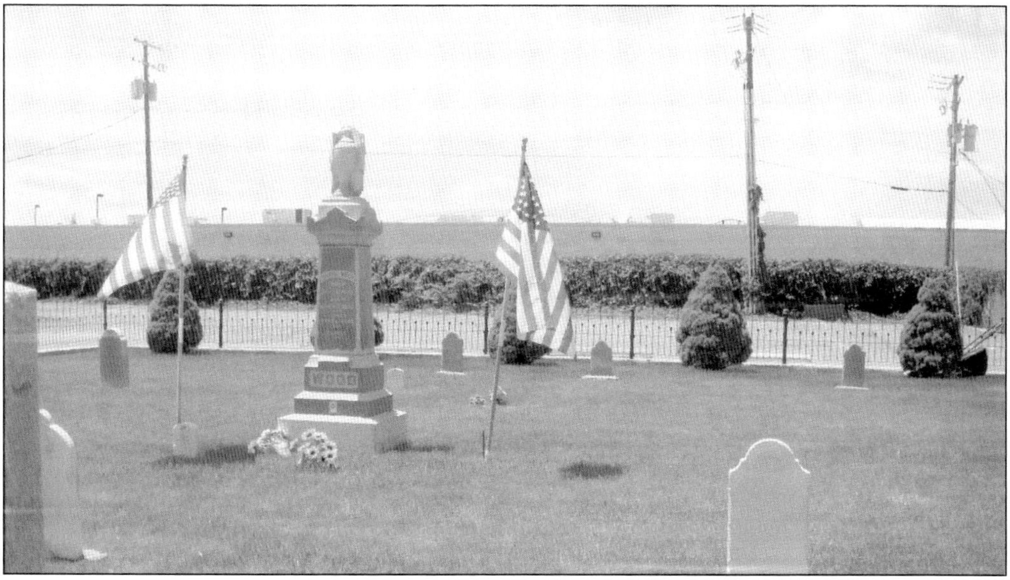

Daniel Wood (1800–1882) is considered the pioneer founder of the town of Woods Cross. He claimed 160 acres of farmland and built a two-story adobe house in 1850. With the crossing of the first railroad through his farm, and the establishment of a station there, Brigham Young dubbed the property Woods Cross. Wood's family cemetery is found in the busy commercial area near 400 South on 500 West in Bountiful.

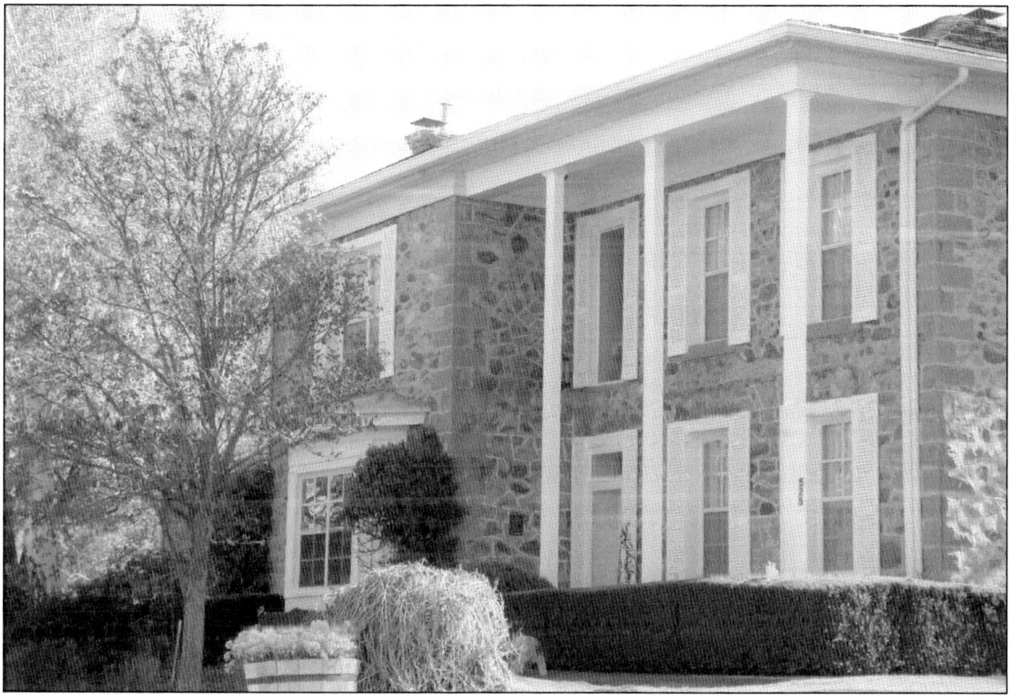

Upon arrival in Centerville from England in 1873, Alwood and Ann Elizabeth Brown purchased 18.3 acres and constructed a two-story log cabin. They planted alfalfa, a six-acre cherry orchard, and a vineyard. The Browns built this beautiful, two-story rock home 12 years later, across the street at 525 East 100 North. The original 20-inch-thick walls still stand strong.

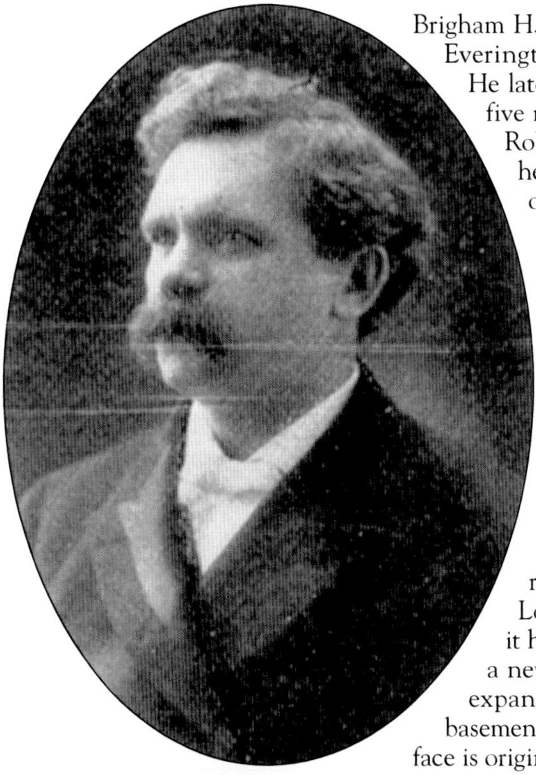

Brigham H. "B.H." Roberts, raised by his mother, Ann Everington, married Sarah Louisa Smith in 1878. He later married two additional women and spent five months in prison for unlawful cohabitation. Roberts was elected to the 56th Congress, but he was refused his seat because of his practice of plural marriage. He became the historian for the Mormon Church and authored several books on pioneer history. (Courtesy Richard Roberts.)

B.H. Roberts, with the help of Charles Duncan, a Scottish stonemason, built this rock house in 1883 for his wife, Louisa Smith. Located at 315 South 300 East in Centerville, it has had three major additions over the years: a new kitchen; a family room; and a two-story expansion on the south end to add bedrooms, a basement storage area, and a game room. The north face is original.

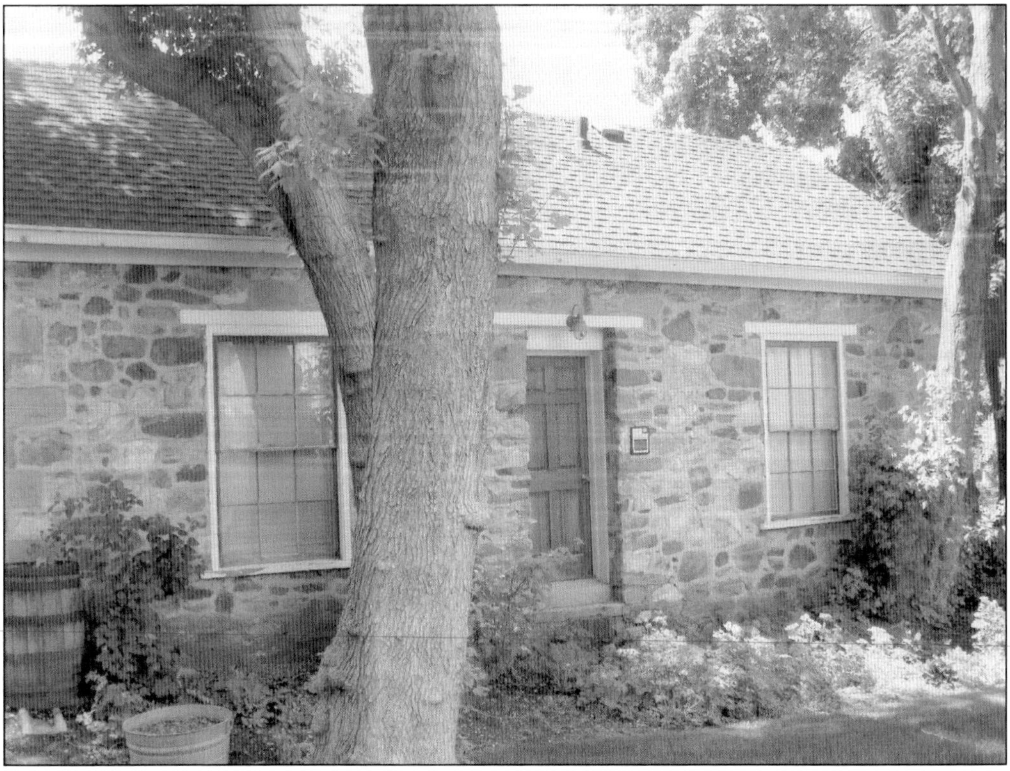

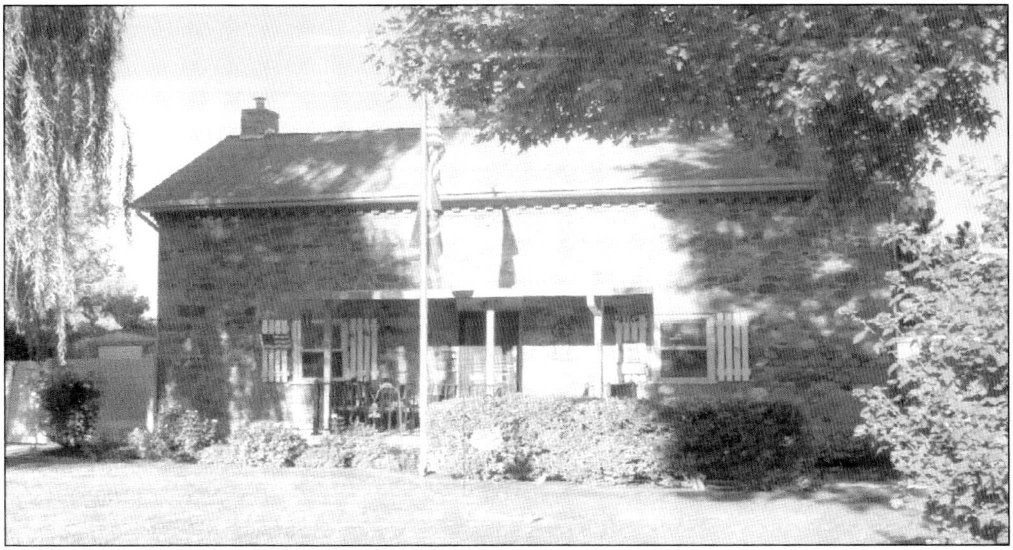

Jeremiah R. Willey, born in 1847 to Jeremiah and Samantha Willey, came to the valley as a child. In 1867, he married Anne Roberts, acquired land on 200 West, and began construction of a rock home in the two-rooms-over-two style of design. This home is dressed with granite quoins made from pieces originally hewed for the Salt Lake Temple. The house still stands at 415 North 200 West in Bountiful.

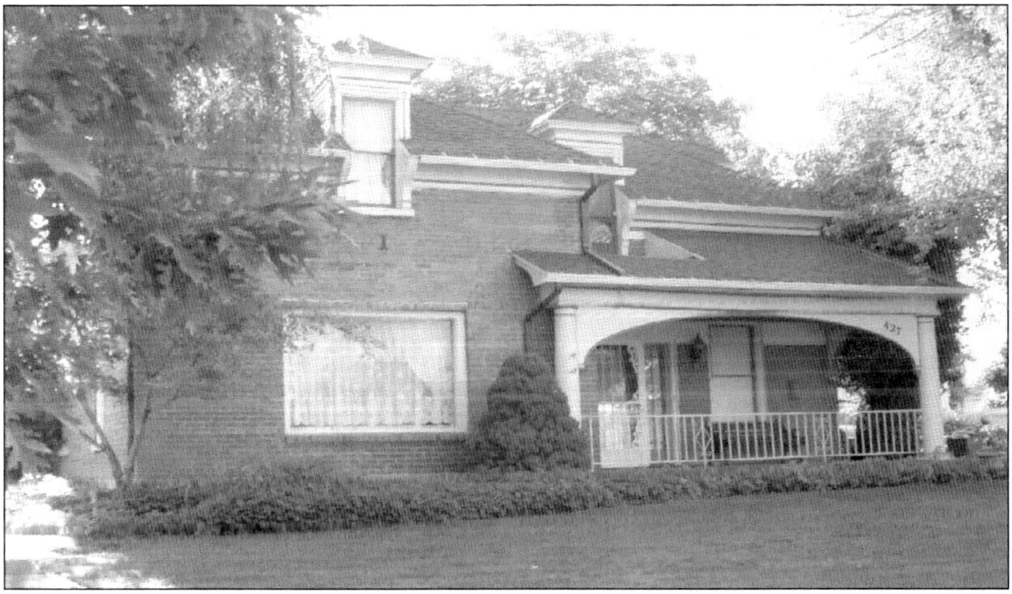

After his father's death, Daniel Davis, for whom Davis County is named, was adopted by Mormon leader Heber C. Kimball and was raised operating the Kimball Mill in Bountiful. In 1890, Davis's son DaKa Davis built this 1.5-story Victorian home at 427 South 100 East in Bountiful with two layers of brick on the exterior and plaster on the interior walls.

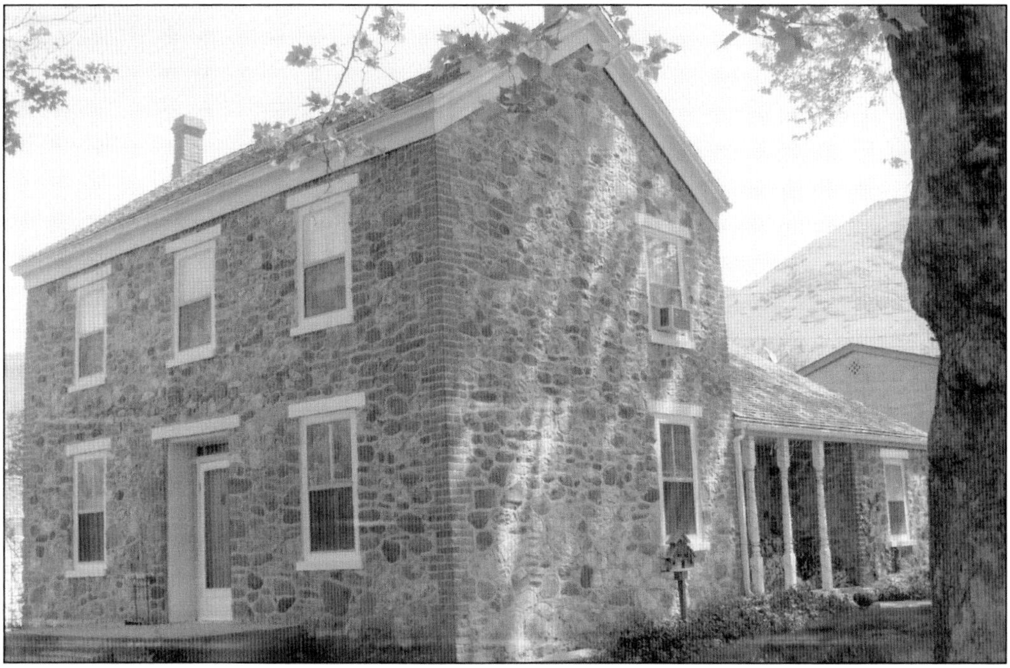

This two-story stone and brick home at 168 North Main Street was built in 1862 by Charles Duncan, a carpenter, and Thomas Whitaker, a cabinetmaker. They used the warmth of the sunny parlor nook to raise silkworms. At maturity, the cocoons were unwound onto bobbins and spun into multistranded silk threads for weaving. Whitaker's wife, Elizabeth, made scarves, vests, and neckties.

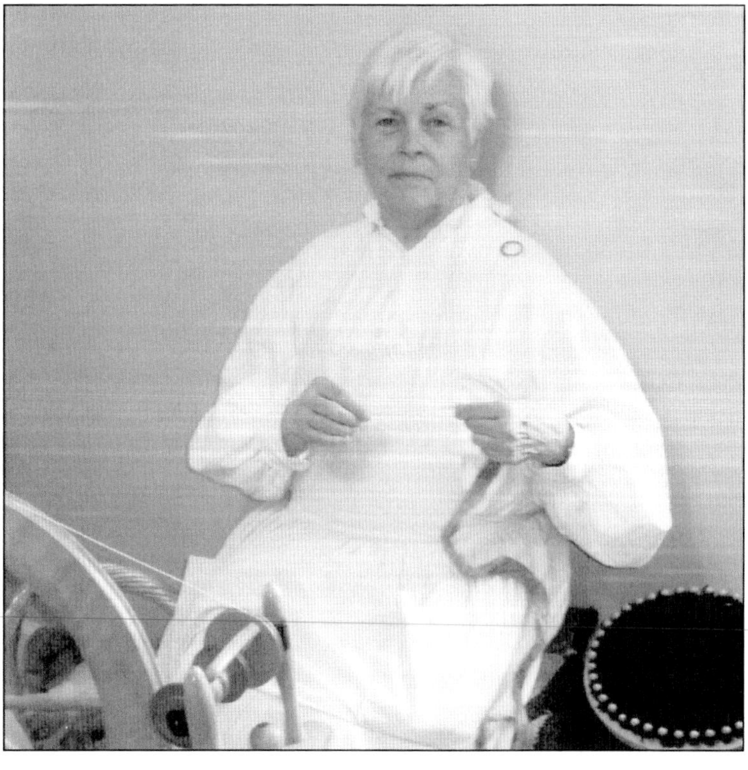

In 1869, Whitaker took a second wife, Hanna Waddoups, who assumed responsibility for raising the silkworms. The Whitaker home was purchased by Centerville City in 1994, and it now serves as a museum and cultural center. It has been restored to its original design and furnished with items from the period. Here, Judy Gunn demonstrates spinning the very fine silk fibers into a thread.

A wood-burning kitchen stove was the center of activity for the early settlers. Shown here in the Thomas Whitaker house, Dorothy Hope begins a meal. Water was heated for Saturday night baths. At bedtime, the fire was steeped with coal to heat the house through the night. Even baby lambs or pigs, chilled in the barnyard, often found themselves warming in front of an open oven.

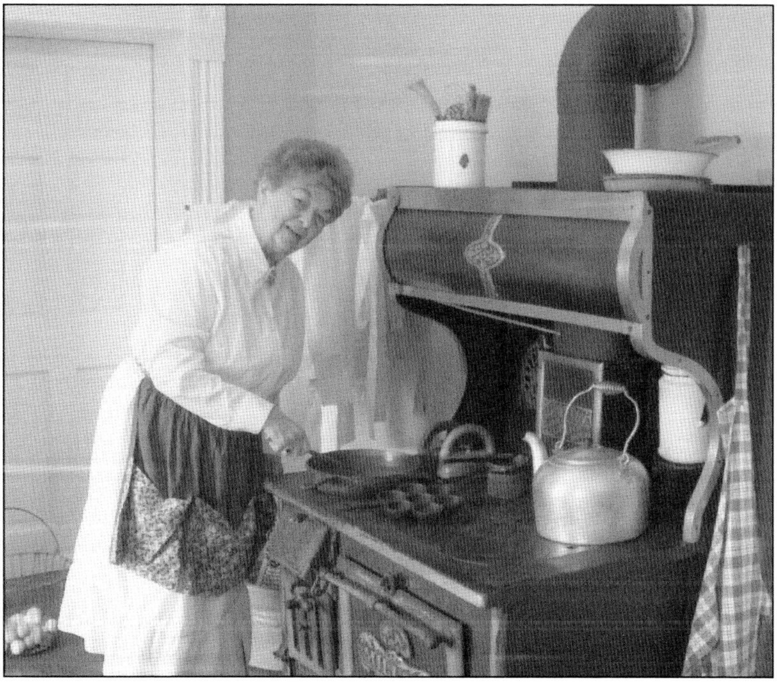

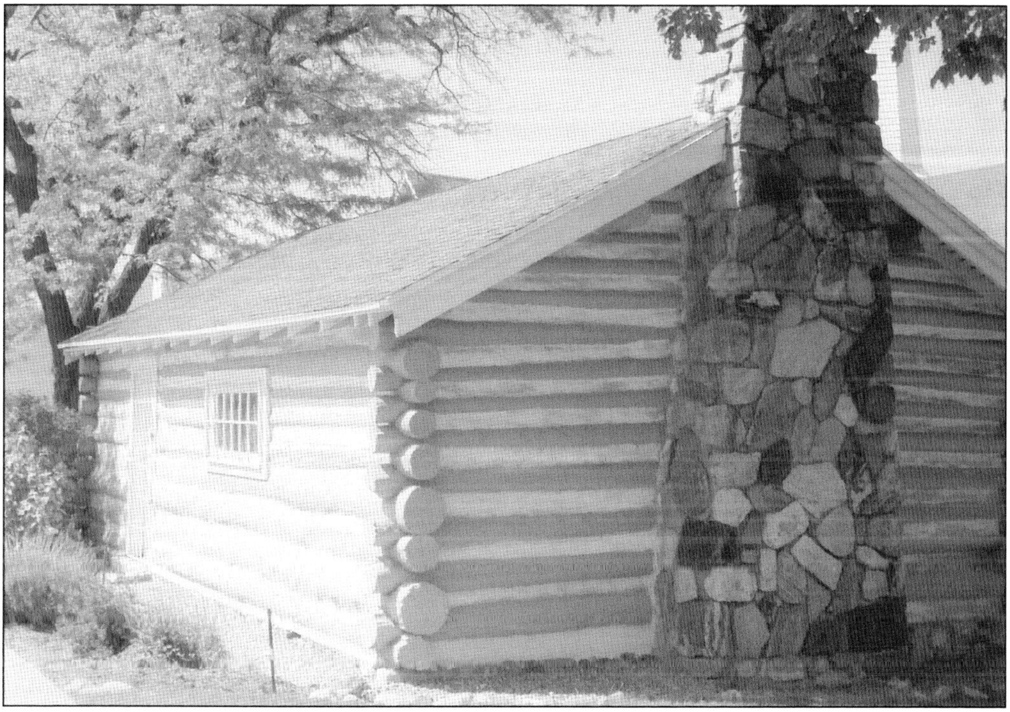

The Pioneer Relic Cabin, located at First North and Third East in Centerville, was built by the Saginaw Camp of the Daughters of Utah Pioneers (DUP) in 1934. It was constructed from the discarded logs from the Alwood Brown cabin and supplemented by old utility poles taken from an abandoned power line along Main Street. The one-room cabin, which preserves historical artifacts and records, is open to the public by appointment.

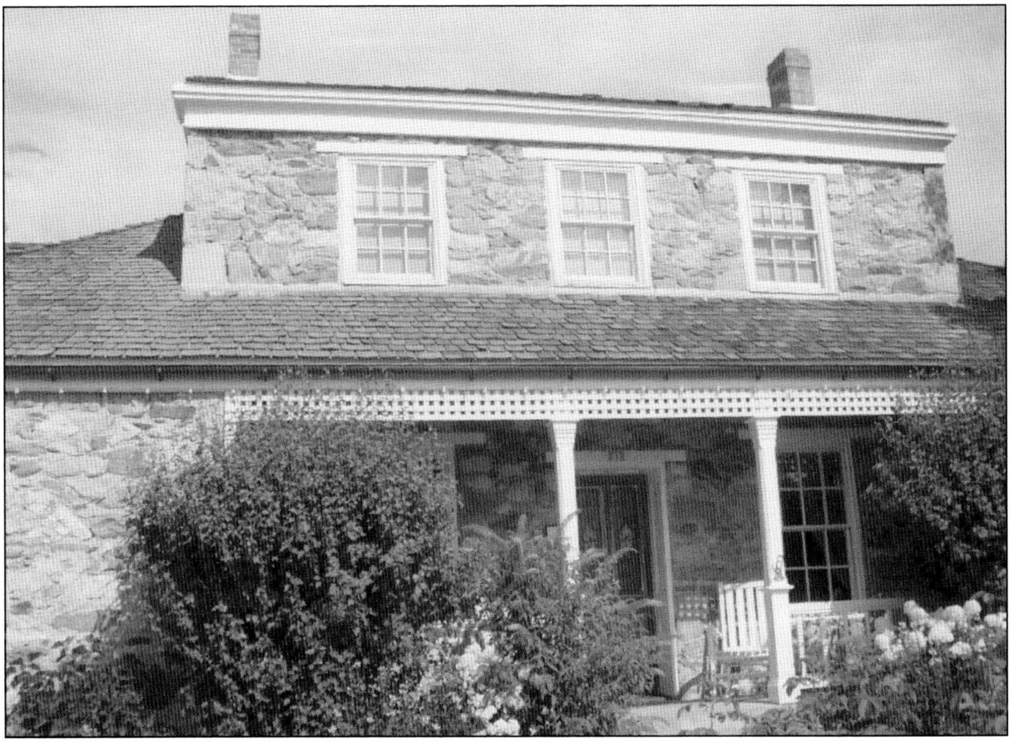

William Capener moved to Centerville in 1875 after the death of his first wife, Sarah. With his second wife, Ellen, he built an unusual two-story home (above) at 252 North 400 East, with a center cell and sloping roof extensions to both sides. Built of native fieldstone, the house included a spacious parlor (below), a kitchen, and five bedrooms. Capener was born in London, England, and trained as a carpenter and cabinetmaker. His grandfather, a minister in the Church of England, encouraged William to join the clergy. Against the wishes of his family, William ventured to America, coming west in 1852. He had five children from his first marriage and eleven from his second. In 2005, during construction of a patio, an old 58-foot well was uncovered behind the house.

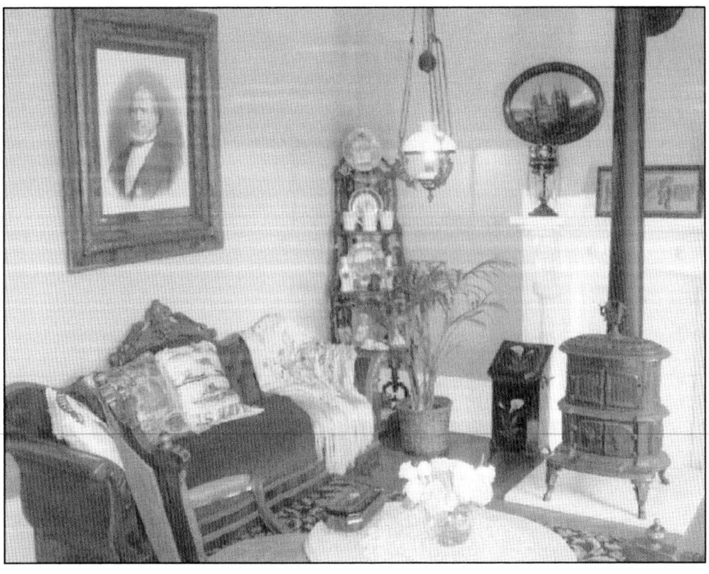

Two

EARLY INDUSTRIES

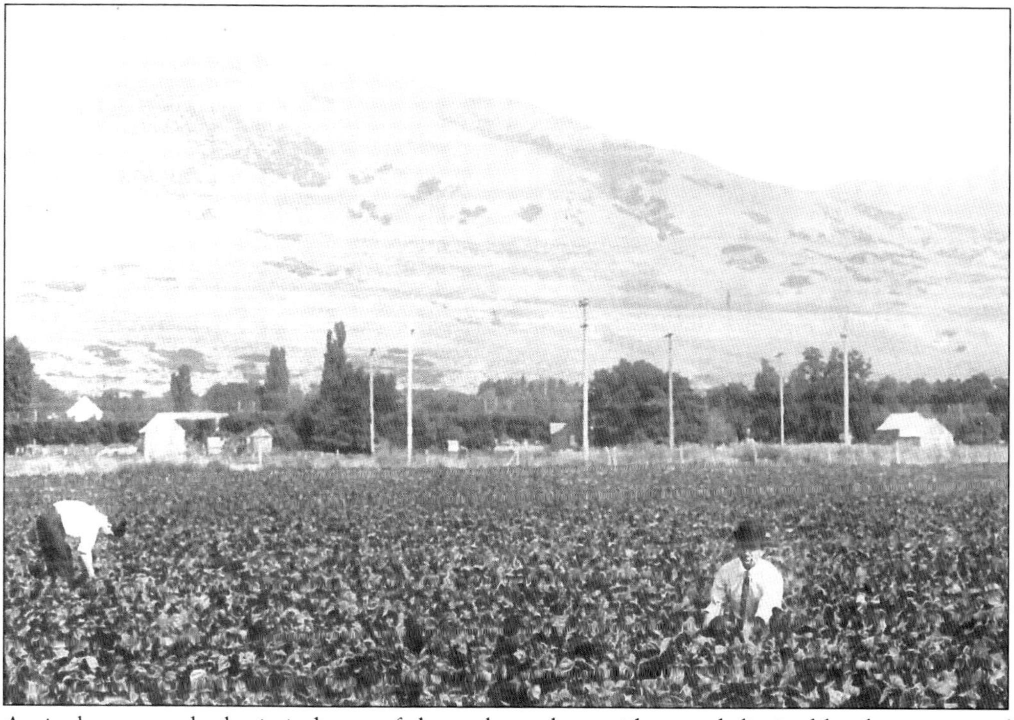

Agriculture was the basic industry of the early settlers, with growth limited by the amount of water available from the small streams. Crops were planted as early in the spring as possible, since the water supply would be diminished by late summer. Potatoes, wheat, squash, and melons were produced and sold to the Salt Lake City markets. The settlers also established orchards of cherries, apricots, apples, pears, and peaches. (Courtesy Kathleen Dalrymple.)

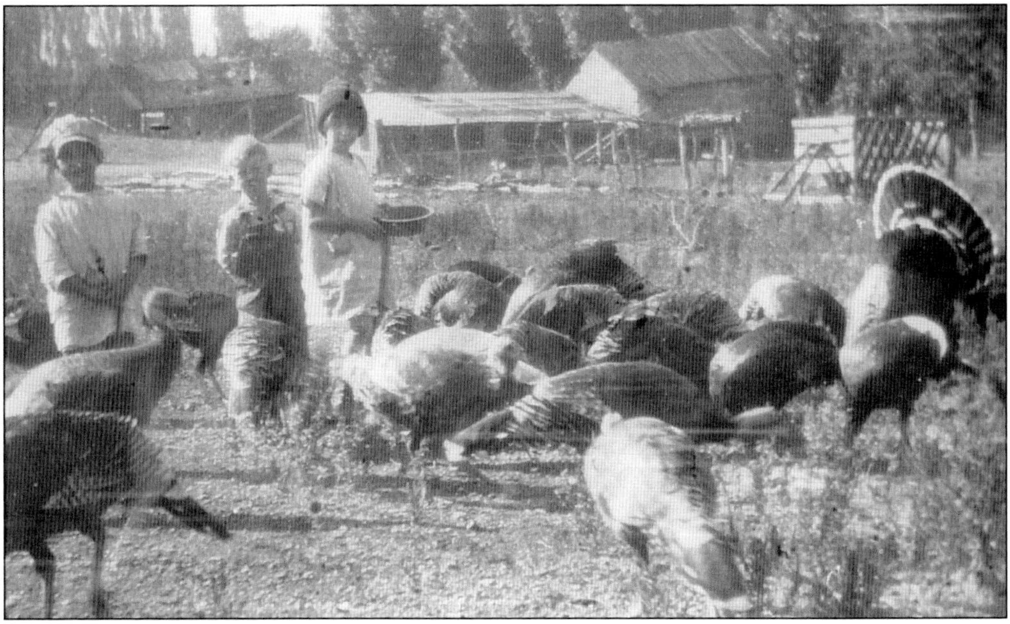

In the early years, each farm was self-sufficient. Residents bartered with neighbors for food and labor as needed. Excess produce, livestock, and grain was traded or sent to market. In this photograph from around 1939, the grandchildren of pioneer Alwood Brown feed turkeys. The blacksmith shop and granary in the background are now part of a home at 547 East 100 North in Centerville. (Courtesy Roxanne Giles.)

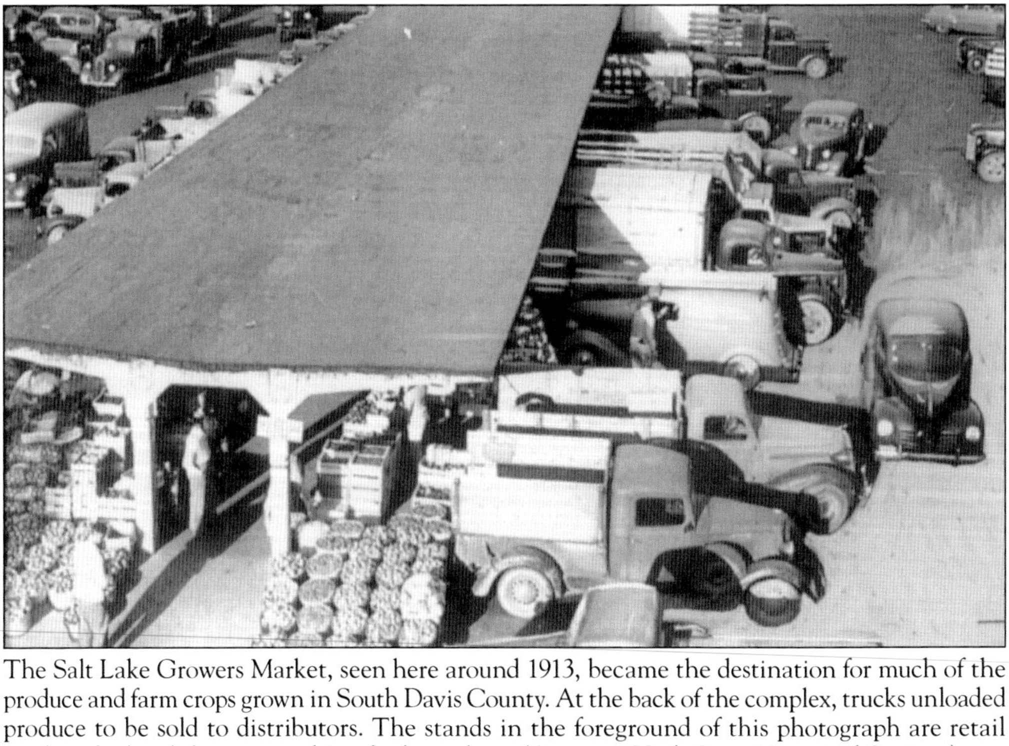

The Salt Lake Growers Market, seen here around 1913, became the destination for much of the produce and farm crops grown in South Davis County. At the back of the complex, trucks unloaded produce to be sold to distributors. The stands in the foreground of this photograph are retail markets for local shoppers seeking fresh produce. (Courtesy Utah State Historical Society.)

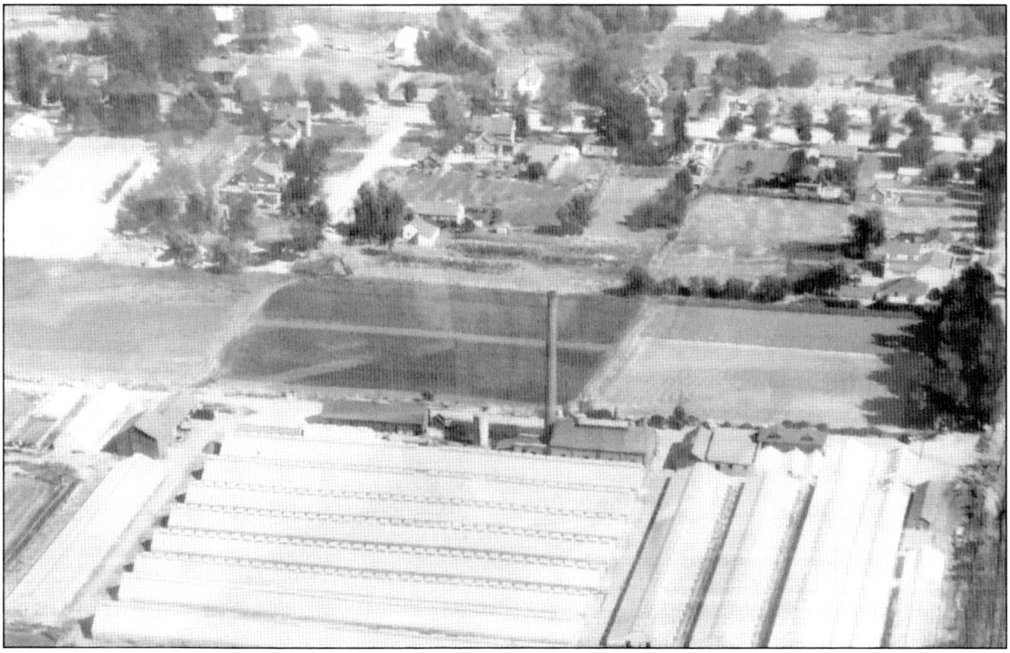

Miller Nursery in Farmington was famous for its long-stem roses, which were exported to eight Western states. The mammoth floral operation grossed nearly $5 million a year and was a major employer for the area, especially at Valentine's Day and during holidays. (Courtesy Farmington Historical Museum.)

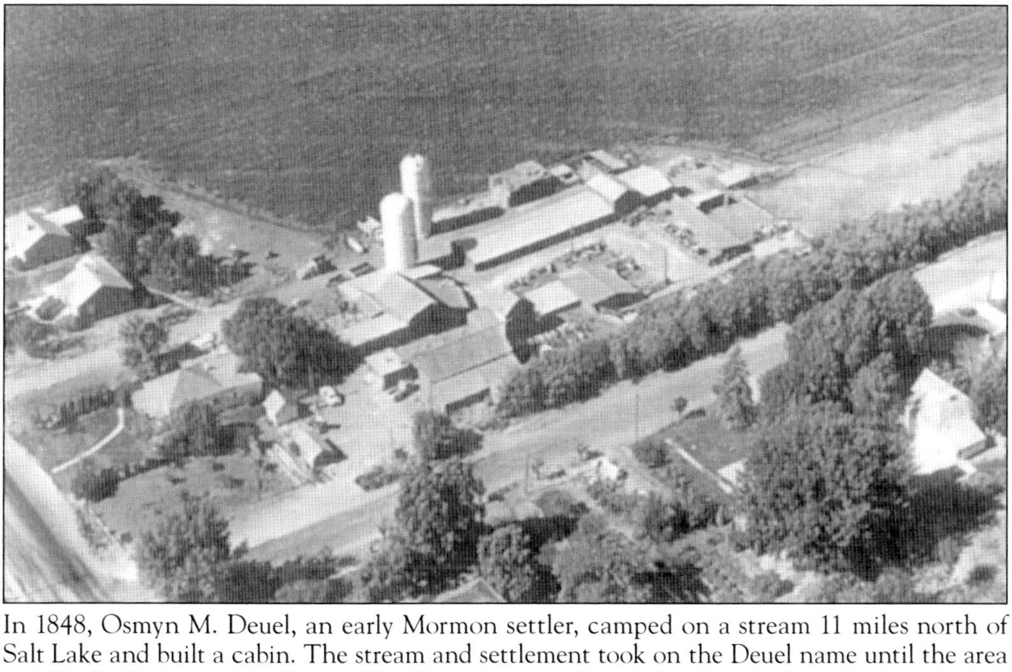

In 1848, Osmyn M. Deuel, an early Mormon settler, camped on a stream 11 miles north of Salt Lake and built a cabin. The stream and settlement took on the Deuel name until the area was finally designated as Centerville. Over the years, Deuel developed a large farm operation, which was later taken over by his adopted son Joseph E. Williams. Deuel died in 1889. (Courtesy Centerville City Historical Records.)

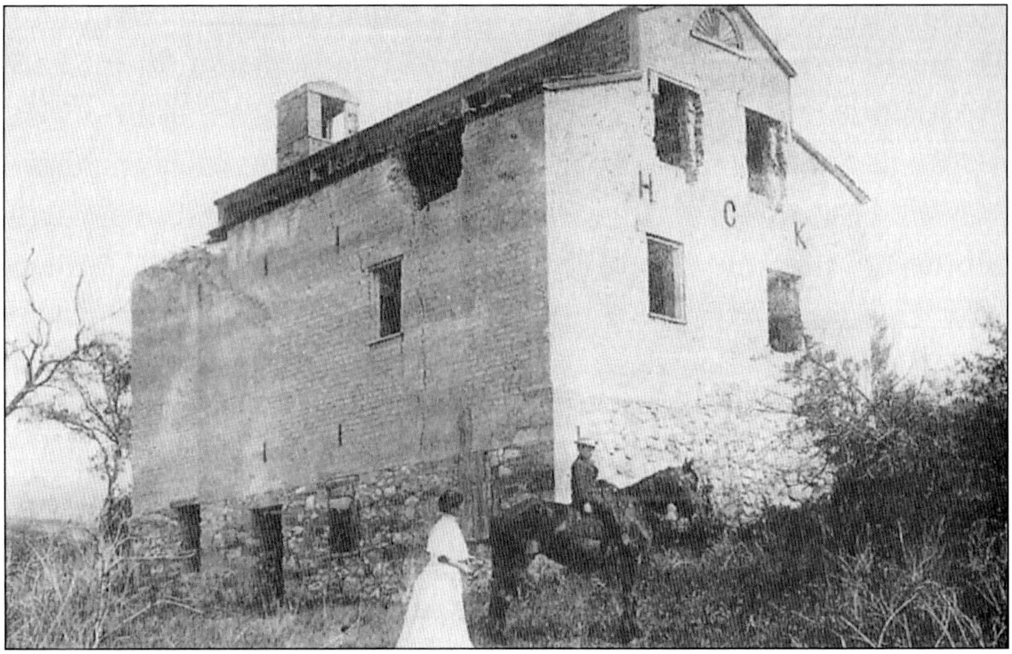

Heber C. Kimball, first councilor to Brigham Young in the Mormon Church, proposed and was granted water rights on Mill Creek for a gristmill in Bountiful in 1851. The ground was cleared by his adopted son Daniel Davis, and the mill was designed and built by Frederick Kesler. The three-story rock mill, seen above in a 1907 photograph, was completed in 1859. It measured 48 feet by 30 feet, the largest mill in the territory. Ice was cut from the millpond during the winter and buried in straw and sawdust in the lower mill for sale during the summer. The pond was used for baptisms by the Mormon Church until the 1890s. A small replica of the mill (below), built by the Daughters of Utah Pioneers, marks the site at 700 South Orchard Drive. (Above, courtesy Utah State Historical Society.)

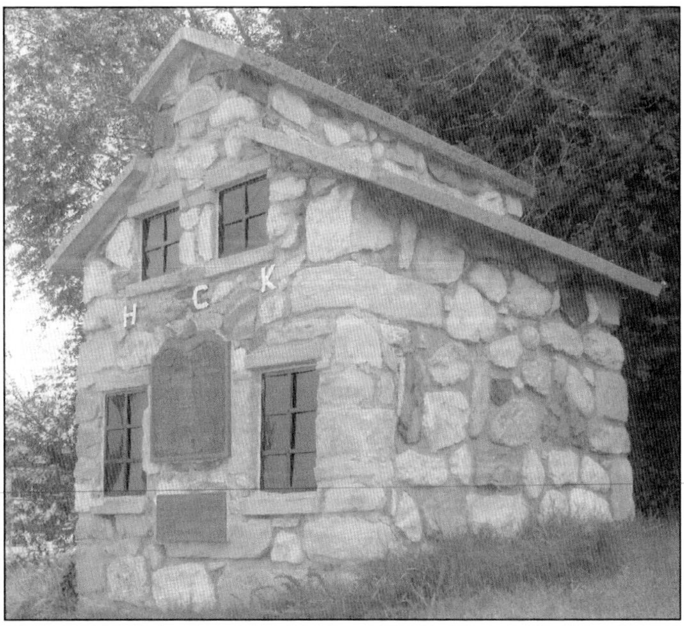

Anson Call (right) moved to Utah in 1848 and was known as a "colonizer of the west," building log cabins in Bountiful while developing his own farm. In 1866–1867, he constructed a gristmill (below) on Deuel Creek at 100 South 700 East in Centerville. Called the "Old Rock Mill," it was driven by an undershot waterwheel, with a retention pond to regulate the depth and flow to drive the wheel. Ice cut from the pond in the winter was stored in sawdust at the cooperative store for sale during the summer. The pond was used for baptisms, as the site of summer strolls, and for rafting. Later, a bakery was located in the lower level of the mill. (Right, courtesy Bountiful History Museum; below, courtesy Kathleen Dalrymple.)

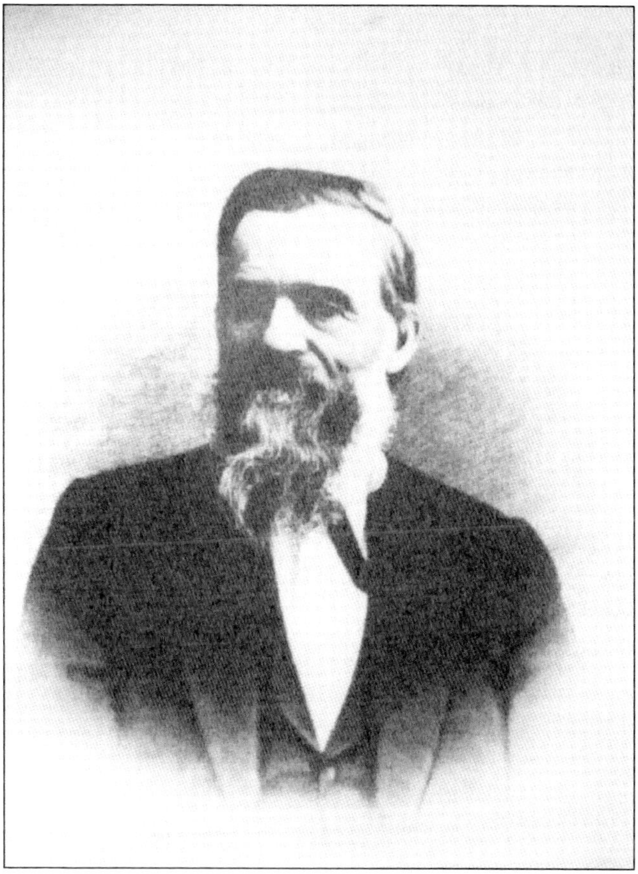

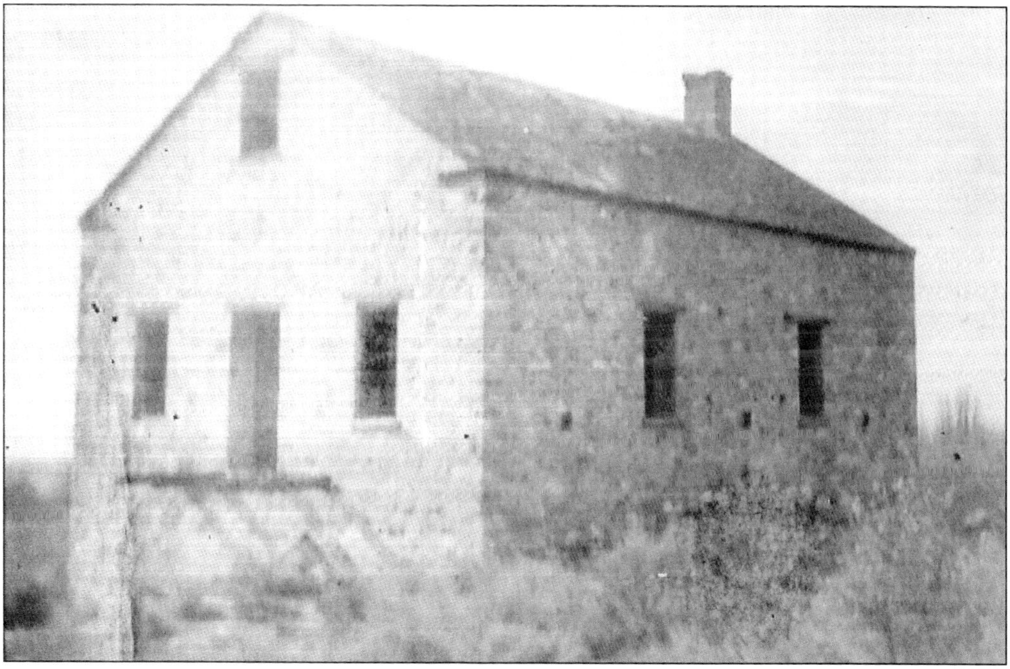

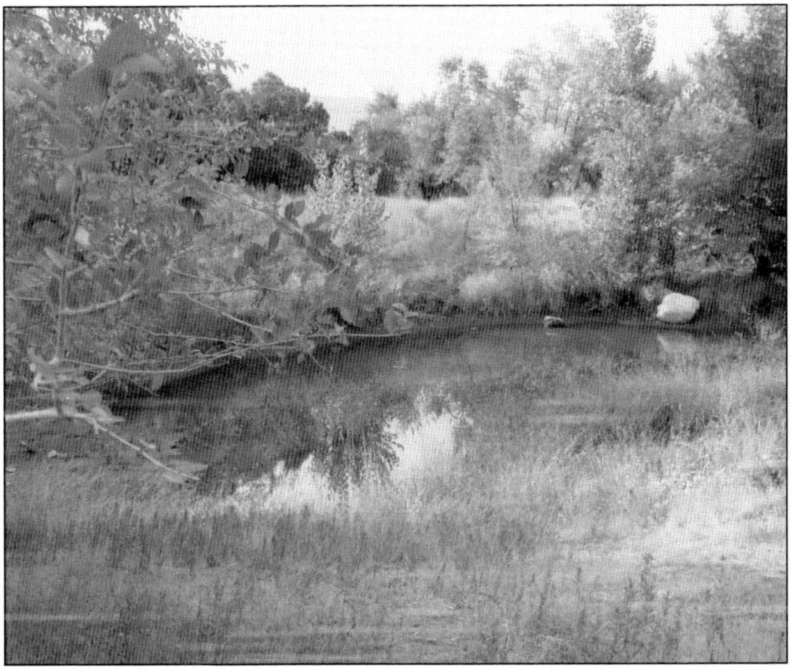

The Anson Call millpond is located at 100 South 700 East in Centerville. Apparently, when the city decided to build a buried water-storage tank as part of the culinary water system, it used the already-excavated millpond area. As a result, the pond located there is slightly farther west and doubles as a debris basin to help prevent flood damage.

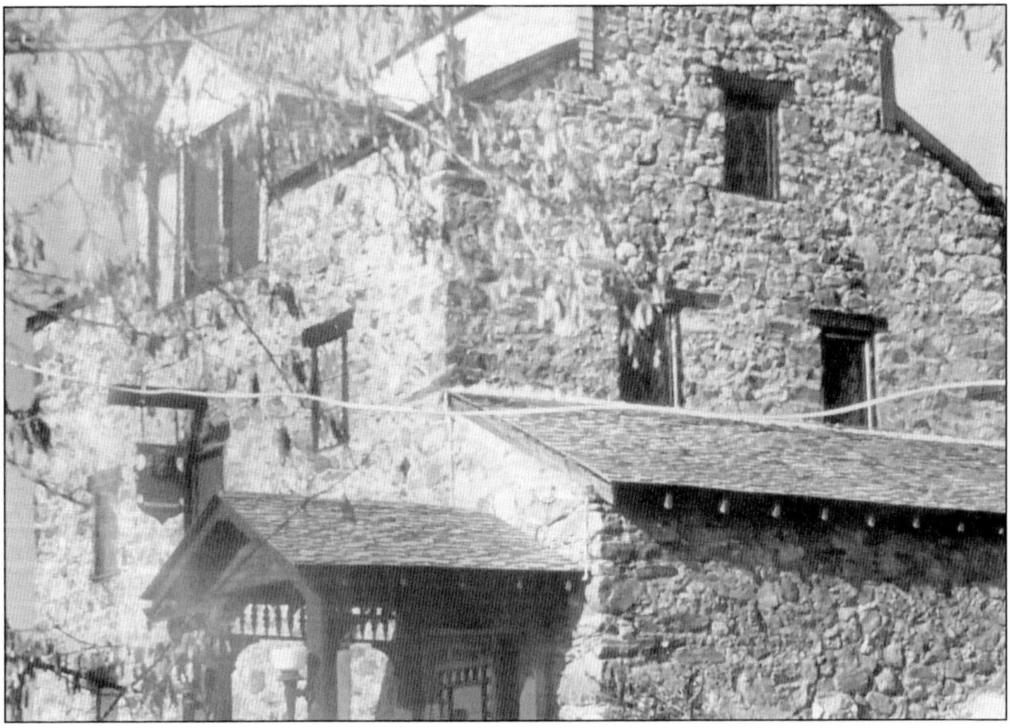

The first flour mill in Farmington was built by Dr. Willard Richards at the mouth of Big Cottonwood Creek. The mill began operation in 1852. It was replaced by a larger, three-story rock structure (shown here) built by his nephew Franklin D. Richards, working with Frederick Kesler. After the mill closed, it became a power plant, then a restaurant, and it is now a private residence. (Courtesy Farmington Historical Museum.)

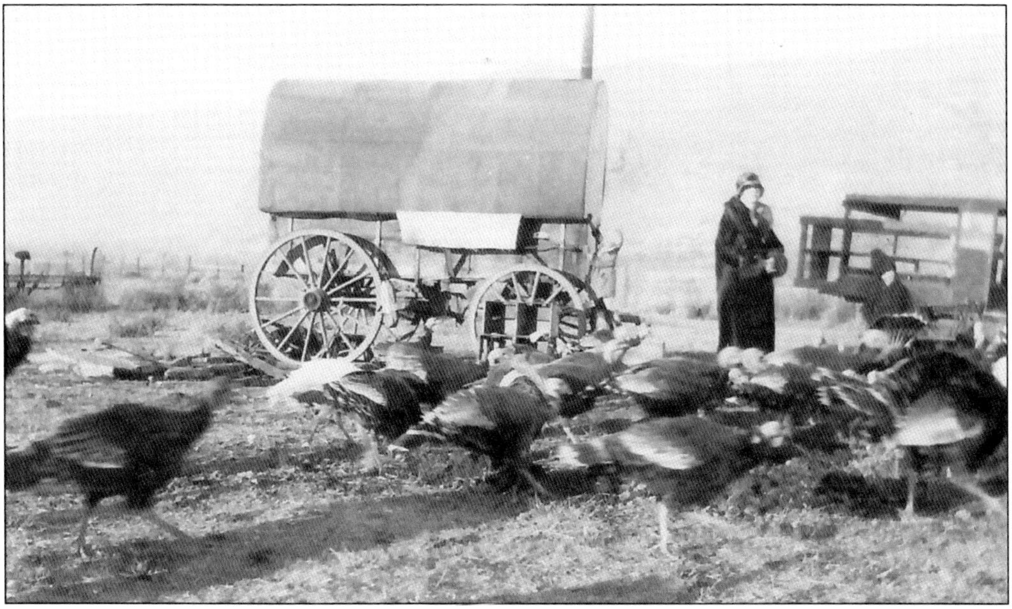

Parked on the Alwood Brown farm in Centerville is a "sheep camp," seen above around 1890. It is perhaps the first version of the modern mobile home. The camp is complete with a stove for cooking and heating, storage cabinets, a washstand, and a bed. No space is left unused. The owners of large herds of sheep would move them from local farms to a range offering good grazing over the summer, often in the mountains. Returning to the valley in the winter, the lambs were born and docked, allowed a few weeks to grow, and then trailed with their ewes back to the summer range. The herder would live in a "camp" for the summer. Supplies were delivered periodically by the owners. The interior of a camp is seen at right. (Above, courtesy Roxanne Giles.)

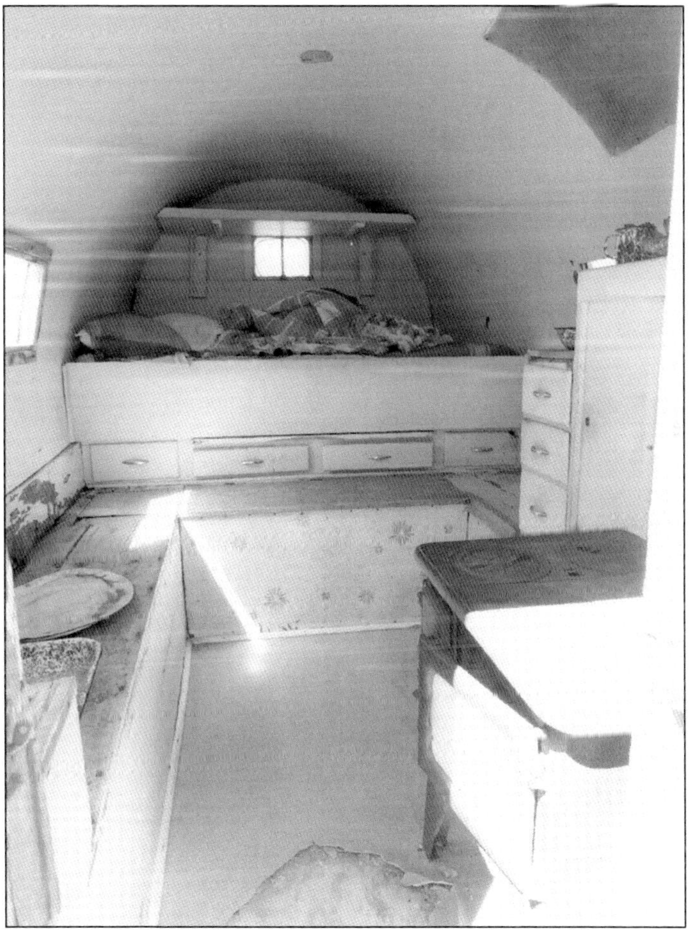

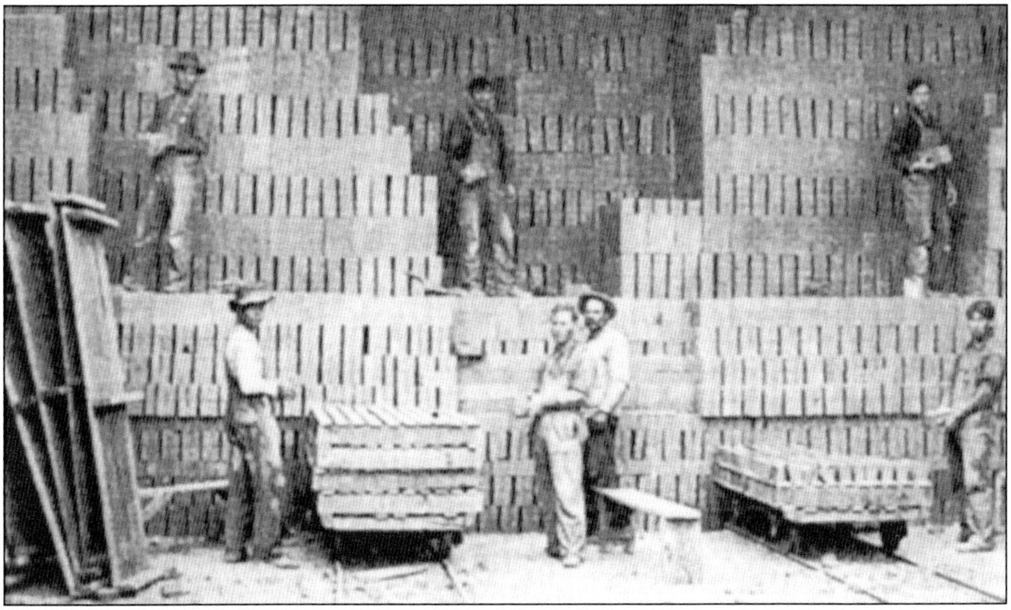

Brick-making was initiated as early as 1852. An area south of 500 South and below 200 West in Bountiful offered an abundance of clay, and it became the location of several brick companies, including Kirk Brick, Improved Brick, and Bountiful Brick. The industry began with sun-dried adobe bricks, but eventually grew to include colored bricks that were cured in kilns. This old photograph shows brick-making operations. (Courtesy Bountiful History Museum.)

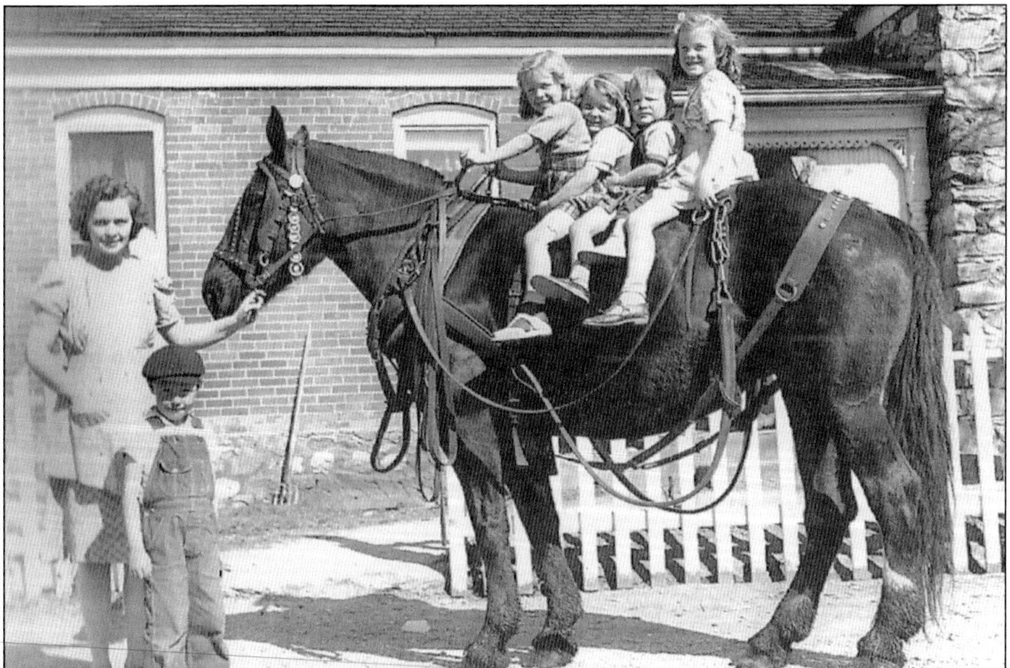

A favorite activity of farm children was unhooking the workhorse for the day and "bumming" a ride out to the barn. Seen here in 1935, Sylvia Tingey and a neighbor boy, Rulon Duncan, stand next to the Tingey children on their horse Bubbles. (Courtesy Nola Tingey Hatch.)

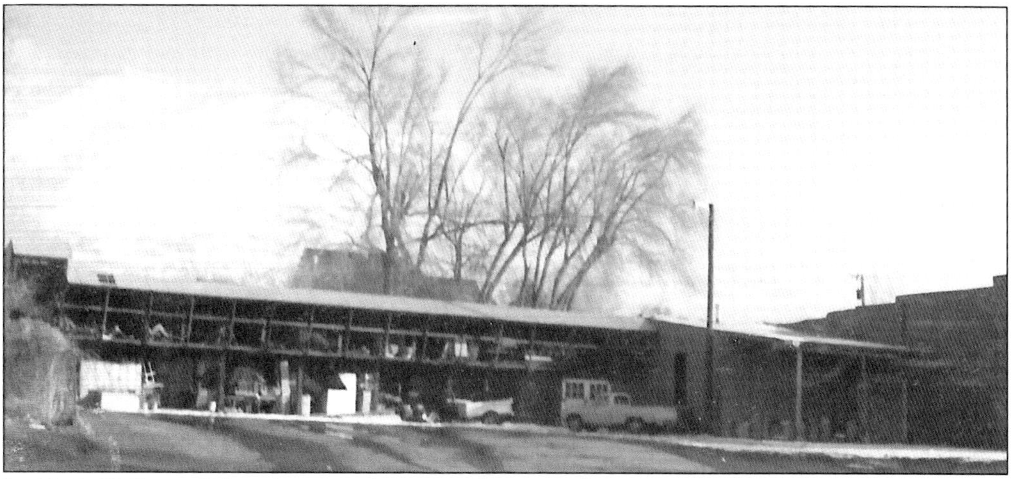

In 1849, William Whipple erected a sawmill in North Mill Creek Canyon. The lumber was delivered to a space adjacent to the local cooperative stores, where it would be sold. A shed was built to protect the lumber at the store in Centerville, making it an early version of the modern lumber businesses. (Courtesy John Hollingshead Jr.)

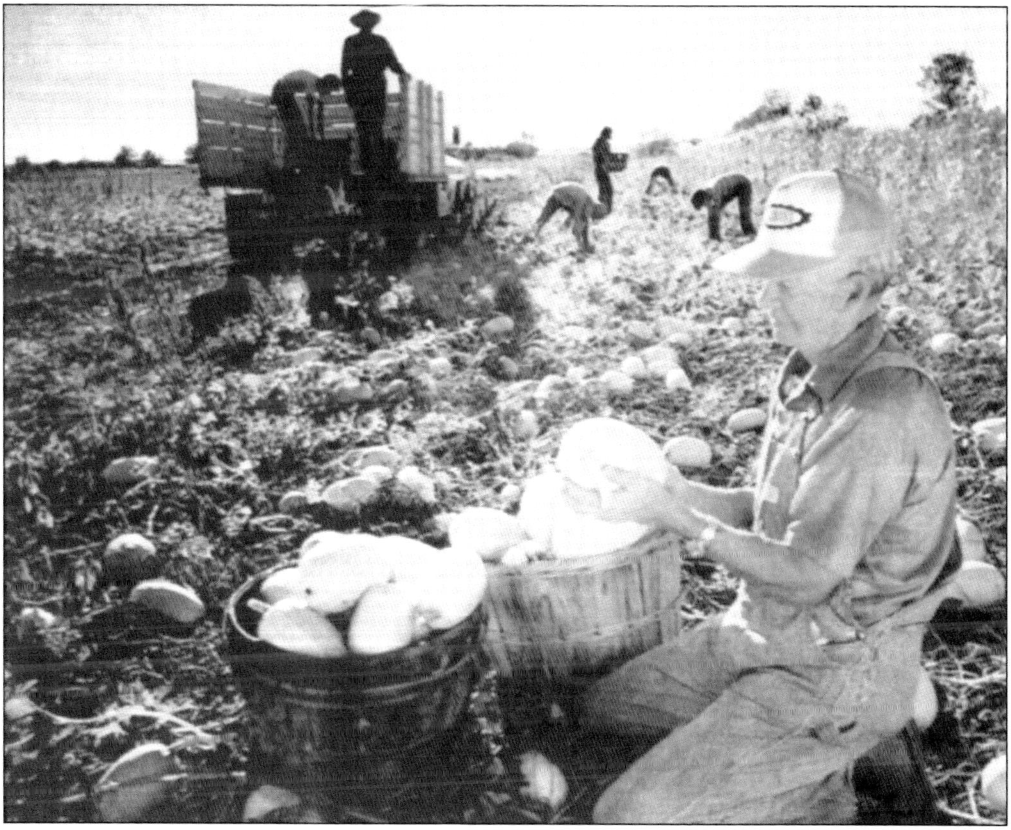

This 1950s photograph shows local farmer Bill Tingey harvesting squash. The image was used as a poster by the Church of Jesus Christ of Latter-day Saints to encourage its members to grow and store food. It was part of the church's welfare program, teaching members to be self-sustaining. (Courtesy Nola Tingey Hatch.)

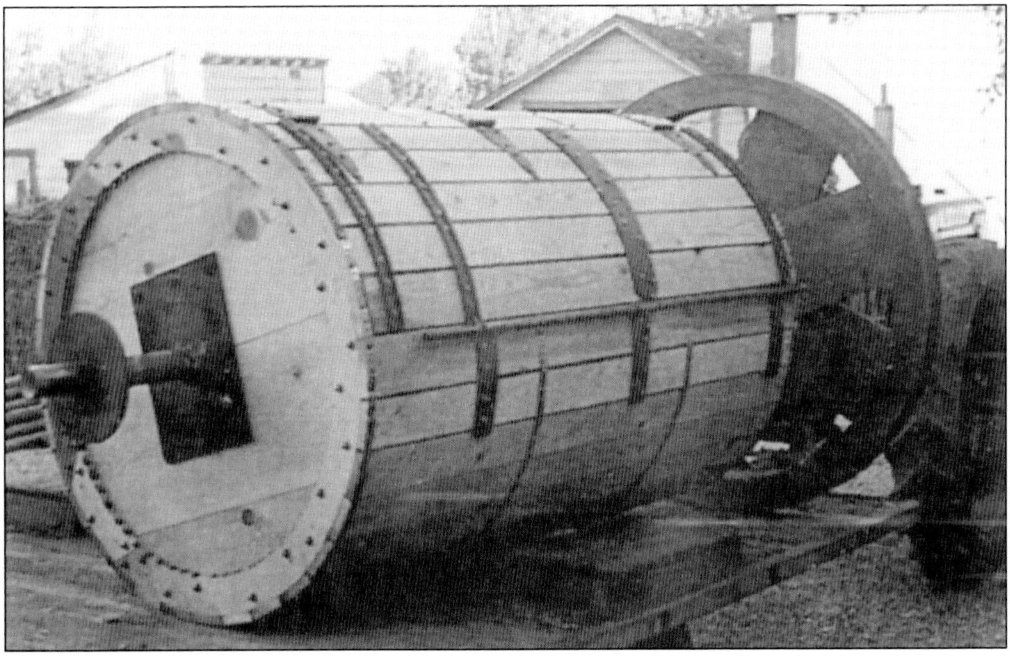

South Davis County was a large producer of vegetables and produce for the Salt Lake City markets. Shown here is a homemade vegetable washer. It was a significant step up from washing beets, carrots, and turnips by hand in a washtub or an old horse trough. (Courtesy Nola Tingey Hatch.)

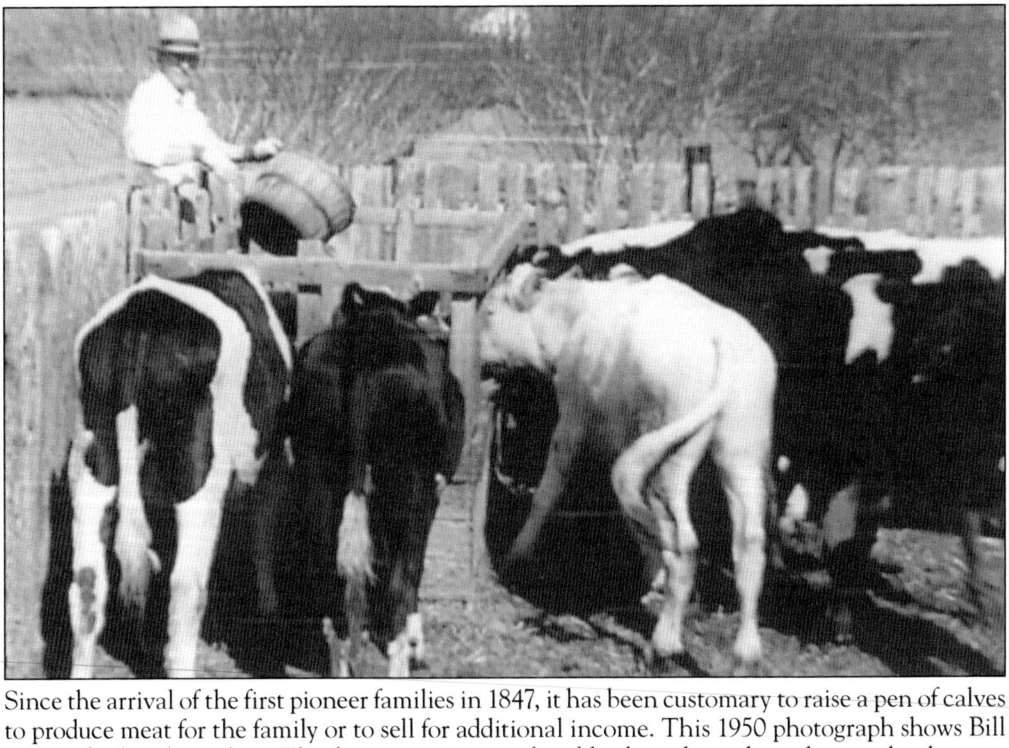

Since the arrival of the first pioneer families in 1847, it has been customary to raise a pen of calves to produce meat for the family or to sell for additional income. This 1950 photograph shows Bill Tingey feeding his calves. The fencing appears to be old split rails, and rough-sawn lumber was used for the feed trough. (Courtesy Nola Tingey Hatch.)

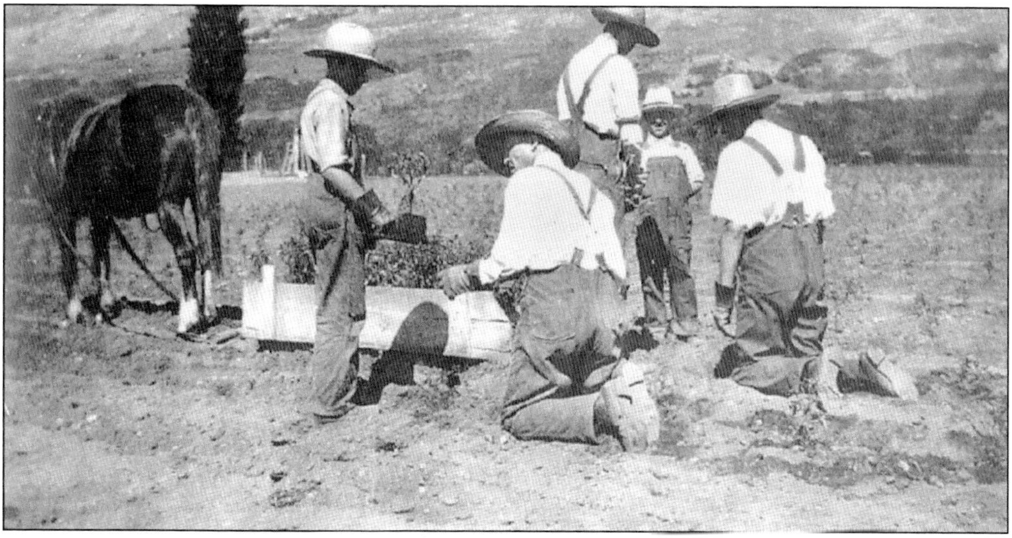

The families in South Davis County, including the children, worked together on the farm, raising vegetables, melons, and orchard fruits. This 1925 photograph shows Tingey family members hand-planting tomatoes in the field. Bedding plants were hauled by horses in the sled along the furrowed rows, with the planters coming along behind. (Courtesy Nola Tingey Hatch.)

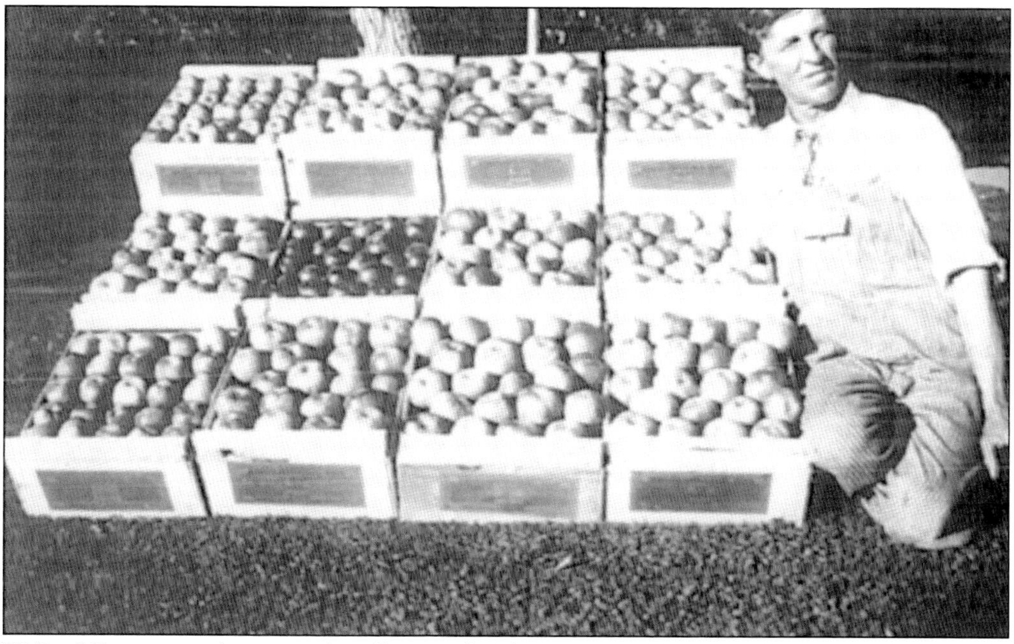

Willard Carr is seen here in 1939 selling apples along Main Street. Others sold cantaloupe along the old highway, hoping to catch afternoon commuters returning from Hill Air Force Base. Such roadside sales were common during the years of the Great Depression. (Courtesy Nola Tingey Hatch.)

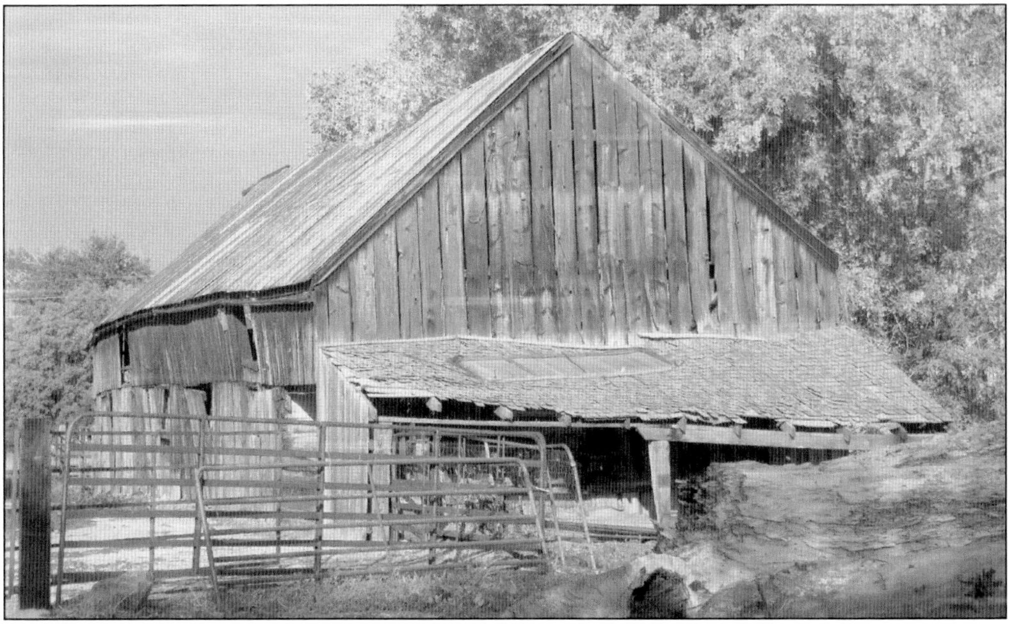

These old barns in Woods Cross tell a story of the early settlers and their homes and livelihoods. Nearly every home had a milk cow and chickens. Beyond that, citizens fell into either of two categories: skilled and professional workers, and those developing agriculture. Many small farms raised various row crops and livestock such as cattle, sheep, beef, and horses. The barns shown here, dating to the 1890s, demonstrate two distinct architectural styles. The structure in the photograph above, with its shed-type roof, was used by those settlers coming from Northern Europe. The barn below shows a classical roofline, as seen in the Eastern United States, including Pennsylvania, Kentucky, and the Ohio River Valley. Many of these barns were built to support milking operations and to store grain and hay.

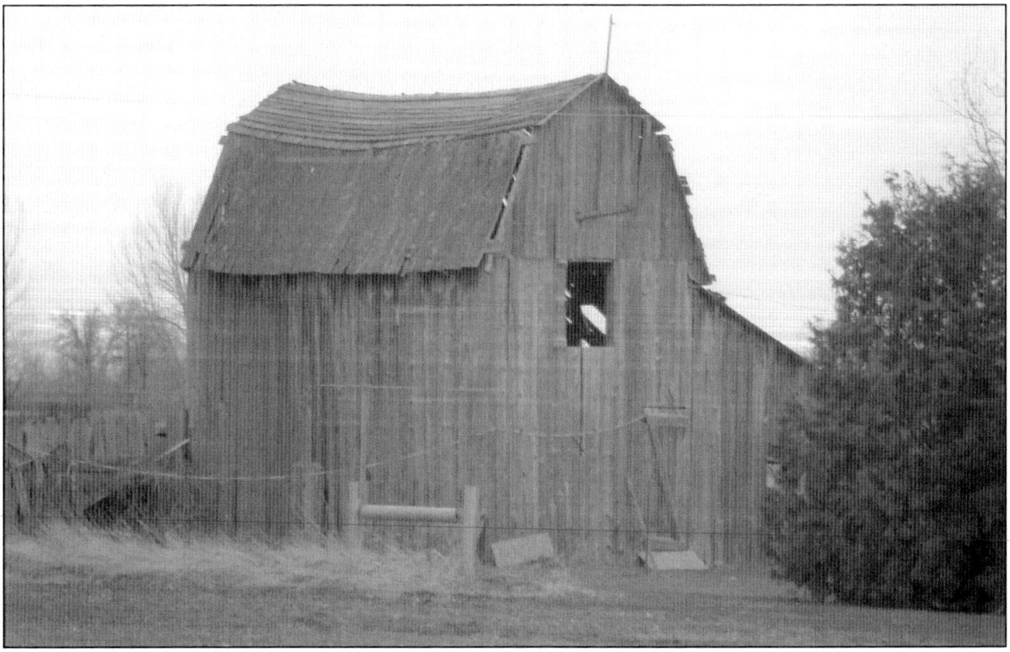

Three

THEY CAME FOR GOLD

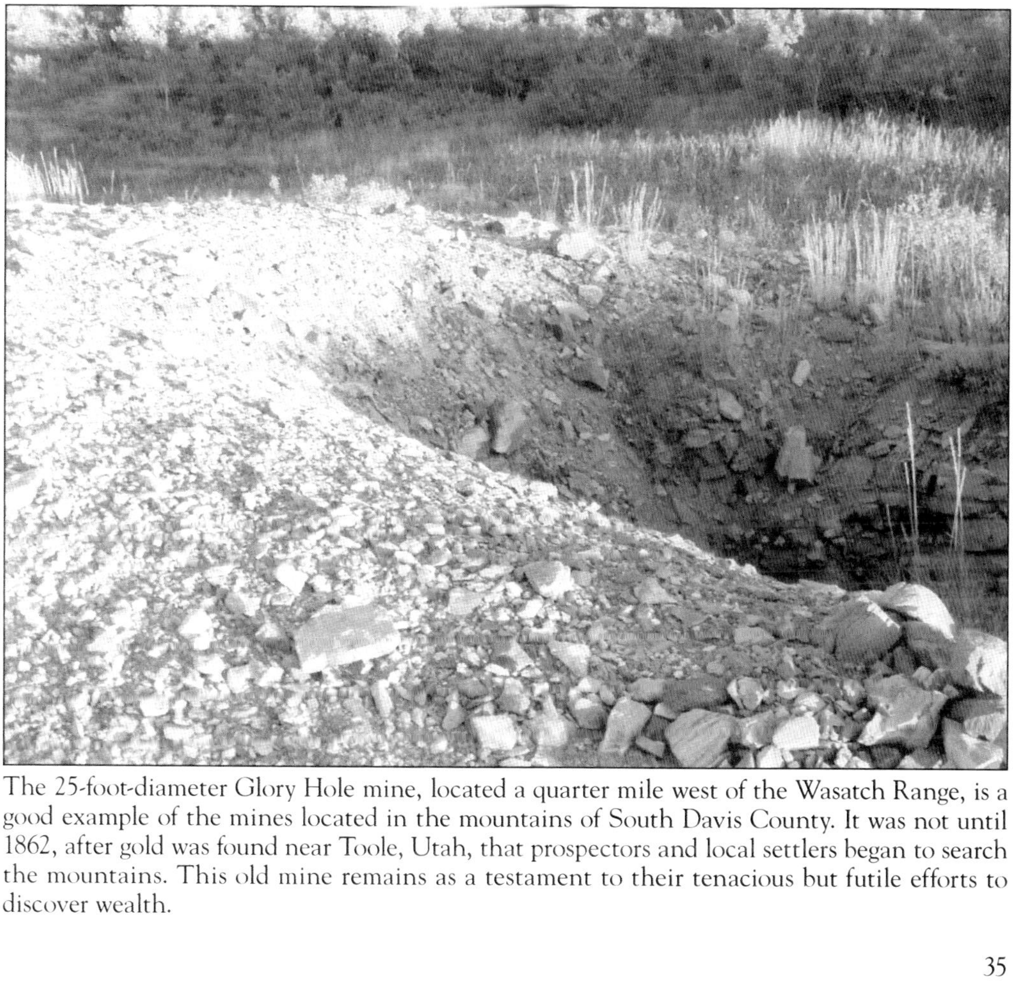

The 25-foot-diameter Glory Hole mine, located a quarter mile west of the Wasatch Range, is a good example of the mines located in the mountains of South Davis County. It was not until 1862, after gold was found near Toole, Utah, that prospectors and local settlers began to search the mountains. This old mine remains as a testament to their tenacious but futile efforts to discover wealth.

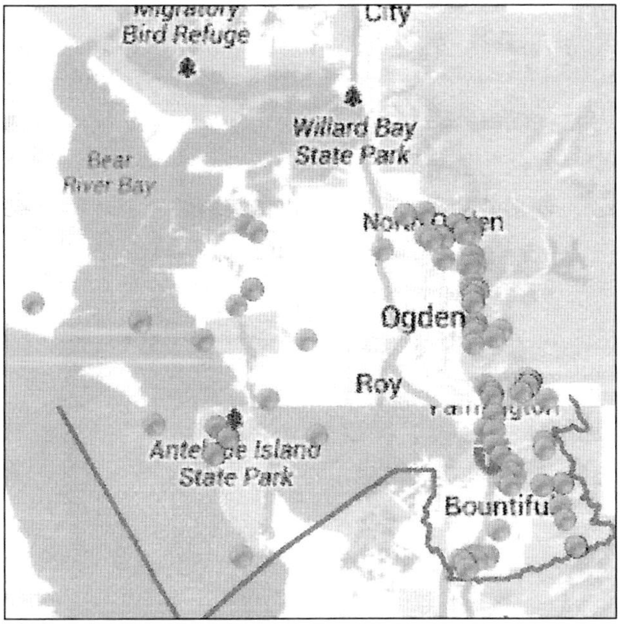

This map shows the mines recorded for South Davis County. Most of the mine sites shown here are sand and gravel pits along the foothills. North Salt Lake had 13, Bountiful had 23, Centerville had 12, Farmington had 12, and Kaysville had 11. In addition, one of the richest copper mines in Utah history was discovered in the 1880s on Antelope Island. After being mined, it was quickly closed. (Courtesy www.usmining.com.)

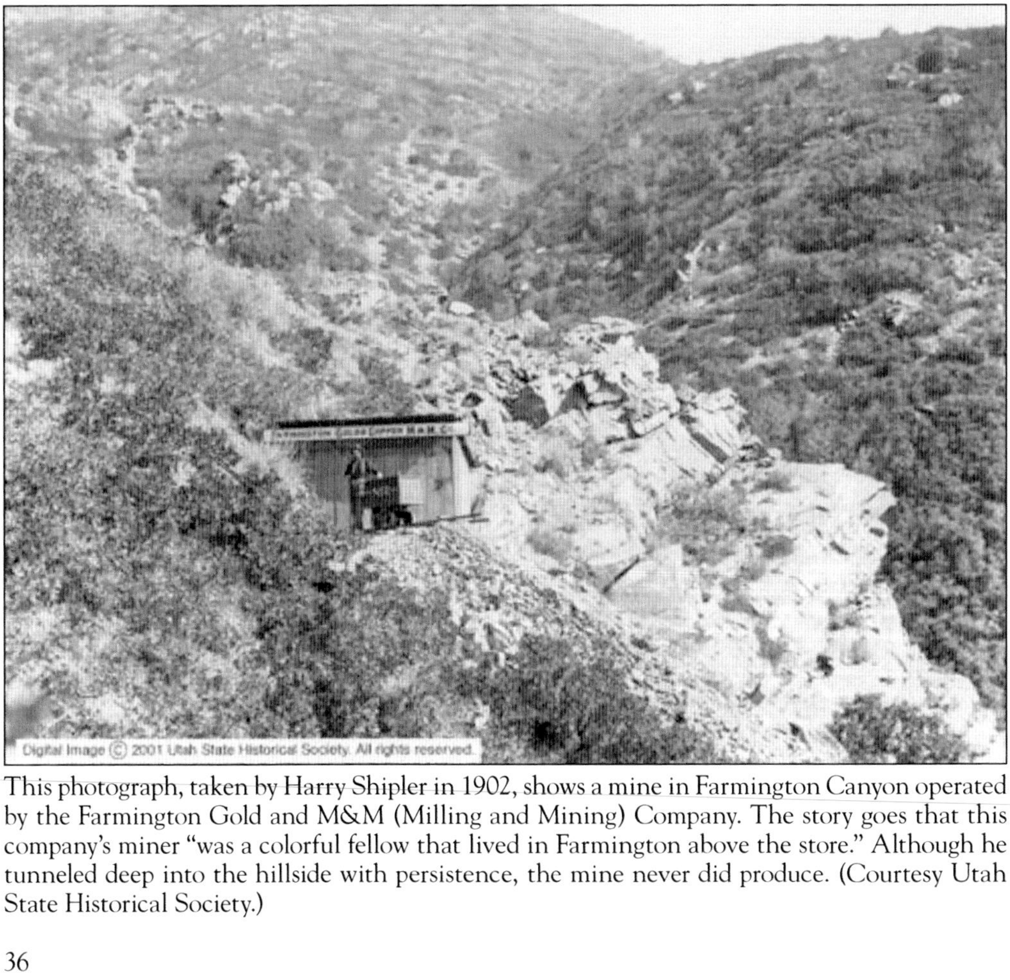

This photograph, taken by Harry Shipler in 1902, shows a mine in Farmington Canyon operated by the Farmington Gold and M&M (Milling and Mining) Company. The story goes that this company's miner "was a colorful fellow that lived in Farmington above the store." Although he tunneled deep into the hillside with persistence, the mine never did produce. (Courtesy Utah State Historical Society.)

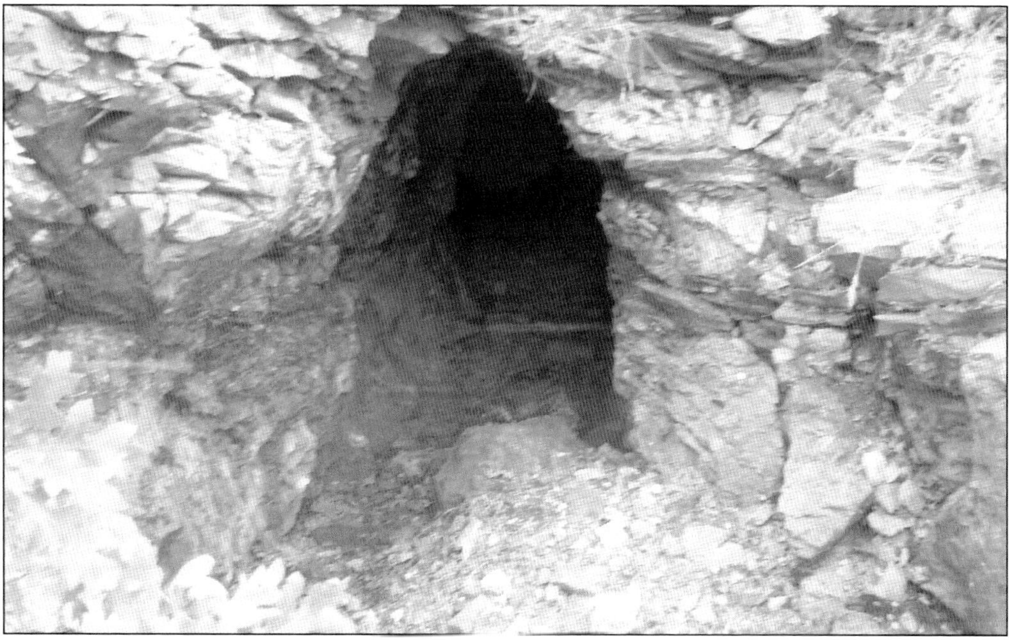

These photographs show examples of South Davis County mines that were dug into the mountains by hand or by using explosives in the 1890s. The tailings piles below each mine and the solid walls exposed inside indicate the huge effort required to carve away a rock face, reducing it to small fragments a few inches across as workers pursued a vein. A cobweb vein of silver and zinc remains exposed at the back of the mine shown above. These abandoned mines remain open for exploration by later generations. Great efforts were expended in the hopes of riches, but such expectations were dashed and lost.

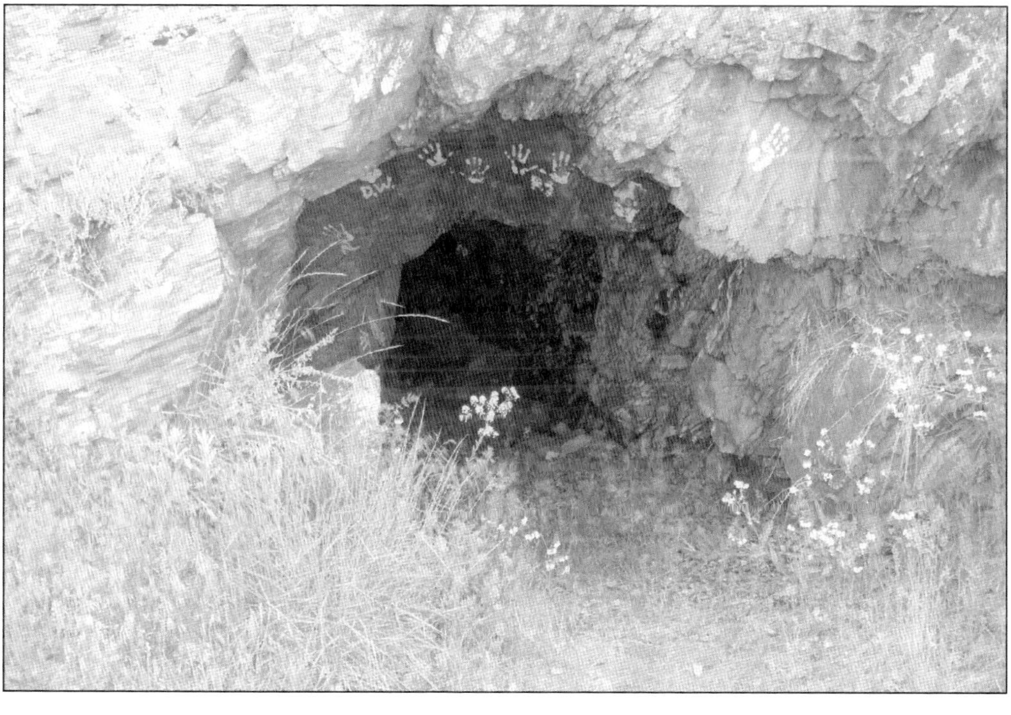

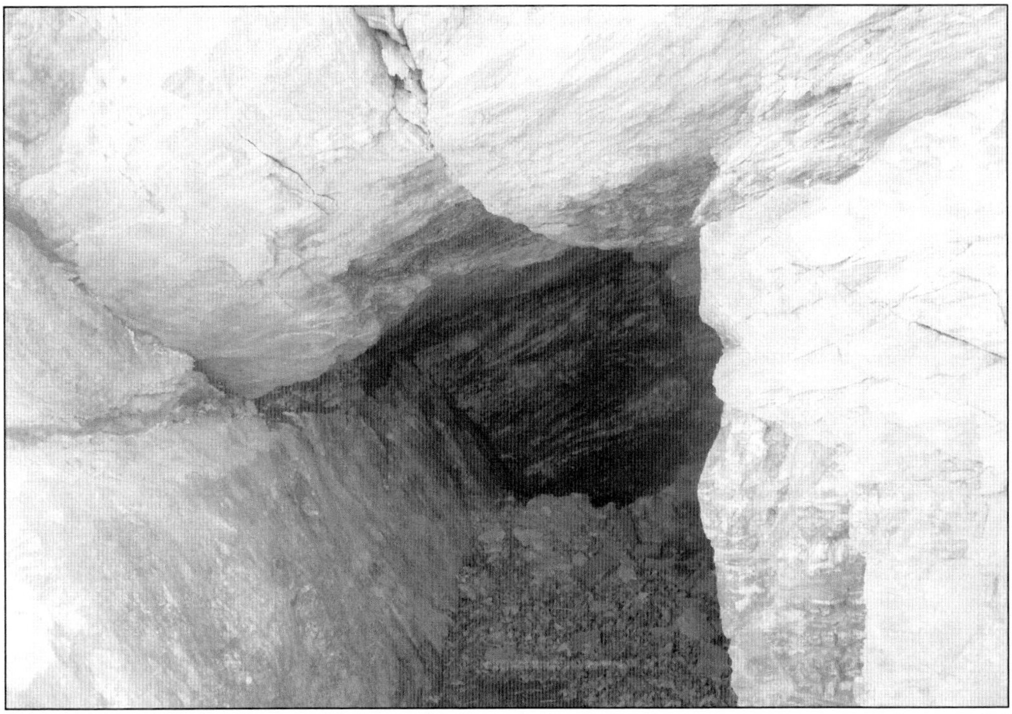

The mine shown above, high on the south slopes of Hogs Back Mountain, was carved into solid granite. Access to the mine is by a sloping face over a six-percent grade—too steep even for horses. This mine was excavated over 40 feet horizontally into the mountain, perhaps with burros and materials lowered down the mountain from above. The back of the mine shows a vertical vein of lead and silver, never expanding in width. The mine remains open, but it is a difficult climb to the entrance. Evidence of the challenges of producing a mine is shown in the excerpts from the *Davis County Clipper* below. The Bucky and Burro mines, accessed from Bountiful, consumed 23 years of efforts before they were finally abandoned.

DAVIS COUNTY CLIPPER reports:

Spring 1896 "*A.L. Buckland filed a claim in Parrish Canyon—copper and silver.*"
August 1902 "*....proving lead, silver and copper on the Morgan side.*"
October 1902 "*500 feet into the Rising Sun prospect tunnel. They hope to intersect the vein in another 25 feet.*"
December 1902 "*Mr. Hilbert went to his mine ....too provisions...*"
February 1903 "*Snow is so deep we can't reach the Buckland Mine.*"
April 1903 "*..... Within 40 feet of the Rising Sun vein.*"
September 1903 "*Alondas and Ross Buckland going back to the mine this week.*"
Summer 1906 "*Pierre Peugeot is developing his Burrow Mine in Sessions Hollow above Bountiful for lead, silver and gold.*" (A mile tramway, 1200 feet of tunnels, seven miles of road, four steel bridges and eight years later—abandoned.)
Summer 1923 A.L. Buckland, "*unable to prove ore greater than 12%, resolved that the venture was unprofitable and moved to Oregon.*" (23 years and 28 claims later—a water wheel, bunk house, blower system, penstock, and kitchen—all abandoned and eventually washed away by the floods of 1930)

(For a half Century the newspaper had frequent comments concerning the mines, but never a "eureka." These records are available in public domain at the Davis County Clipper Archives.)

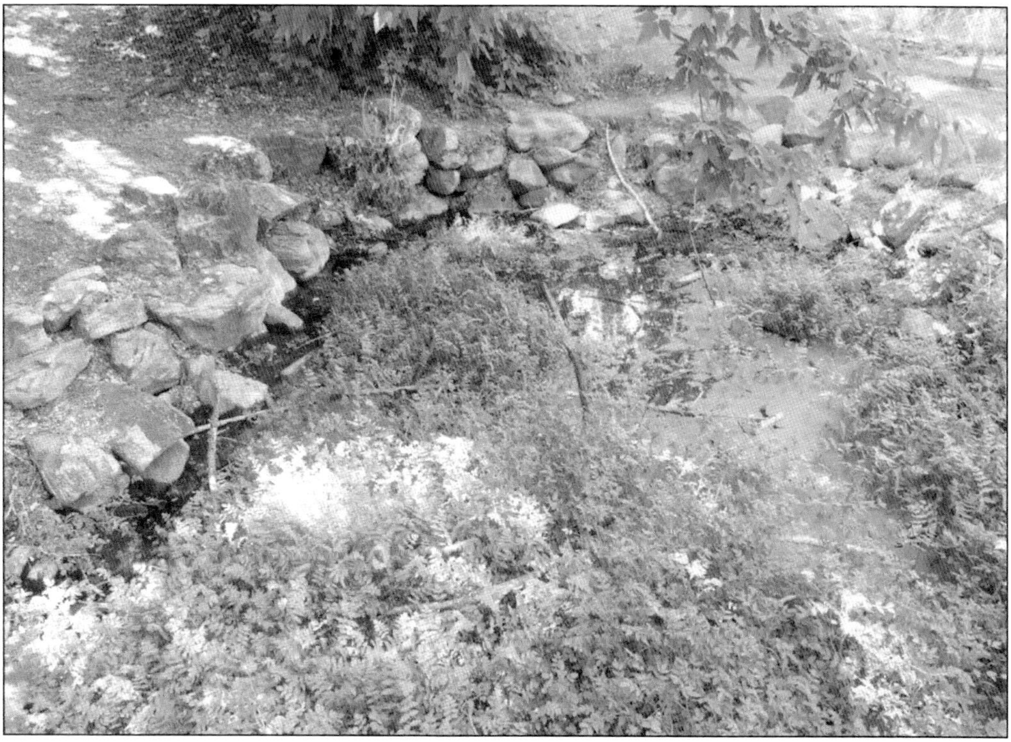

These two prospecting digs on Big Mountain, above Bountiful, are typical of many of the mines claimed through the end of the 1800s. Eastern investors were eager to cash in on the gold and silver strikes, which were making many rich in just a few short years. It was thus common to make a dig, such as those shown here, file a claim, and sell shares to unwary investors. There are hundreds of such dry mines, which probably lined the pockets of bogus prospectors with gold.

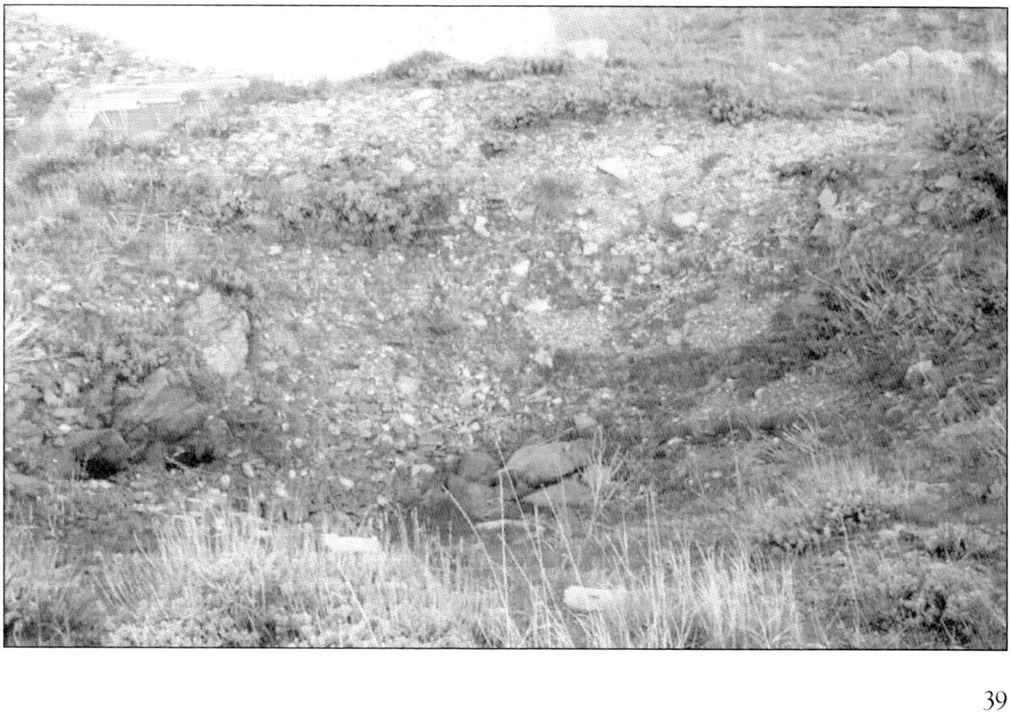

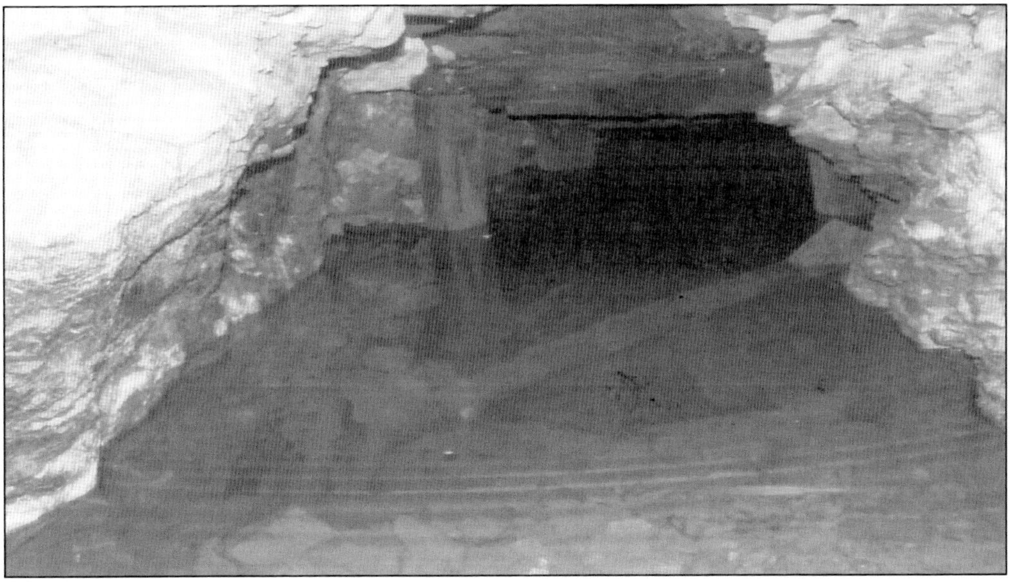

This old mine, on the south slopes of Hogs Back Mountain, dates to around 1880. Dubbed the King mine, it is a good illustration of the condition of many such sites. Looking in from the mouth of the mine, one can still see the shoring of heavy timbers, still present but slowly crumbling. Over time, this mine has filled with water and become a dangerous site to explore.

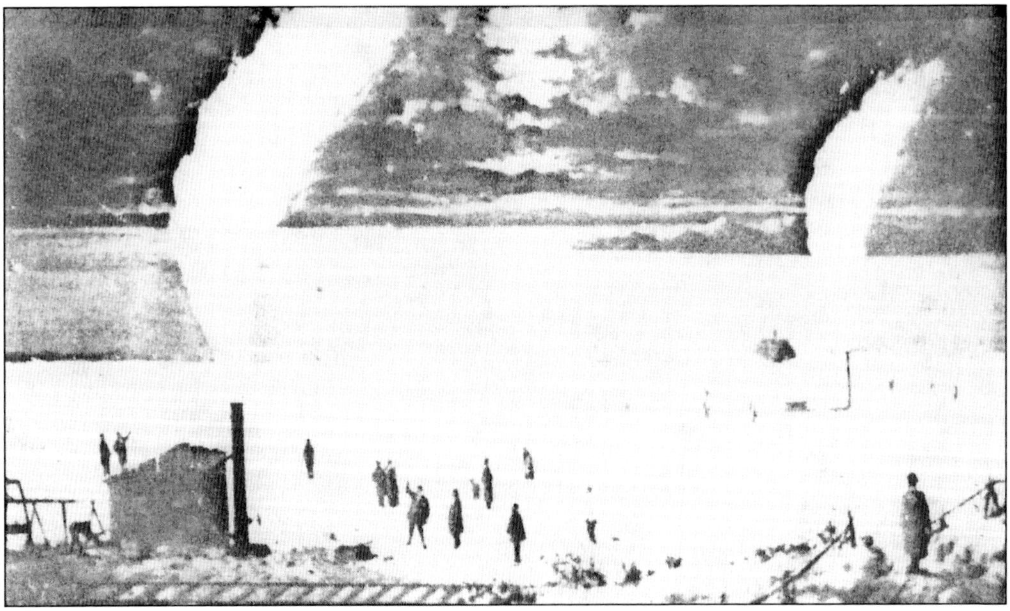

In 1883, while digging an artesian well, George Chase and Ephraim Garn discovered natural gas on the lakeshore near Farmington. The American Gas Company bought the rights 10 years later and, in February 1895, began to provide fuel to Salt Lake City and the Ogden Gas & Electric Company. By 1898, the gas played out and the wells were capped. It had most likely been marsh gas. (Courtesy Utah State Historical Society)

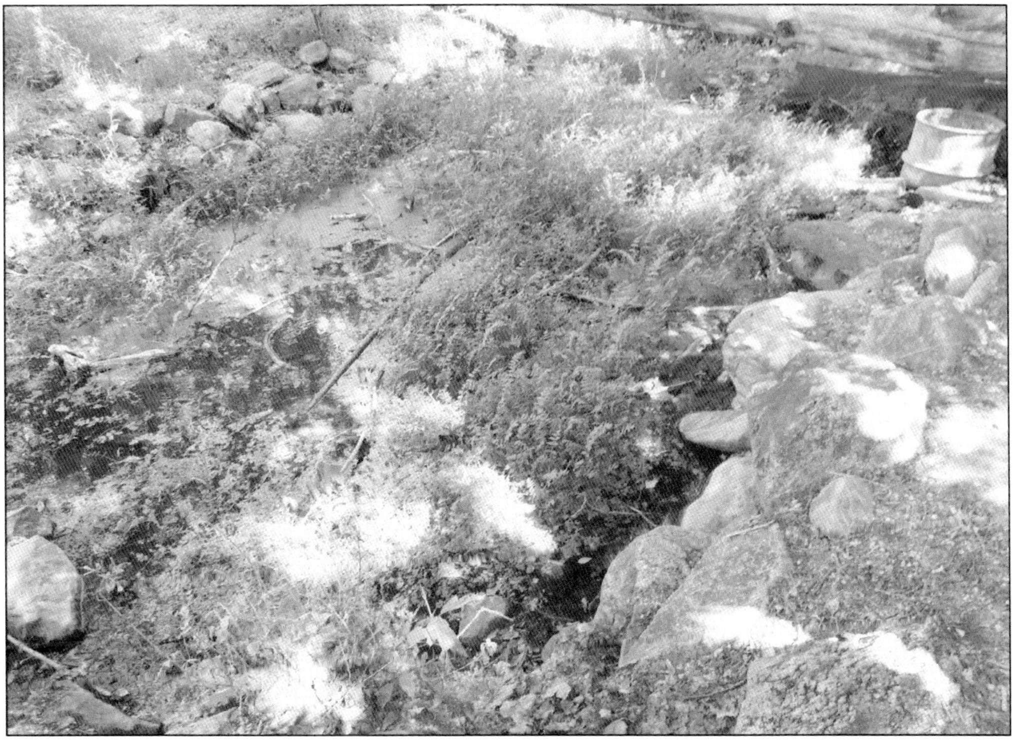

On the face of Hogs Back Mountain, a short distance above Aqueduct Maintenance Road, is an old mine that is still not totally closed. The face of the mountain above the mine has been removed down to solid rock, as seen in the photograph above. The dark space at the bottom of the cut is the opening to the mine, shown in a closer view below. Pursuing a dream of gold and silver, workers mined directly into the mountain. Little mineral value was found, but the water in small flows seeped into the mine. The focus then turned to discovering a new source of water for irrigation—but that, too, never panned out.

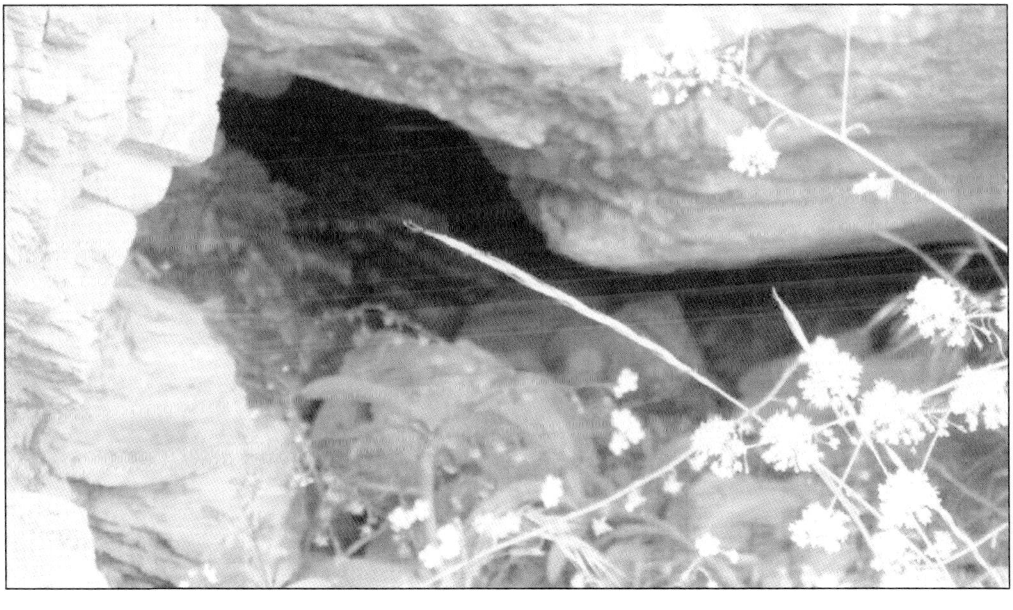

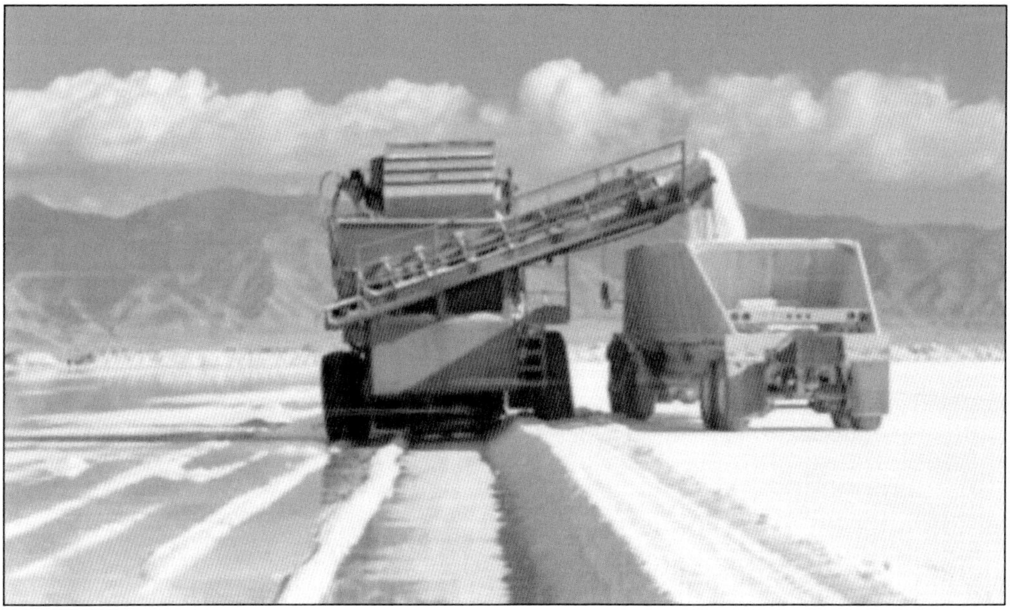

An important mineral found in South Davis County is salt from the lake. Explorers John C. Fremont and Kit Carson reached this area in 1843. Fremont recorded, "We boiled down five gallons of lake water to yield fourteen pints of very fine clean salt." The salt operations have moved to the south side of the lake, where Morton Salt Company and others produce clean table salt. (Courtesy Morton Salt Company.)

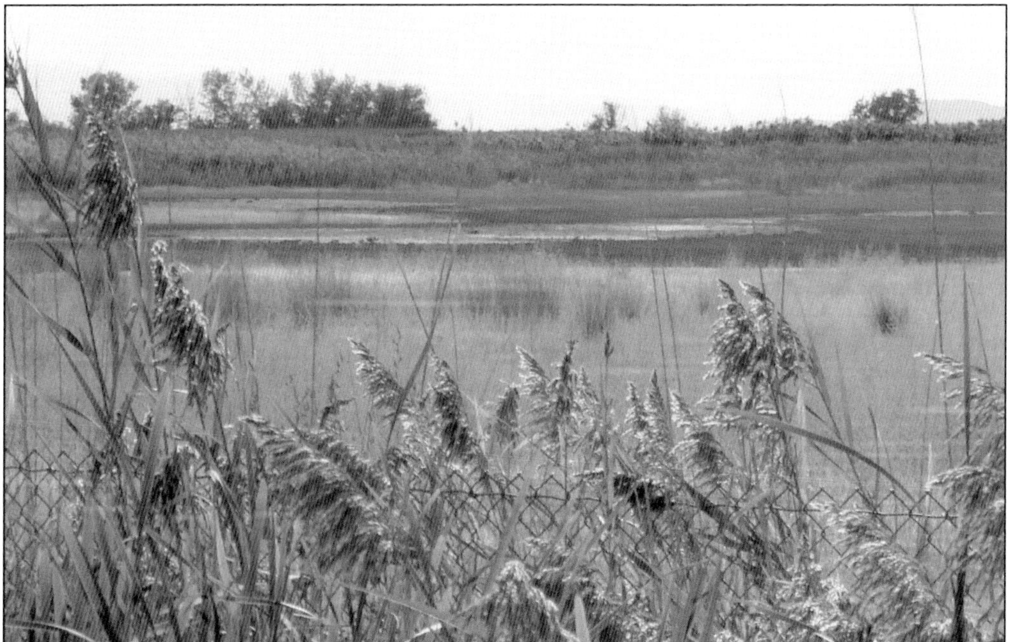

Dikes were built to allow the eastern portion of Farmington Bay to retain freshwater. Organized under the State Division of Wildlife Resources, a protected area of 18,000 acres of marshland is now managed for the nesting and protection of waterfowl. Over 200 species of birds have been identified along the shorelines and on the lake.

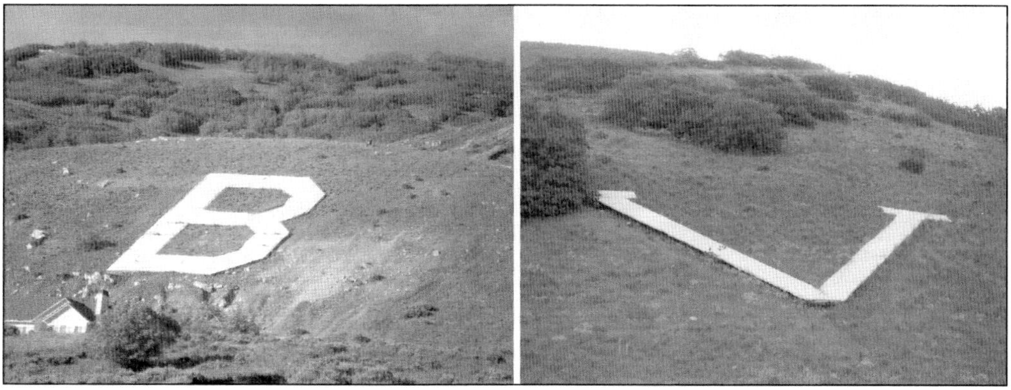

In the 1970s, Viewmont and Bountiful High Schools placed these markers high on the western mountainside. They are visible from anywhere in the valley and to travelers on Interstate 15, which extends the full length of South Davis County. Whether the large letters represent the school names or the mascots—the Vikings and Braves—does not seem to matter.

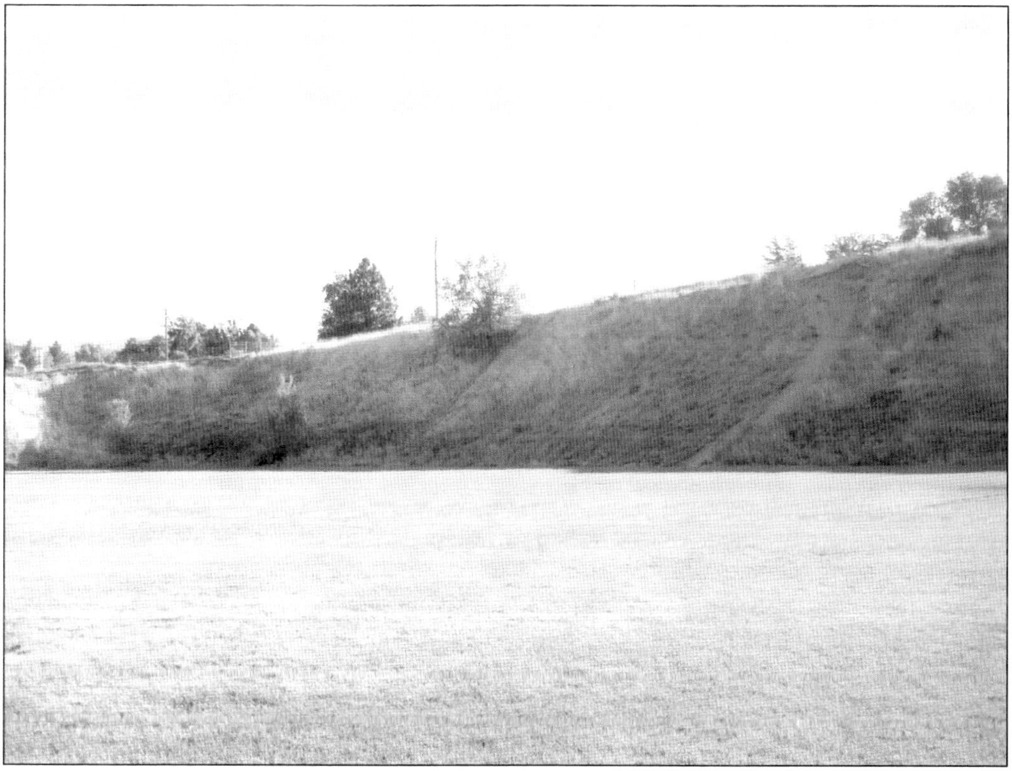

The Foss Lewis Construction Company, founded in 1938 by Foss Sessions and Irene Denning Lewis, was a well-known sand and gravel quarry. It operated for 62 years, filling crossings on Davis Boulevard, building roads, and selling aggregates. Overtaken by residential growth, the quarry site is now a beautiful city park at 2575 South Davis Boulevard in Bountiful. It was one of 41 sand and gravel mines opened in South Davis County.

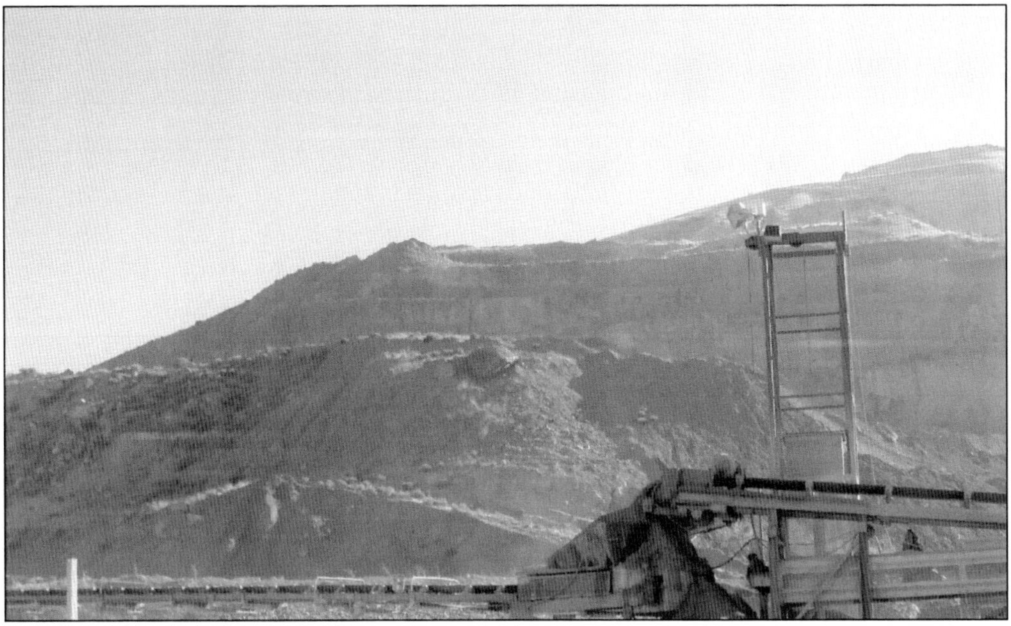

The largest quarry operation in the valley is located at 1810 North Beck Street. Now operated by J.B. Parsons and Staker Paving and Excavation, the facilities have mined away the entire west end of a mountain. Freeway and road construction has depended heavily on this quarry to obtain sufficient aggregate to build bridges, overpasses, and on-ramps, and to raise the highway to avoid drainage or flooding problems. In preparation for the 2002 Winter Olympics, a major construction effort involved widening and building new freeways. A city rail system was constructed to carry people from the downtown venues to the University of Utah stadium and the Olympic Village. A steady stream of trucks hauled material from this Beck Street quarry to lay the road base, provide concrete, and produce asphalt paving.

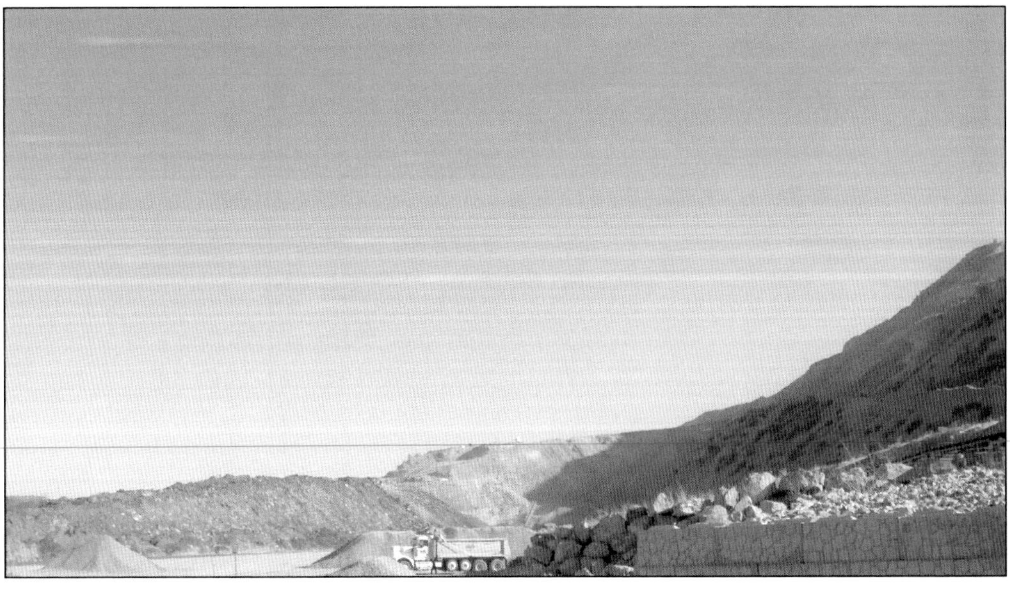

Four

Main Street and Merchants

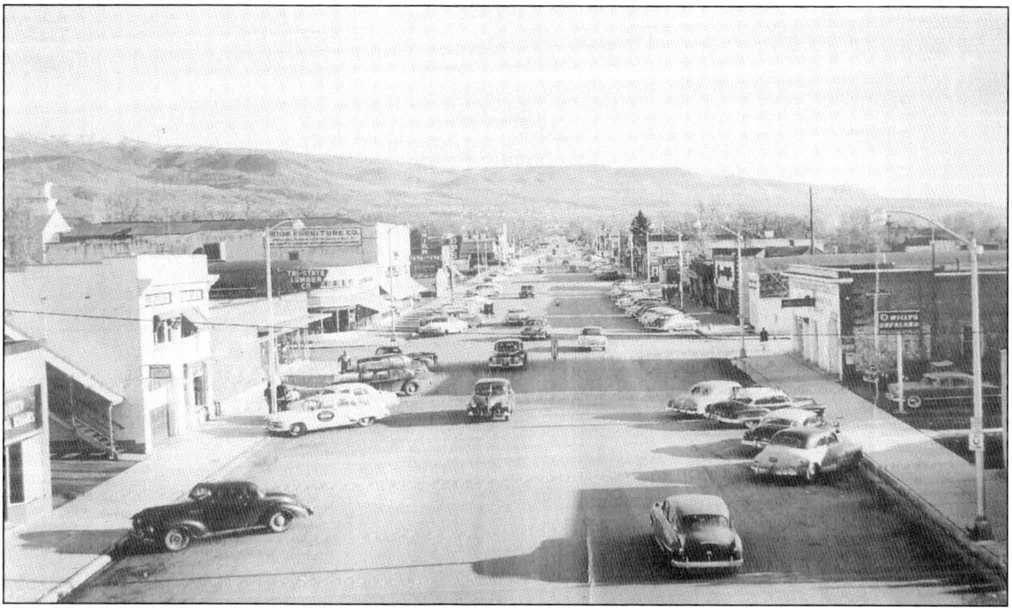

A century after the first pioneer settlers arrived in South Davis County, there were four main commercial settlements: Bountiful, on the south; Centerville, a few miles north; Farmington, which became the county seat; and Kaysville, which was originally an extension of the grazing areas of Farmington. This photograph looks south down Main Street in Bountiful around 1948. (Courtesy Bountiful History Museum.)

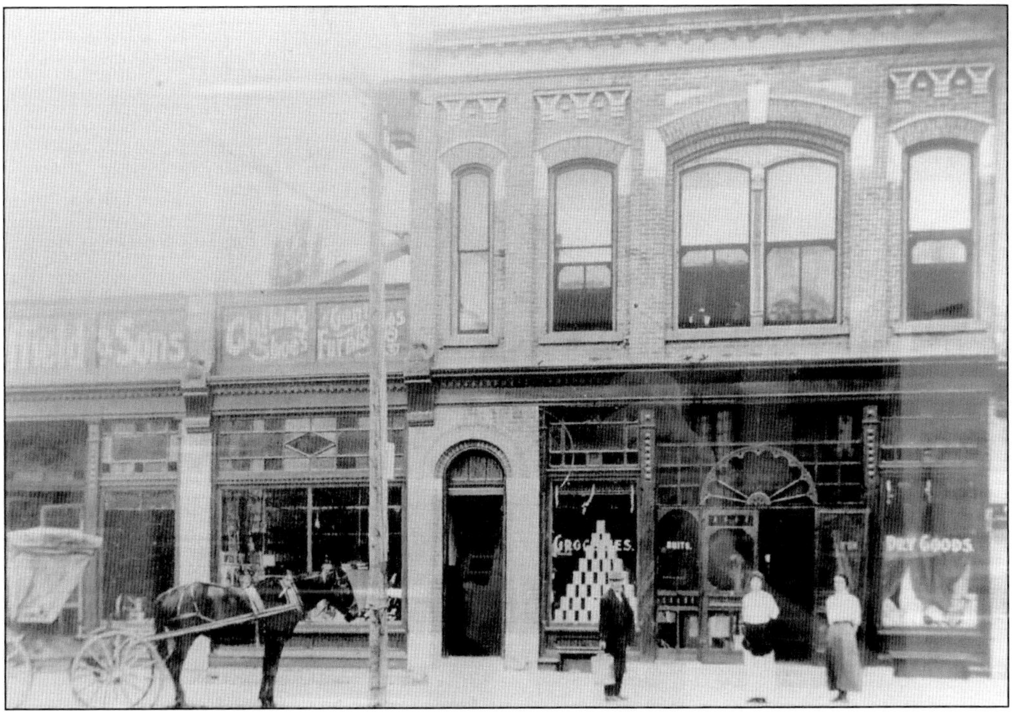

The settlers along North Cottonwood Creek were divided into two wards of the Mormon Church in 1851. The south ward became known as Farmington, and the northern portion became Kaysville. The photograph above, taken around 1890, shows Main Street in Farmington and Schoffield & Sons Mercantile. This store carried a large variety of household goods, grocery items, clothes, and hardware, all under one roof. Whether a shopper was looking for a bucket of paint or a new pair of overalls, it could be found at the mercantile. The photograph below, looking north along Main Street in Kaysville around 1922, shows similar commercial services. (Above, courtesy Farmington Historical Museum; below, courtesy Kaysville City Records.)

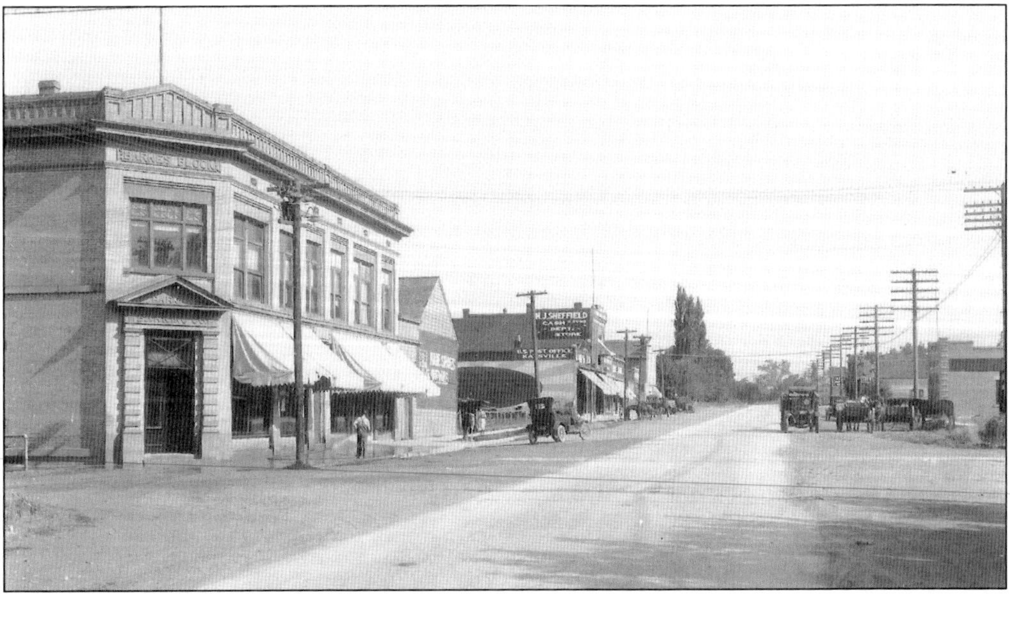

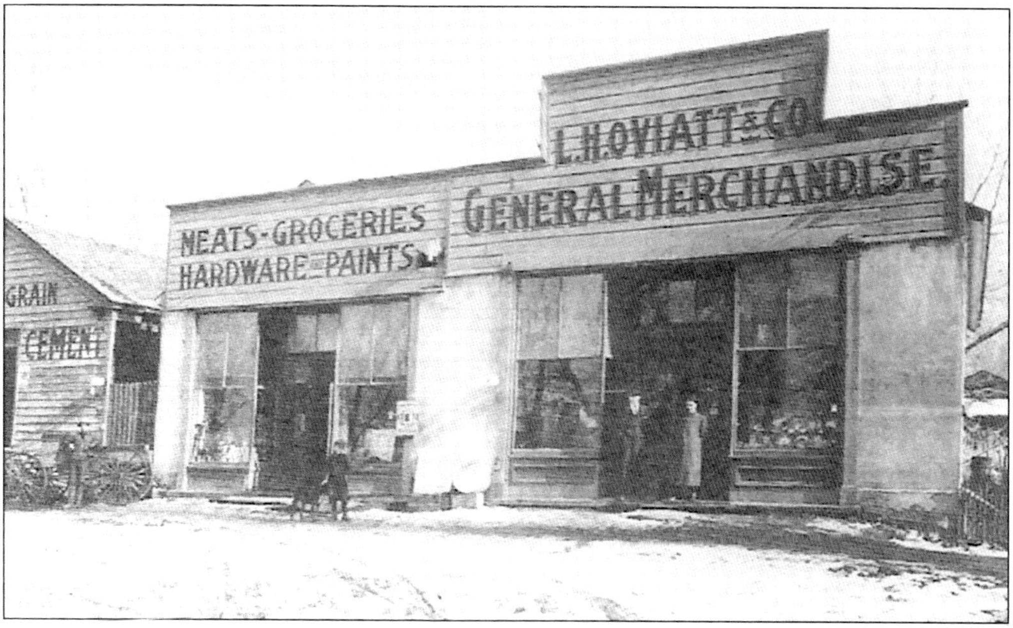

Vital to Main Street and community development was the general store. The L.H. Oviatt & Co. store (above) was located in Farmington in the 1860s. Similarly, the Co-op Store in Centerville (below), built around 1865, was central to the community. The general store became the exchange center for butter, eggs, cheese, garden vegetables, and fruit. One early journal records children receiving two eggs each from their mother to exchange for a candy stick at the store. It was also a place to catch up on local news. Each store provided a space where one could post a notice of events or a change in church meeting schedules. (Above, courtesy Bountiful History Museum; below, courtesy John Hollingshead Jr.)

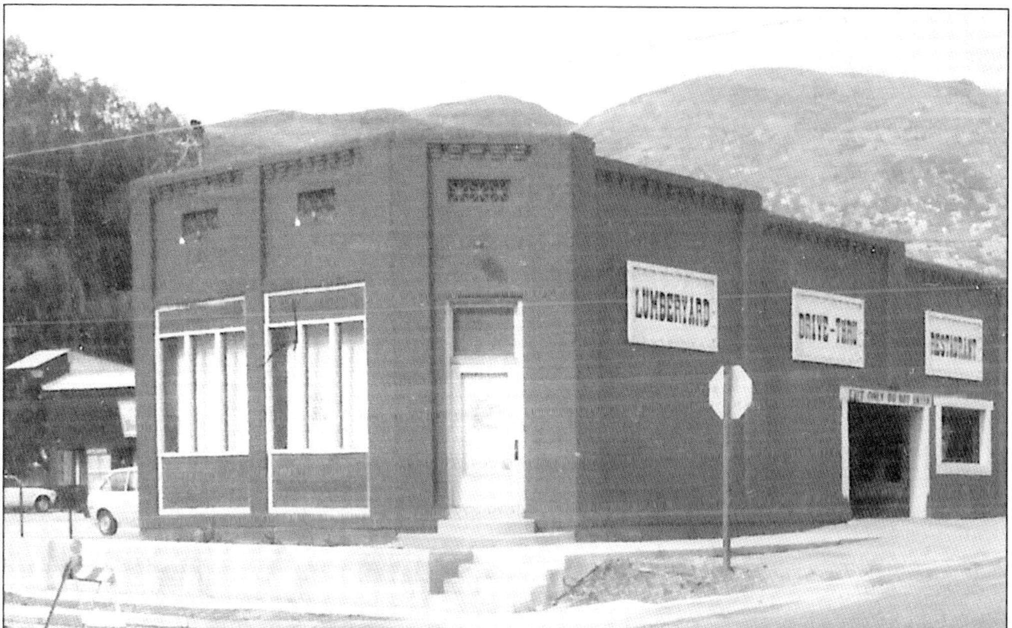

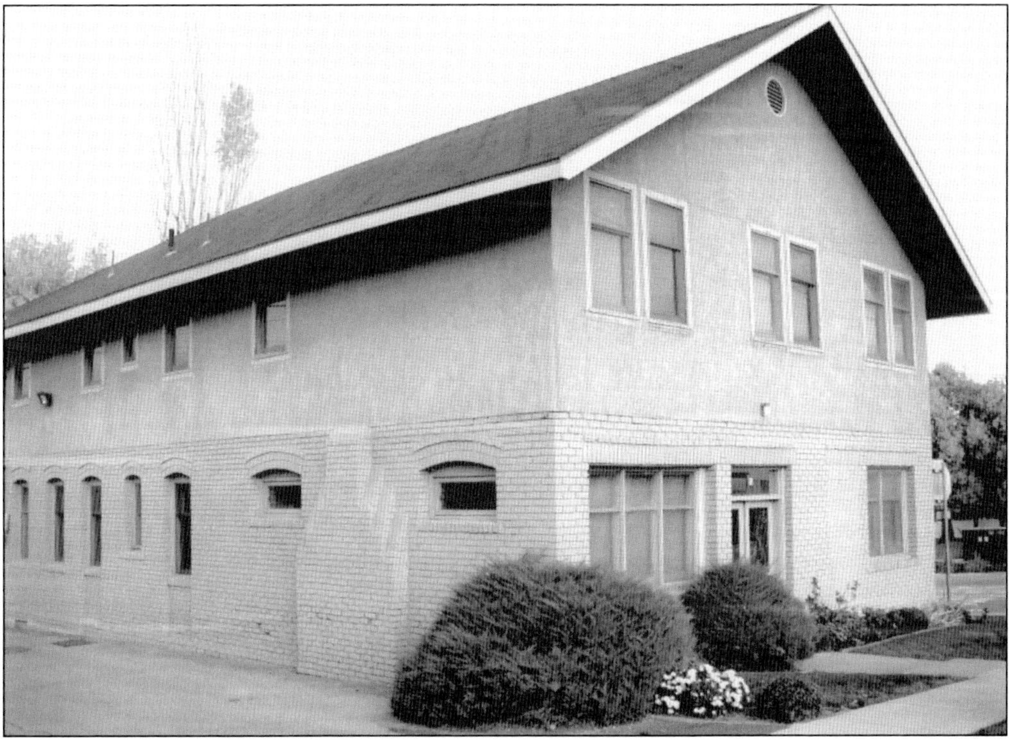

The St. Joseph Roadhouse, on the corner of Main and Center Streets in North Salt Lake, was constructed in 1917. It was originally used to house workers of the Bonneville Irrigation System. Here, they could get a good meal, a shower, and a bed for the night. It was later purchased by S.L. Union Stock Yards as a hotel for businessmen and cattlemen. It is now used as an apartment building.

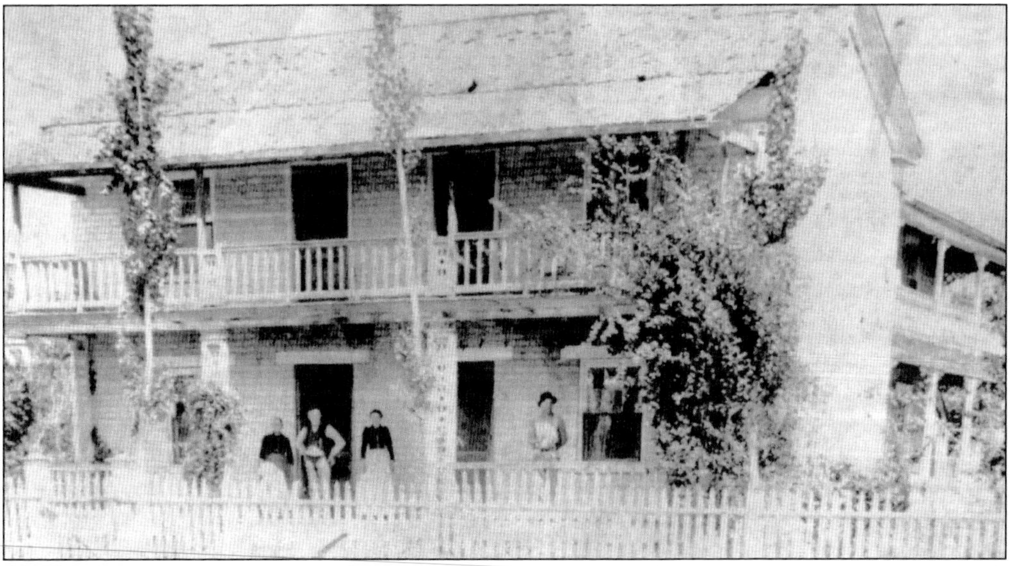

The Haight Hotel in Farmington, built around 1869, was one of the first stopover sites between Salt Lake and Cache Valley and even into southern Idaho. Travelers could rent a room, receive a meal, make repairs if needed, and have their horses watered, fed, and stabled. For a lower fee, a traveler could elect to park his wagon and sleep next to it. (Courtesy Farmington Historical Museum.)

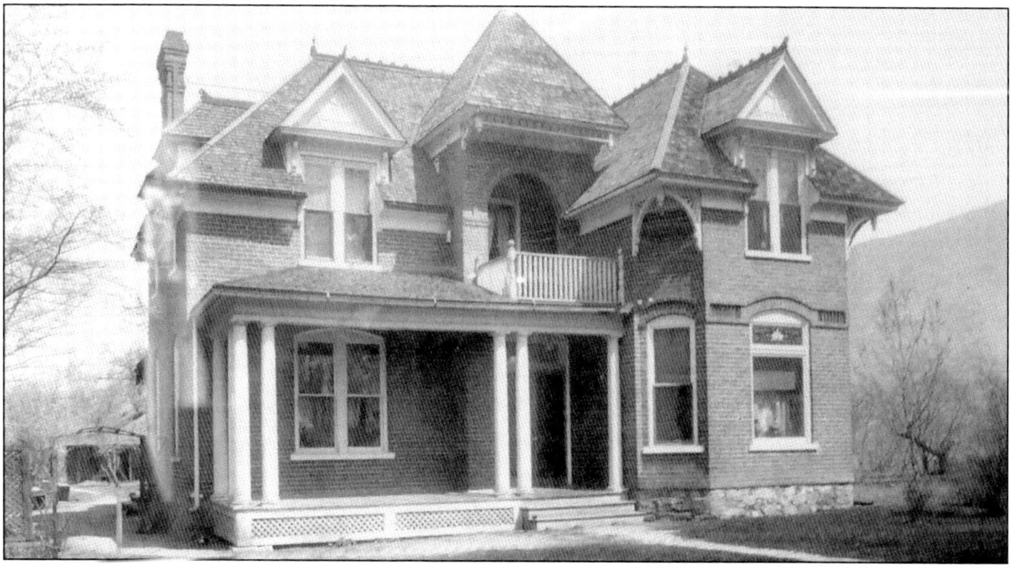

The Joseph S. Clark home in Farmington, at 340 West State Street, was built in 1912. As the oldest son, Joseph Clark was charged by his father to hold the family together, creating what is often called Clark Lane. The property remained in common for many years, and all of the family shared in the work and benefits. This residence is an example of the early mansion-style homes.

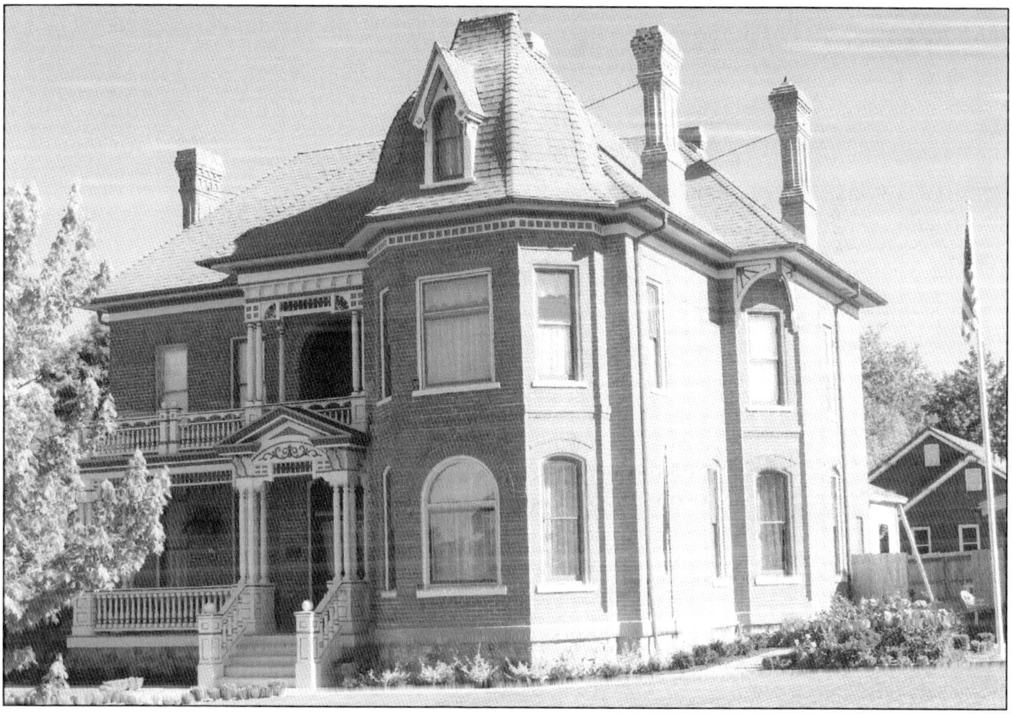

The brick George Moroni Barnes home in Kaysville, constructed around 1884, is an excellent example of Victorian architecture. Designed by William Allen, it stands as a monument to its original owner. Barnes, born on March 6, 1860, became a leading businessman, founding the first bank in Kaysville, Barnes Bank. It is located at the southwest corner of 100 West and Center Street.

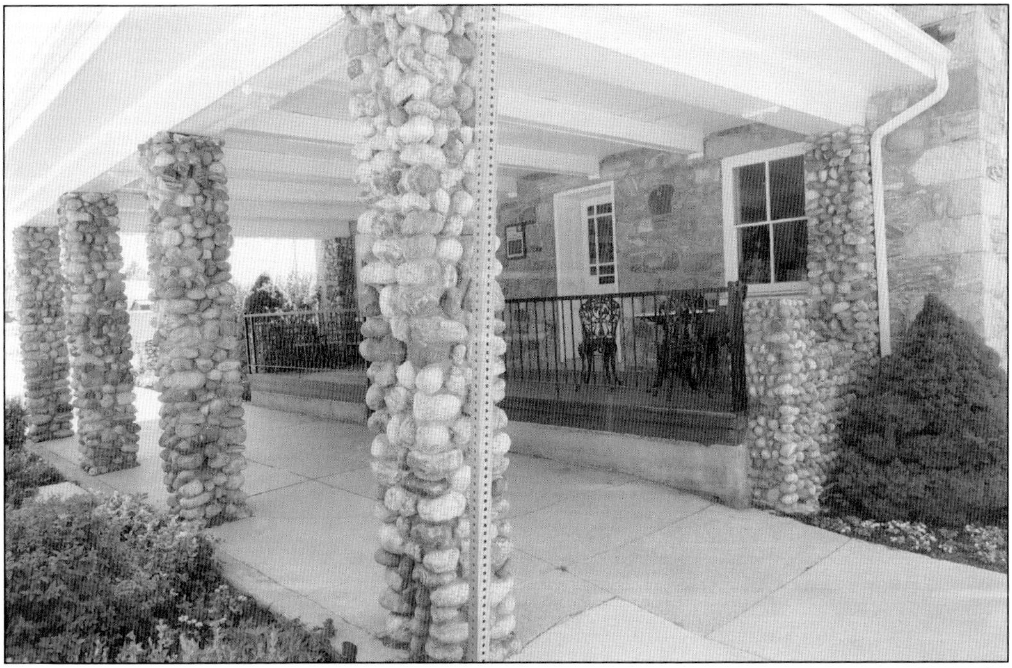

The Rock Hotel in Farmington, at 100 East State Street, was built around 1860 as a private home for Thomas and Elesta Hunt. Upon their death, it was converted to a hotel. The porches on the north and east were added in the early 1900s. Hyrum Van Fleet purchased the hotel in 1908. After a major fire, it was renovated and doubled in size. It was referred to as the "Honeymoon Hotel," because newlyweds could walk 50 yards from the courthouse and spend their honeymoon there.

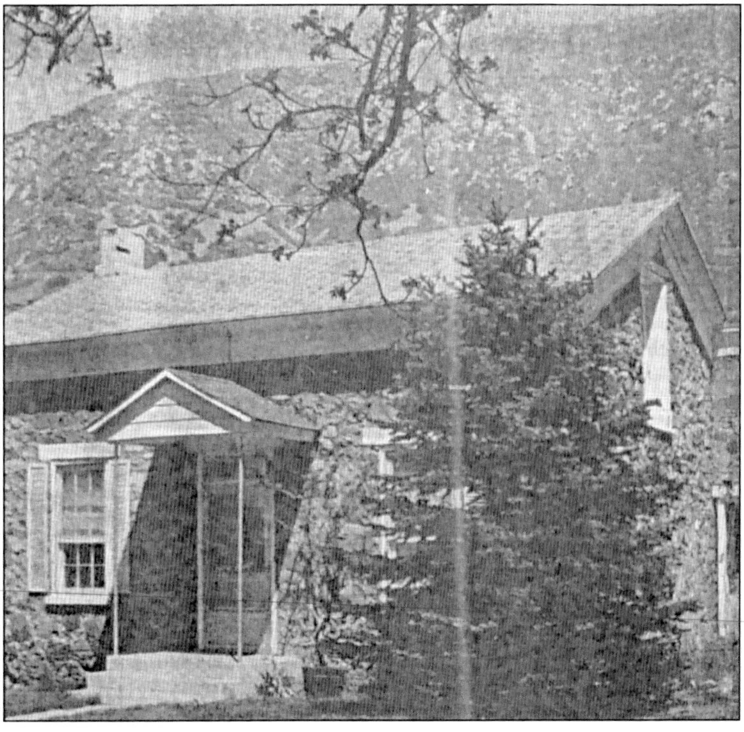

This home at 79 South 100 East in Farmington was built of native rock by Hector Haight in 1872. Haight was the first settler in Farmington. A Mr. McKay later married Sarah Wiseman and occupied the home as a personal residence. He started salt production west of Farmington. Using evaporation ponds, he scooped up the dry salt to sell. (Courtesy Farmington Historical Museum.)

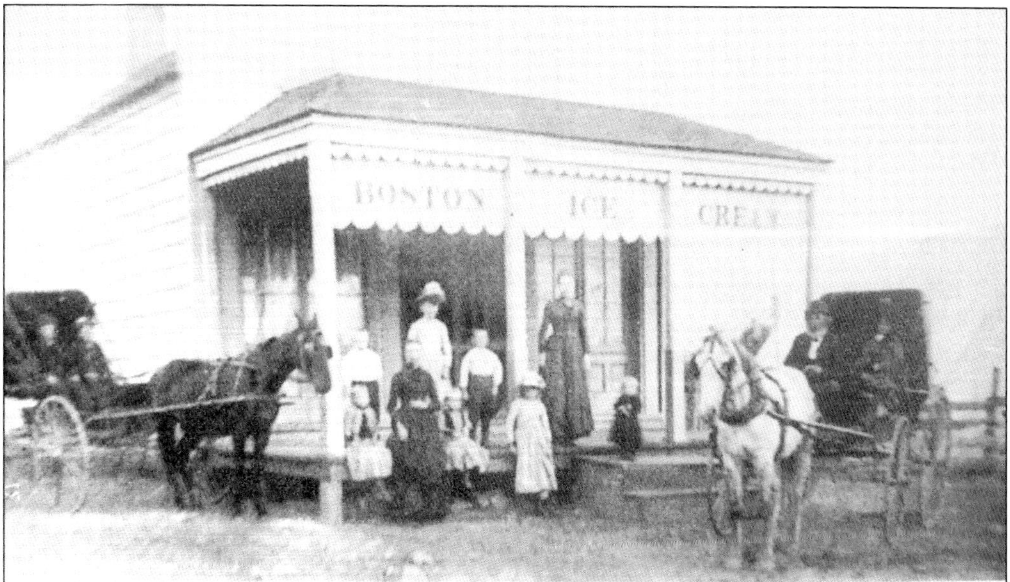

Boston Ice Cream Parlor - 1916
South east corner of 1st north & main street

Originally, this building was the Boston Ice Cream Parlor, operated by Lewis Barton in 1880. It was located at 100 North Main Street in Kaysville. Later, it became Horace Lewis's photography studio and then the Jed Sessions Barber Shop. (Courtesy Kaysville City Records.)

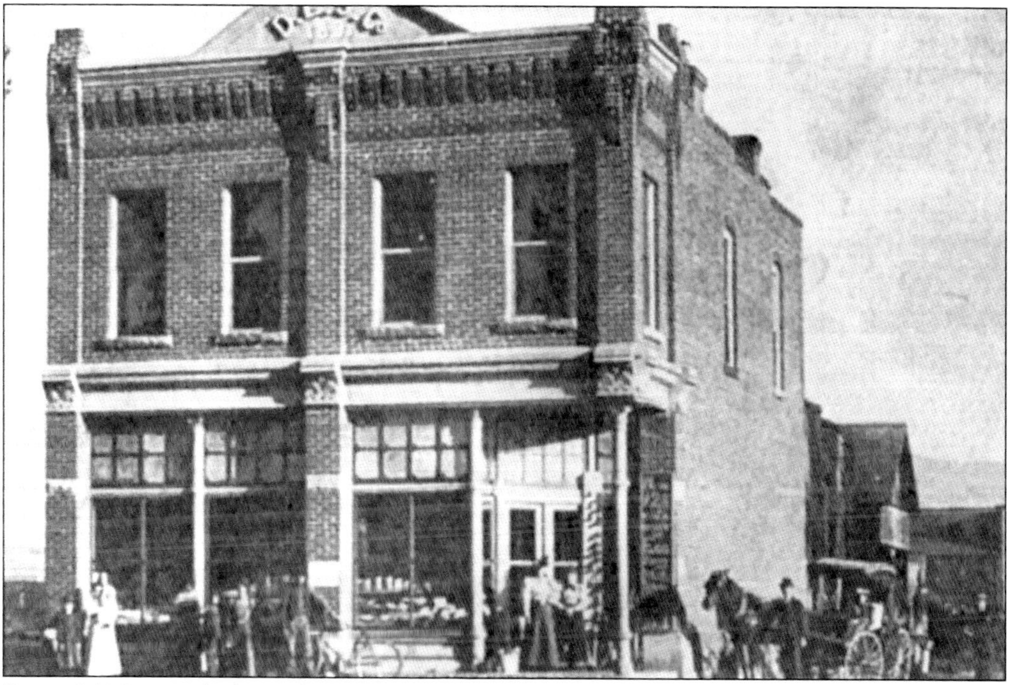

Bountiful Mercantile, located at 800 West and 500 South in Woods Cross, was built by the Deseret Livestock Company as a service for its employees and the residents in the area. It handled general merchandise and was a trade center for locally produced products. The original frame building was replaced with this brick structure in the early 1900s. (Courtesy Bountiful History Museum.)

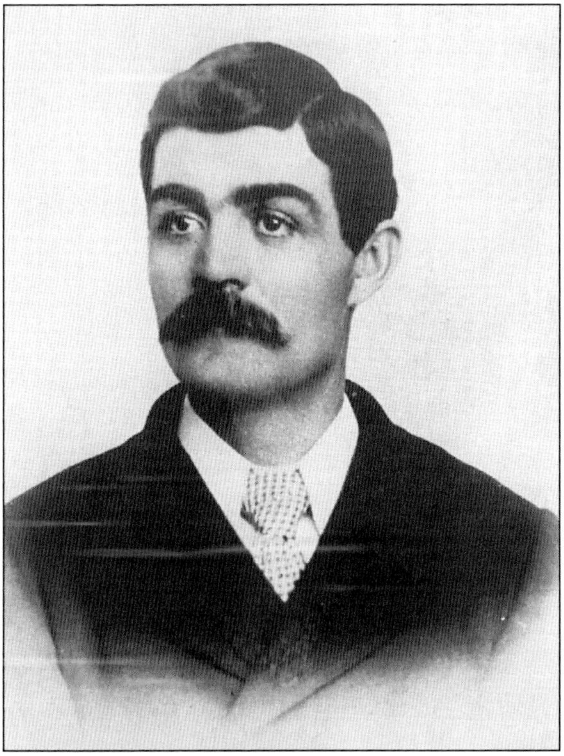

Walter Rampton (left) was born in Bountiful in 1866. He joined the fife-and-drum band, playing the fife. He paid for his lessons with vegetables from the garden. Rampton married May Rosetta Dustin, and they moved to Farmington in January 1890. Having been trained in his father's blacksmith shop, he worked as a blacksmith at various sites in Nevada, California, and on the Lucin Cutoff during construction of the railroad across the Great Salt Lake. In 1908, his wife inherited some land in Farmington, where they built a drugstore. Walter Jr. graduated from pharmacy school, and he and his father worked together in the store (below) until 1919. Walter Sr. (left) was known to the children as Grandpa Rampton. He produced homemade ice cream of various flavors, which he allowed the children to sample. (Both courtesy Farmington Historical Museum.)

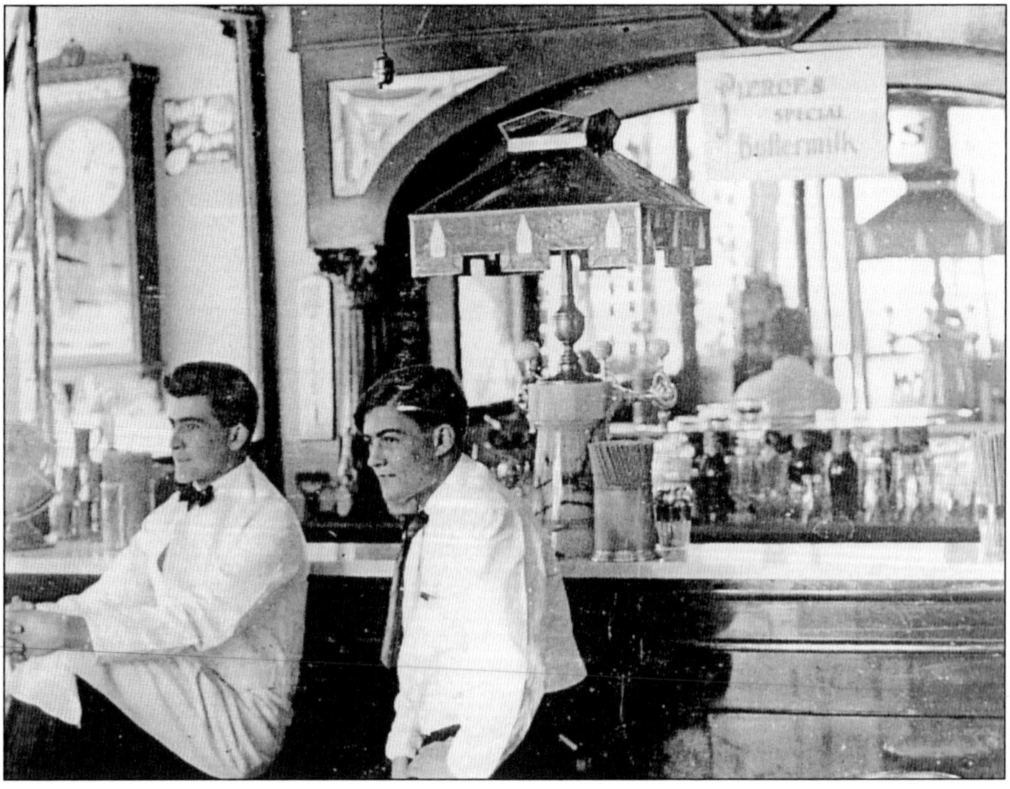

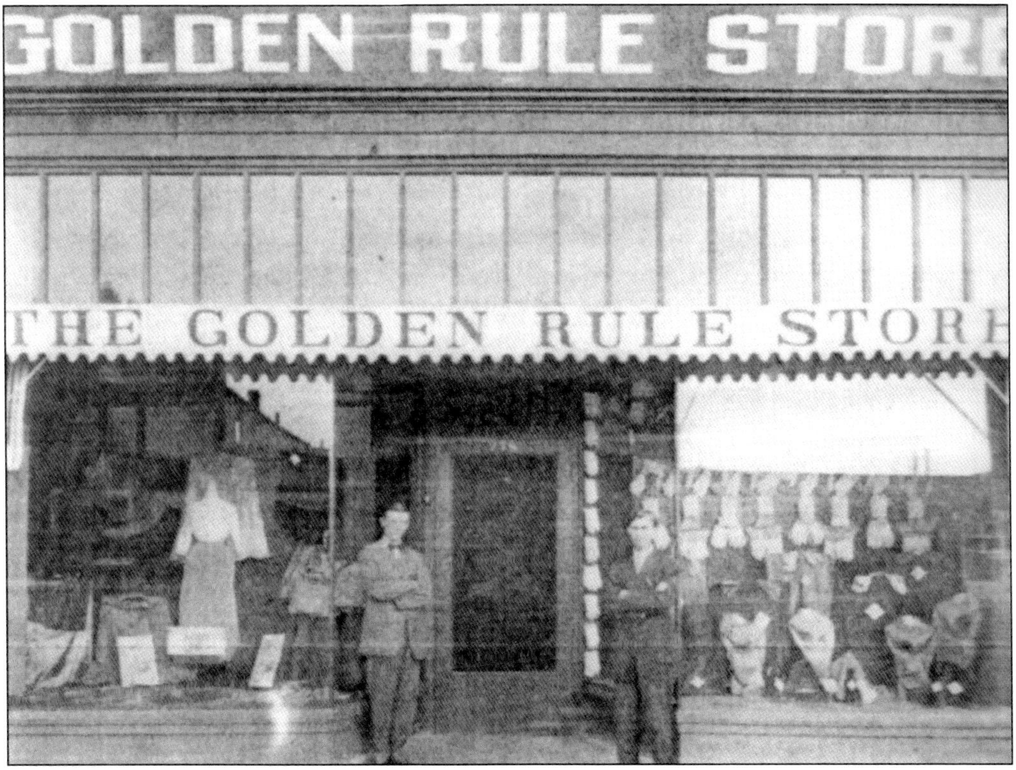

James Cash Penney, 27, opened his first store, the Golden Rule Store, in Kemmerer, Wyoming, in 1902. Finding success, he moved to Utah and opened a second store between 100 and 200 North on Main Street in Bountiful in 1910. (A claim is made that the second store was built in Eureka, Utah.) In less than a year, it moved to the southeast corner of 100 South and Main Street (above). Three years later, the store's name was changed to J.C. Penney Co., after the owner. The rest of the story is well known, as the business grew into a major chain with thousands of retail stores worldwide. The photograph below shows the store after it moved to 145 South Main Street. (Both courtesy Beverly Nowak.)

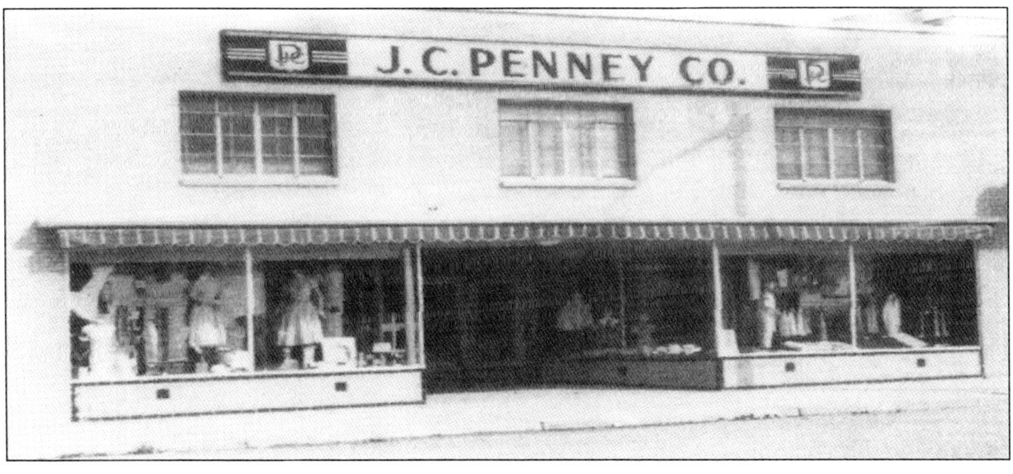

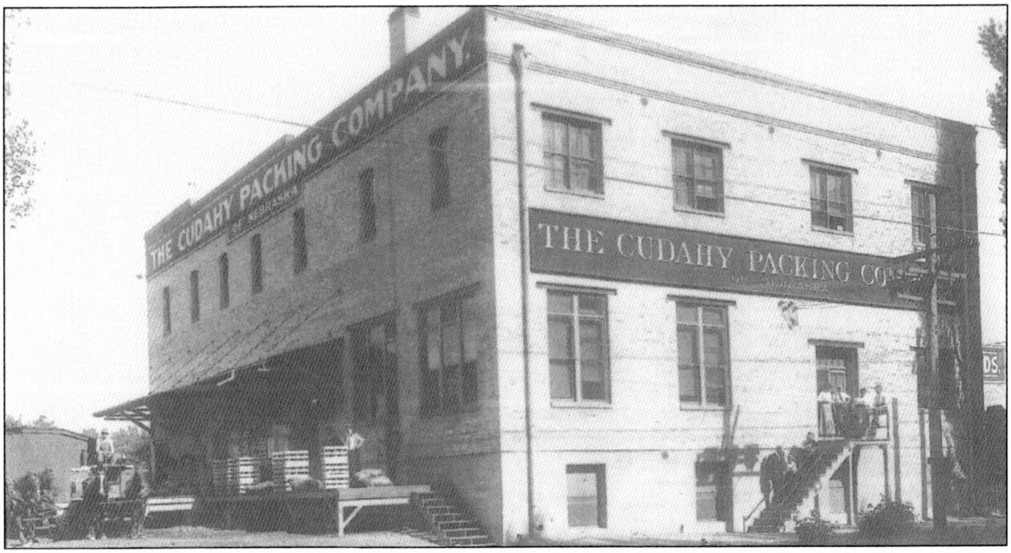

The Cudahy Packing Company was located near the livestock auction yards in North Salt Lake. Originally located farther up the hillside, the new plant (above) was built in 1916 on Center Street, just below the railroad tracks. It was a very successful operation, specializing in sausage and processed meats. Product was shipped all over the country until changing times and techniques caused the plant to shut down in the 1970s. The building has since been torn down, and the surrounding area has been incorporated into the North Salt Lake Industrial Park. The photograph below shows the "Sausage Crew" around 1916, displaying various products created in the plant. (Both courtesy City of North Salt Lake.)

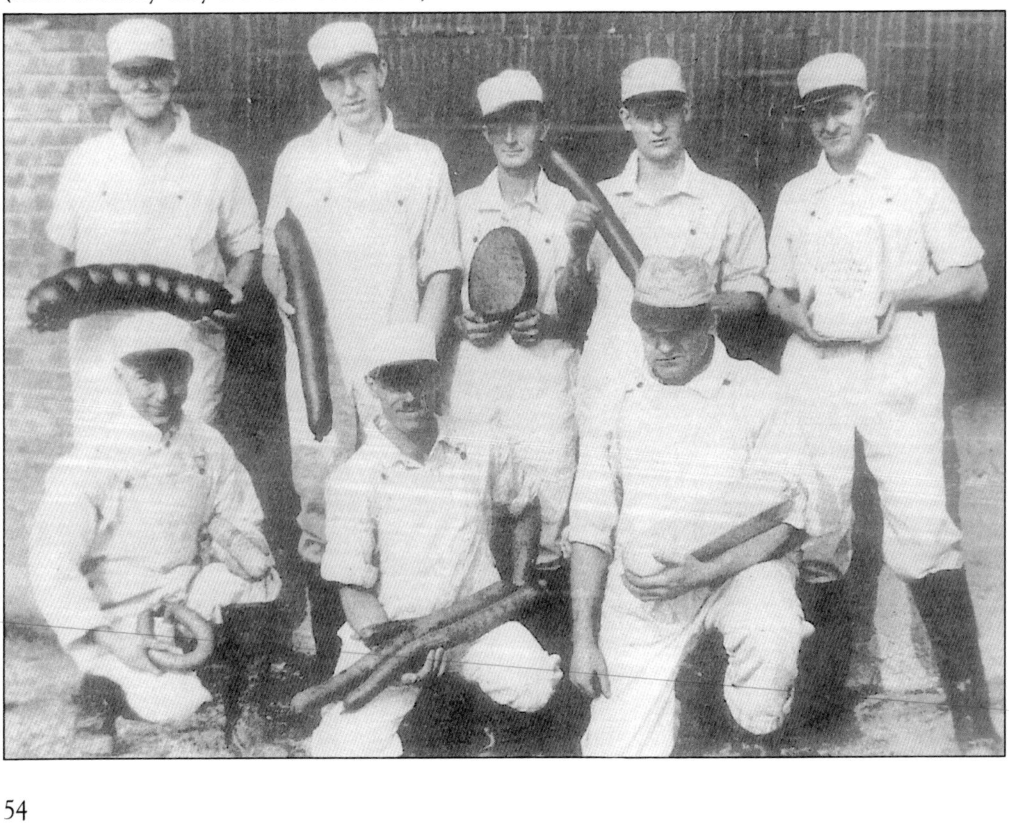

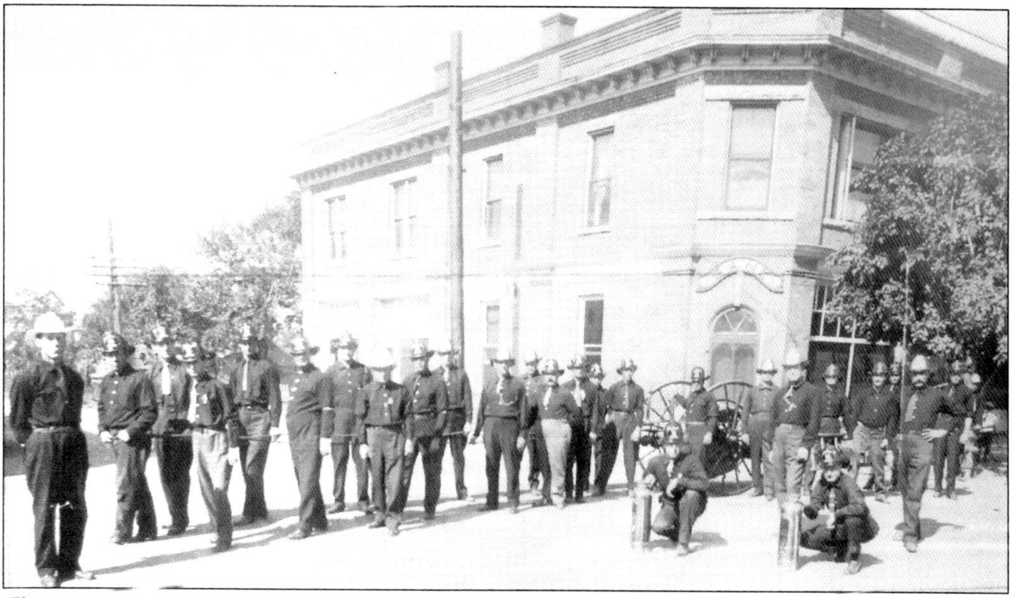

The Bountiful Fire Department shows off its newest equipment. Note the uniforms and hard hats. The fire wagon in the right center could be pulled to the location of the fire and used to pump water. Irrigation ditches were common throughout the community. (Courtesy Bountiful History Museum.)

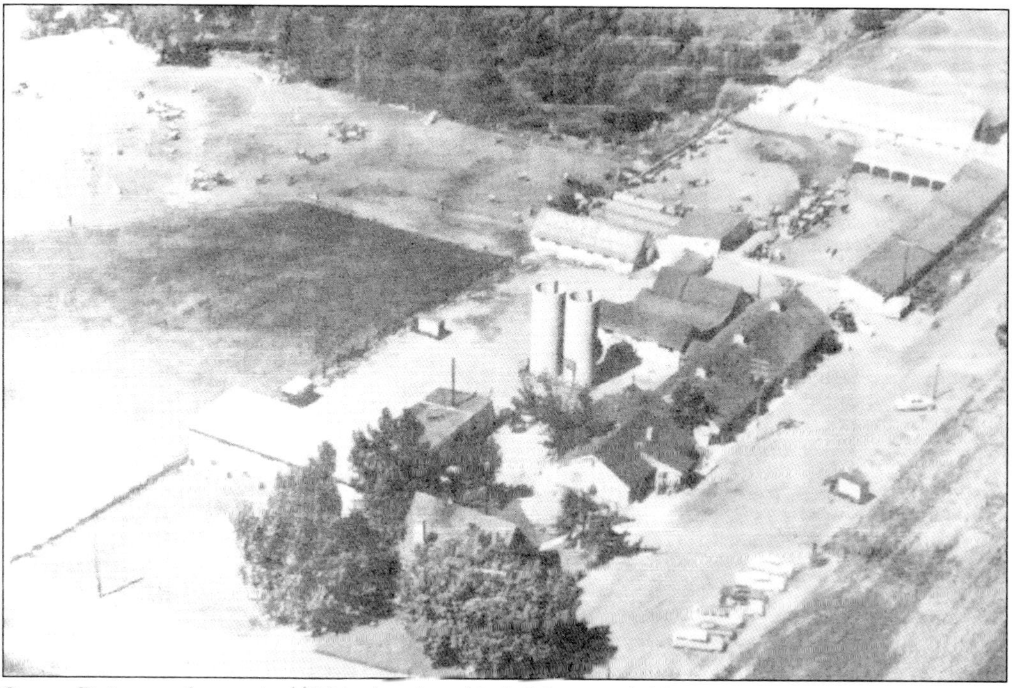

Smoot Dairy was begun in 1930 by brothers Ned, Edgar, and Alma Smoot on a 20-acre parcel of land east of Main Street, near 1000 North in Bountiful. In 1935, it moved to 1900 North Main Street in Centerville, and the name was changed to Smoot Bros. Jersey Farm. In 1963, the facility burned down, a result of an electrical short during an east wind. Nearly 200 cows perished in the blaze. (Courtesy Centerville City Historical Records.)

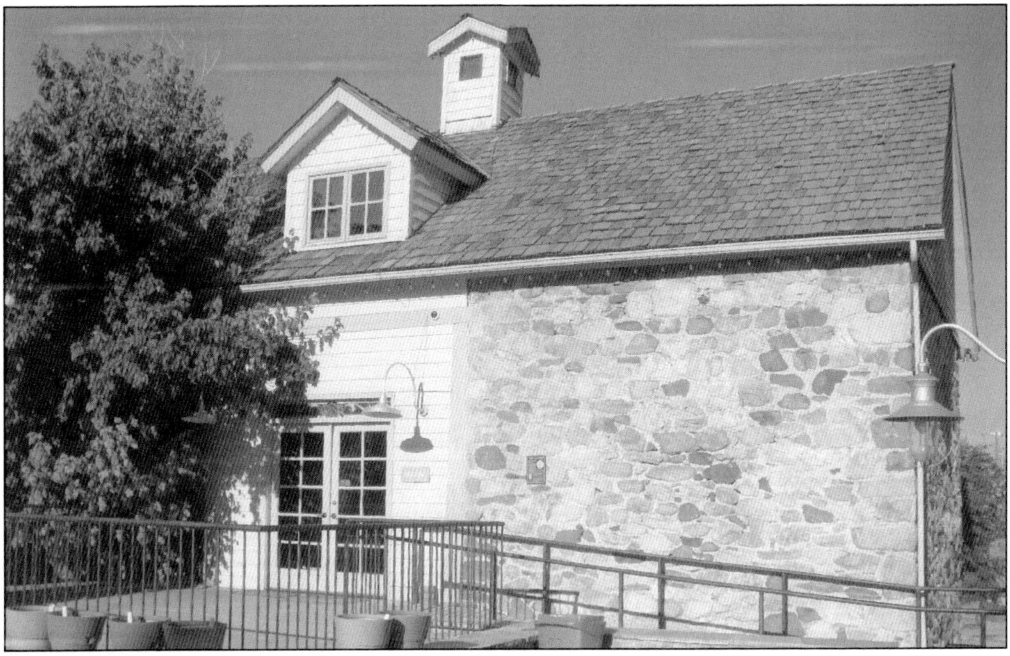

This old barn was constructed in 1850 by a Vermont farmer named Daniel Carter, who came to the Salt Lake Valley by wagon train. Located at 299 North 200 West in Bountiful, the home is claimed to be the oldest existing structure in Bountiful still on its original site. It has been converted into a small commercial shop and an apartment.

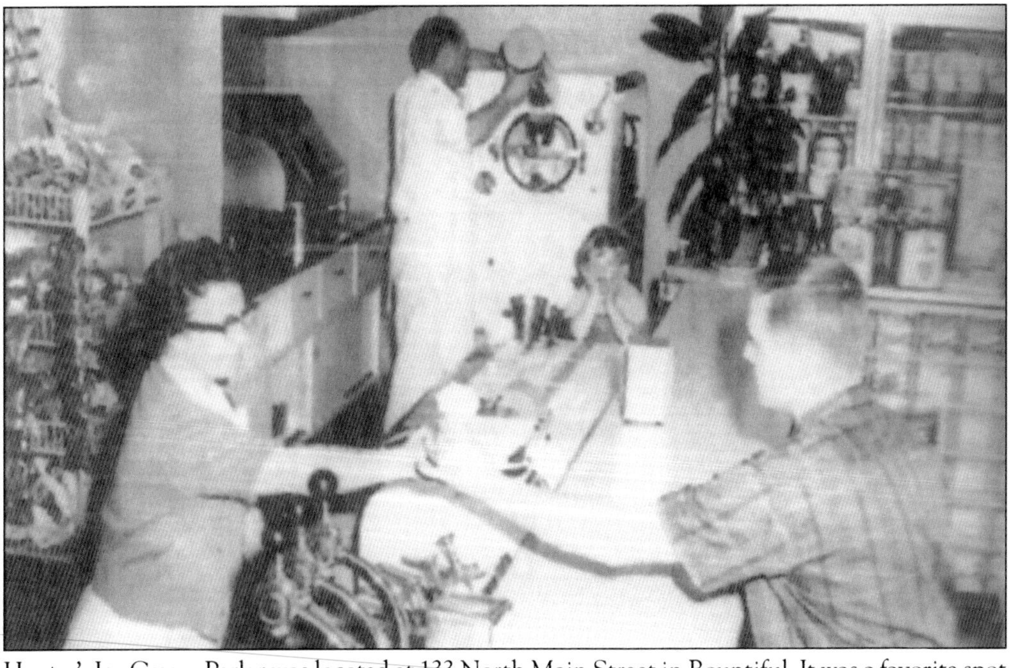

Hunter's Ice Cream Parlor was located at 133 North Main Street in Bountiful. It was a favorite spot to take a break and enjoy ice cream made and sold on-site. The business was owned and operated for 23 years by James Hunter and Parley M. Pratt before they sold it. It was later destroyed by an explosion and fire thought to be caused by arson. (Courtesy Beverly Nowak.)

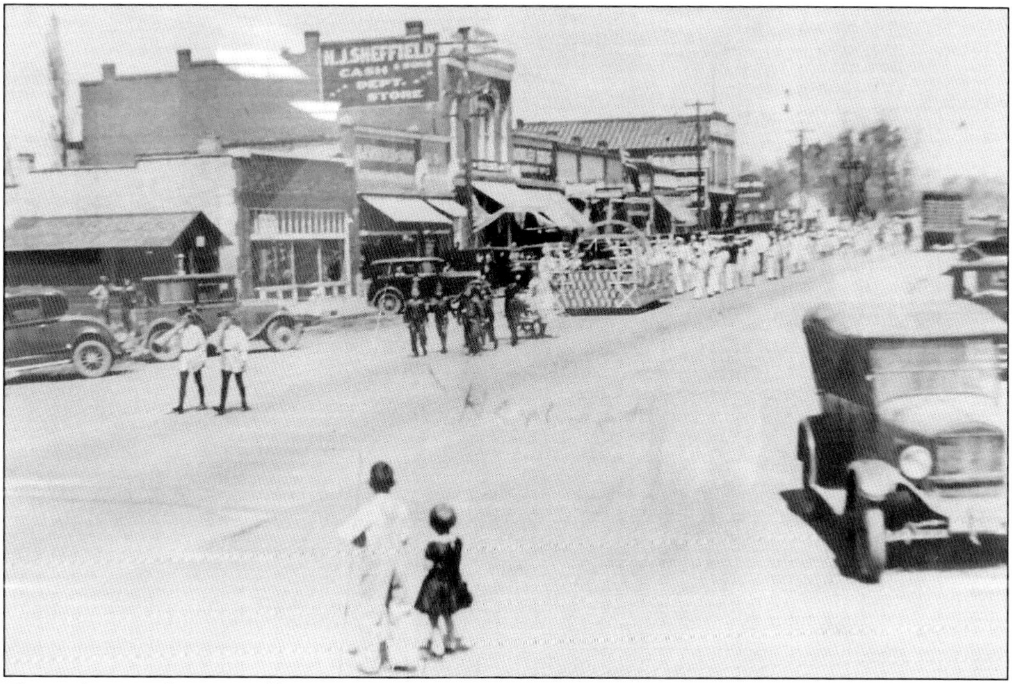

Shown here is the Kaysville Fourth of July parade around 1924. The parade was the largest event held in the community each year. Many local residents participated by making floats or dressing up as pioneers and other figures and marching in the parade. (Courtesy Kaysville City Records.)

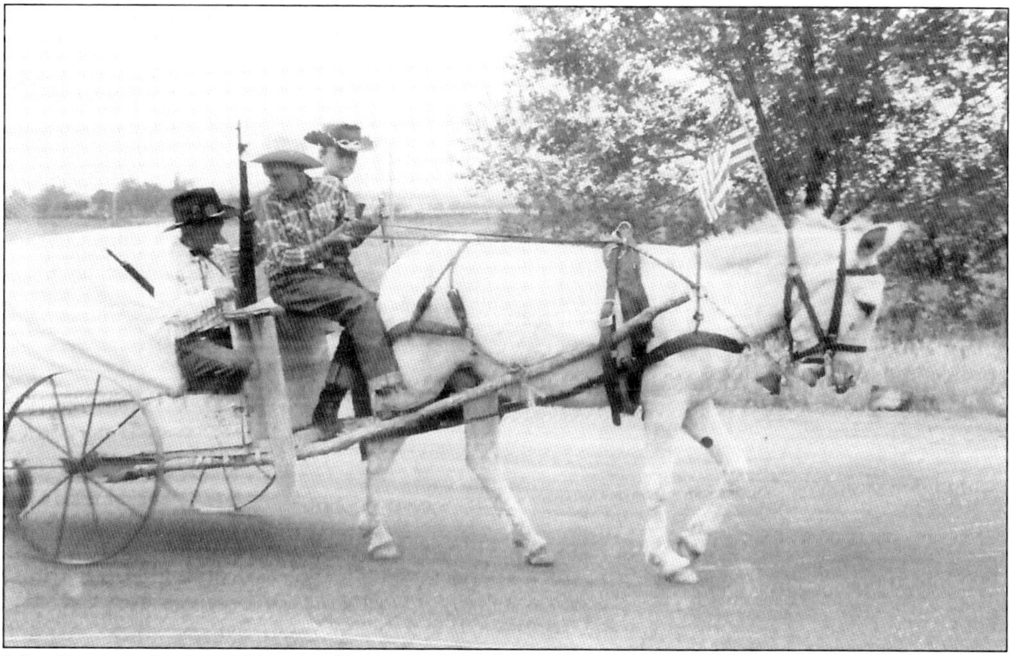

John Brown's donkey Whitie pulls Brown's grandchildren in their covered-wagon cart in a Fourth of July parade down Main Street in Centerville in 1938. The gentle-natured animal seemed to enjoy the attention of the youth and was often borrowed to give buggy rides or to be ridden bareback. (Courtesy Mark Giles.)

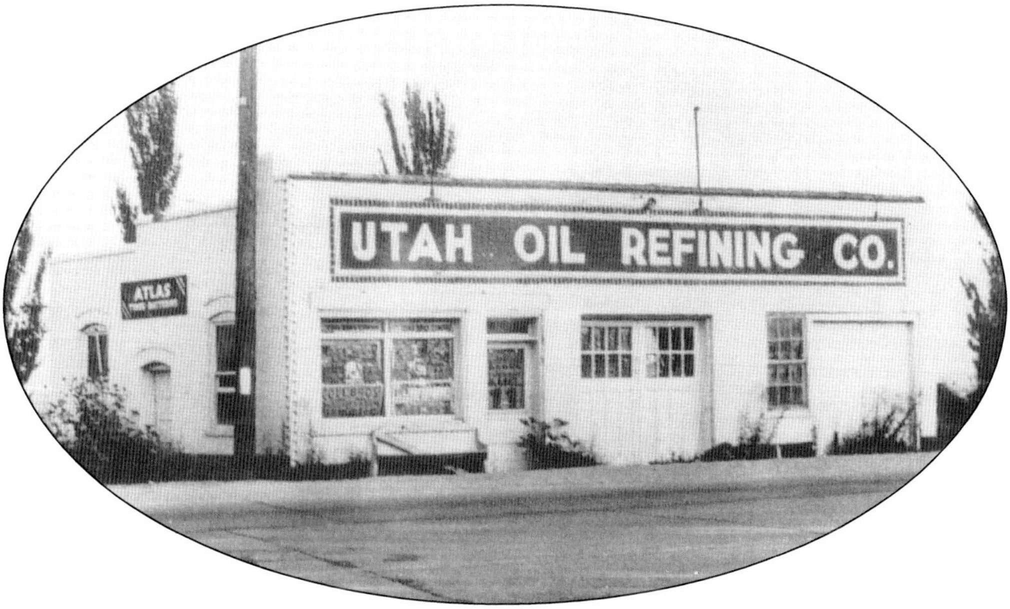

The building in the photograph above was constructed at 71 North on Highway 89 in the early 1900s. It was built by George Gwynn and Claude McNeil to house their auto repair business. A hand-cranked gas pump stood in front of the building. Displays of oil cans and other car parts stood out front. Over time, the business was acquired by the Utah Oil Refining Co., one of the earliest refining businesses in South Davis County. Since that beginning, several refineries are now located in southwestern Davis County. The largest is likely the Holly Refinery (below), at 500 South, west of the railroad tracks in Woods Cross. (Both courtesy City of North Salt Lake.)

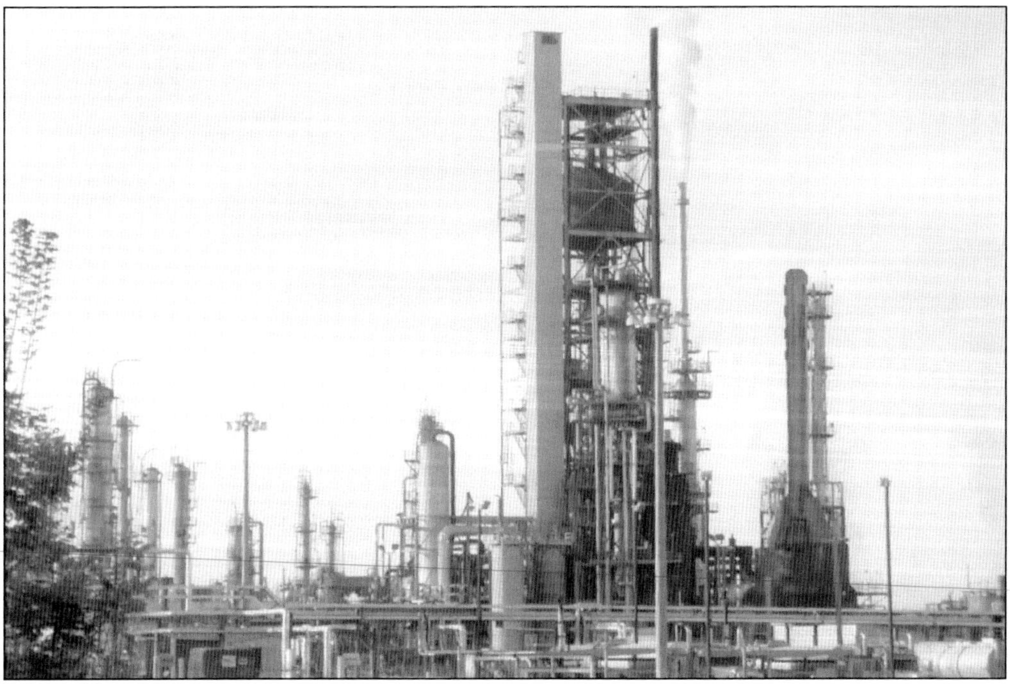

Five

Government and Law

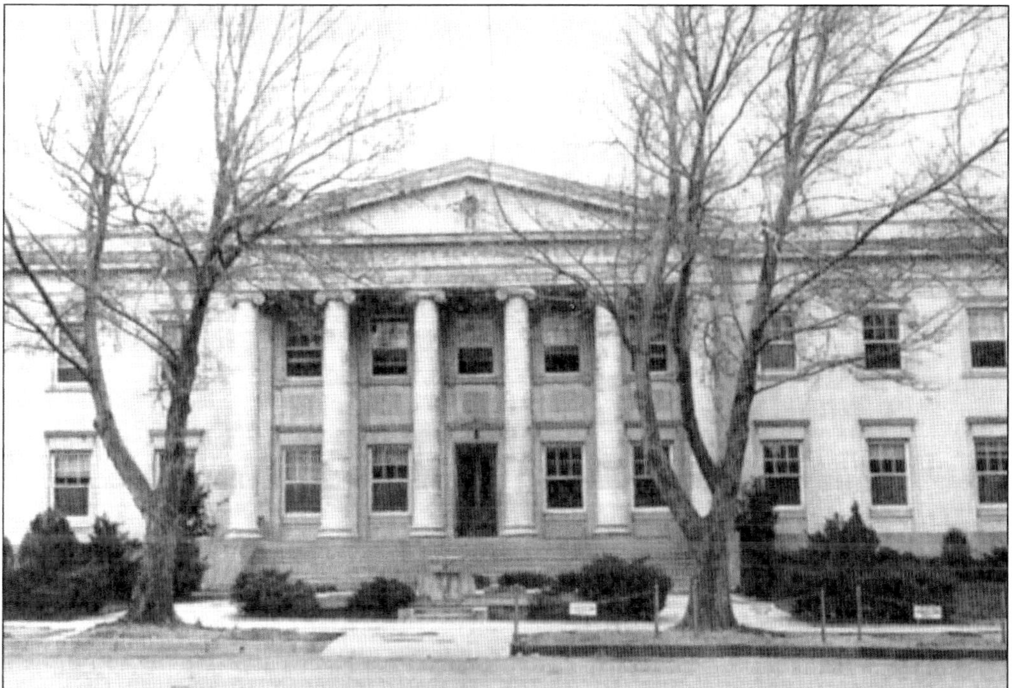

An adobe courthouse and community center was constructed in Farmington in 1855. It was used for dances, social activities, and band practices, and it served as the government offices. The county is directed by a panel of commissioners plus other elected officials. The original building was demolished in 1890. The Memorial Courthouse, shown here, was built in 1931–1932 as an expansion of the replacement courthouse. (Courtesy Farmington Historical Museum.)

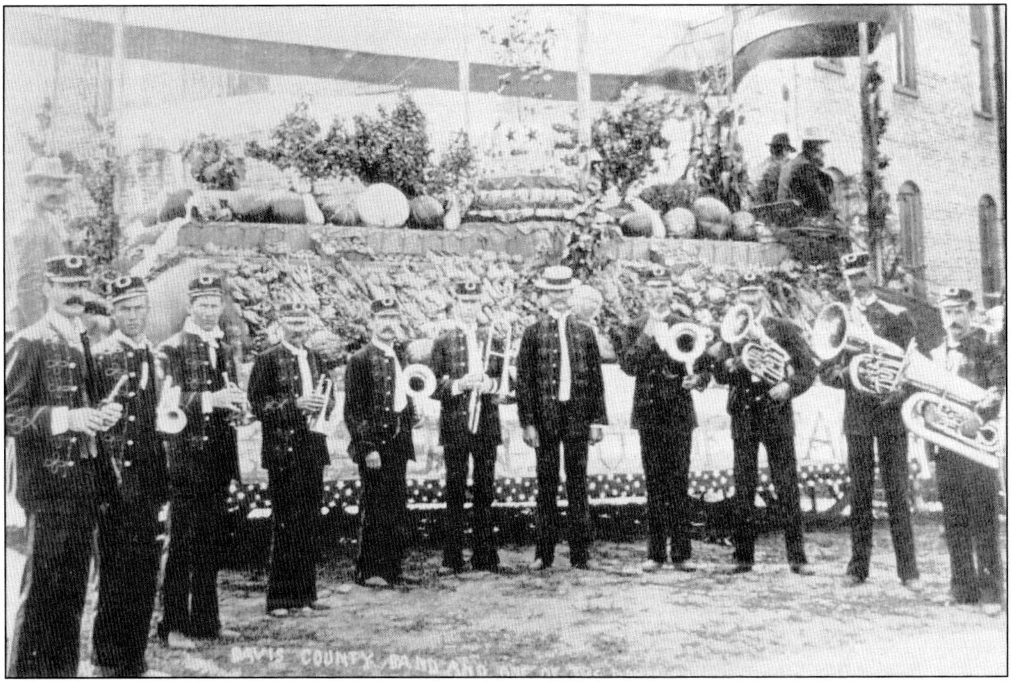

The Davis County Band performs in front of a large float in 1897. The band played at political rallies, Fourth of July celebrations, and various significant events, such as the dedication of the new county courthouse (see page 59) in 1932. (Courtesy Farmington Historical Museum.)

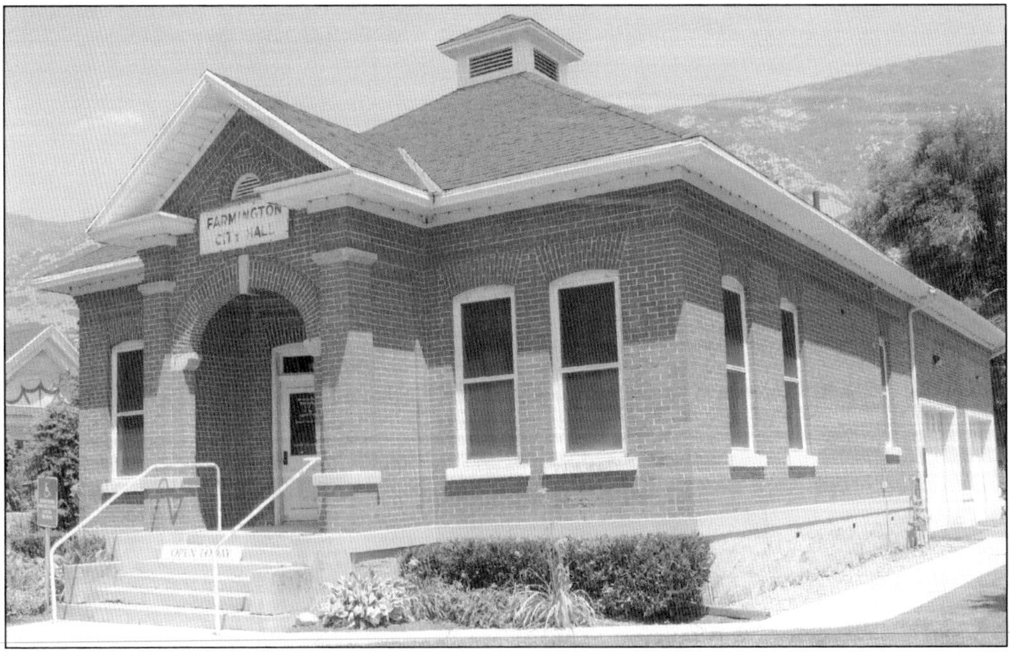

Constructed in 1907, this building was the stake president's office for the Mormon Church, serving all of Davis County. After the stake was divided in 1915, this building was purchased by Farmington City, becoming Farmington City Hall in 1917. In August 1970, the city hall moved to a new site, and this became the Farmington Historical Museum on July 9, 2004.

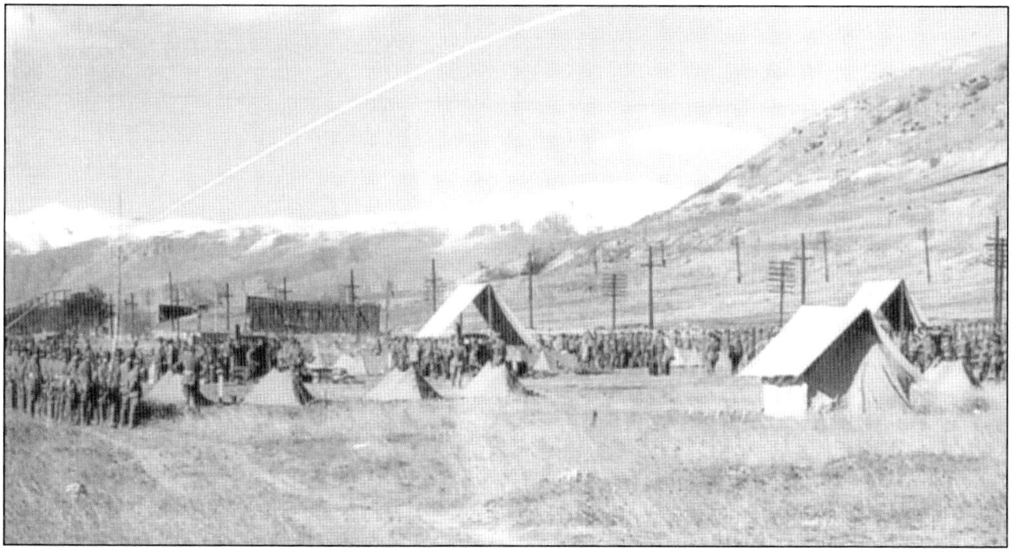

With the prospect of the United States entering World War I, a US Army training site was established in North Salt Lake around 1915. Located near the current Staker Paving Company on Highway 89, hundreds of soldiers were bivouacked and received training in preparation for combat there. (Courtesy City of North Salt Lake.)

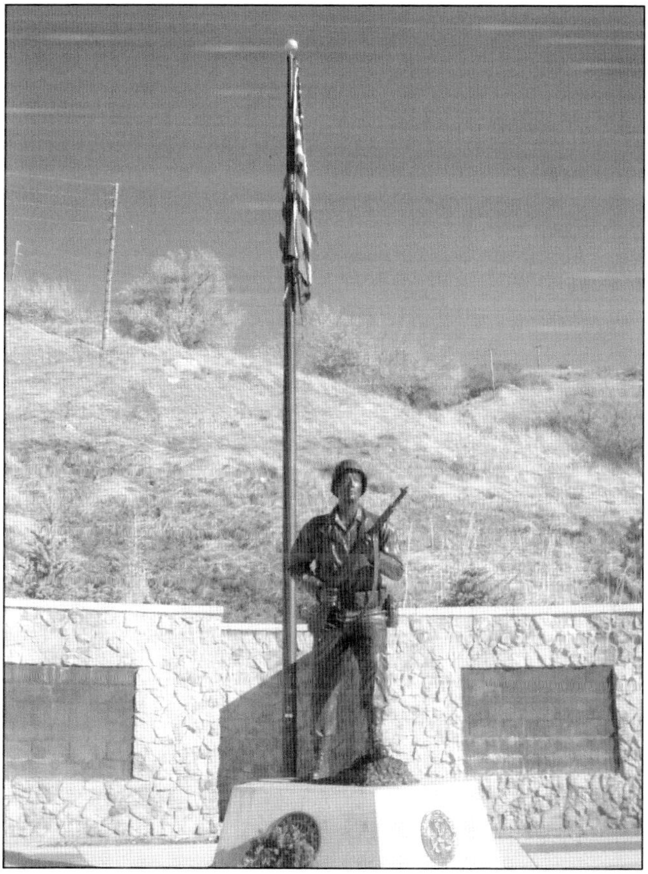

The War Memorial in Centerville is a reminder of the many soldiers that left their homes to serve in the military, many to fight wars abroad. Both men and women proudly served, and some gave the ultimate price for their country's freedom. South Davis County residents have served in all of the nation's wars since the Utah War of 1857–1858.

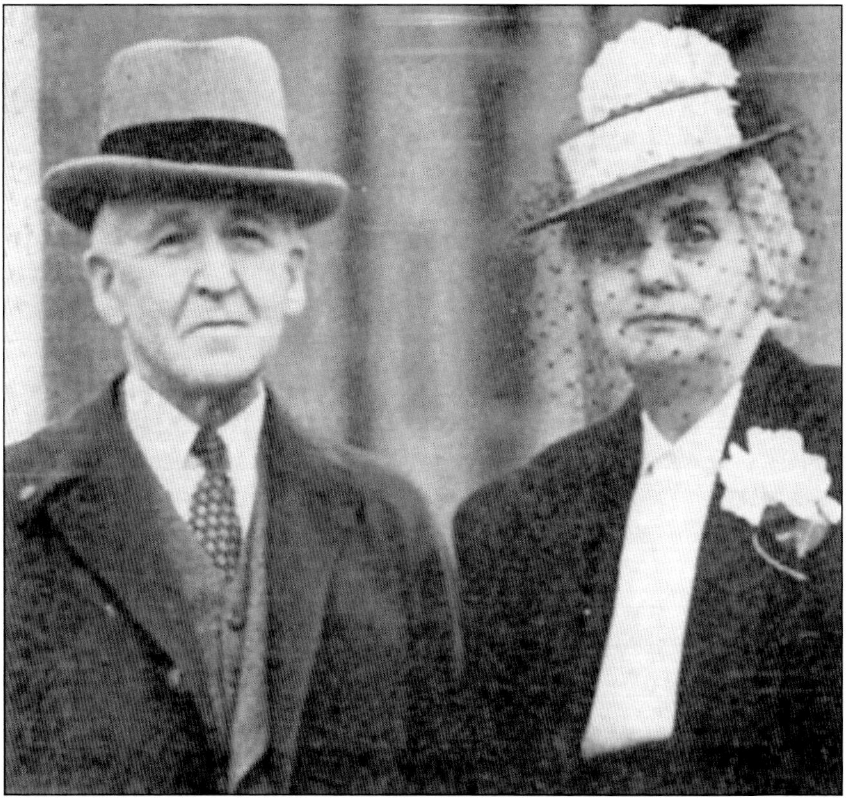

Henry Blood was born and raised in Kaysville. In 1932, he ran as a Democrat for the office of governor and became the seventh governor of the state. He won a second term in 1936 and served until 1941. As governor, he was known for his policy of "pay as you go." Through difficult financial times in the United States, Blood kept Utah solvent—slashing spending, establishing public-works programs, and cutting the size of state departments. Henry and his wife, Minnie, (above) were the first to live in the governor's mansion, which was donated by the Kearns family to the state in 1937. Their home remained in Kaysville, where they built a large Victorian-style house (below) at 96 South 300 West. (Above, courtesy Kaysville City Records.)

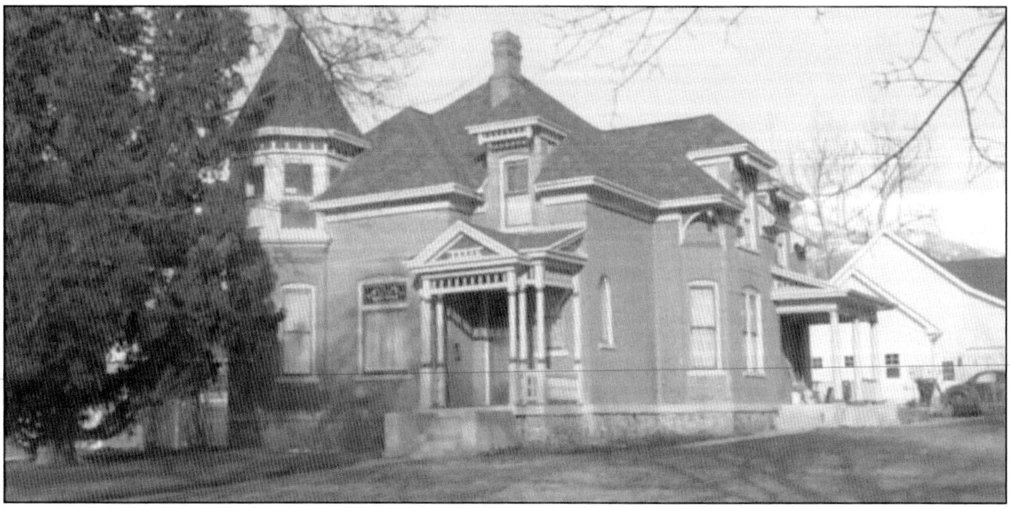

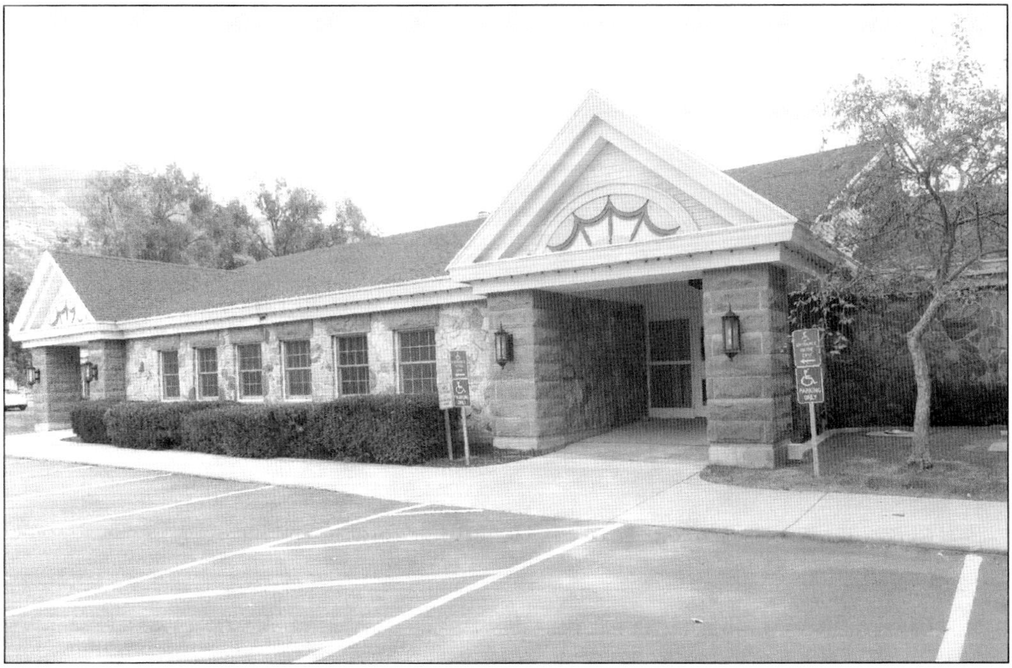

Farmington, a cattle-grazing area settled by Horton Haight, was selected as the seat of government for Davis County in 1850. The City of Farmington was incorporated in 1892, with a population of 1,180 residents. The Farmington City Hall (above) was constructed in 1970 and used until 2010. It was a significant improvement and expansion over the old, compact facility. However, as the community continued to grow rapidly, it soon proved inadequate. A new building (below) was constructed in 2004 at 160 South Main Street. The structure incorporates modern and traditional architectural themes. The modern interior features glass and marble. The old facility is now used by the Davis County School District.

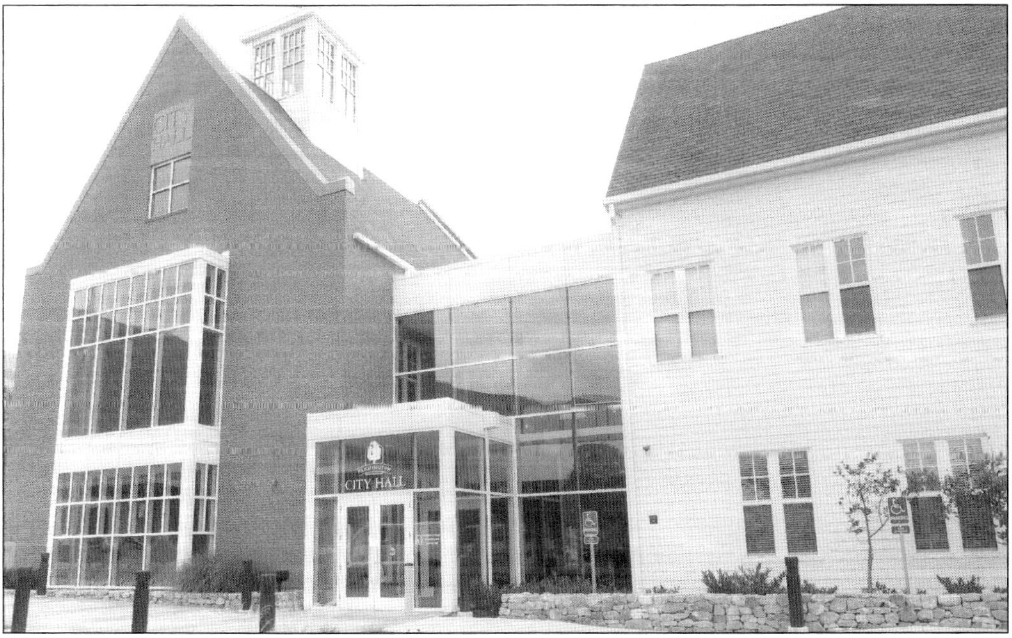

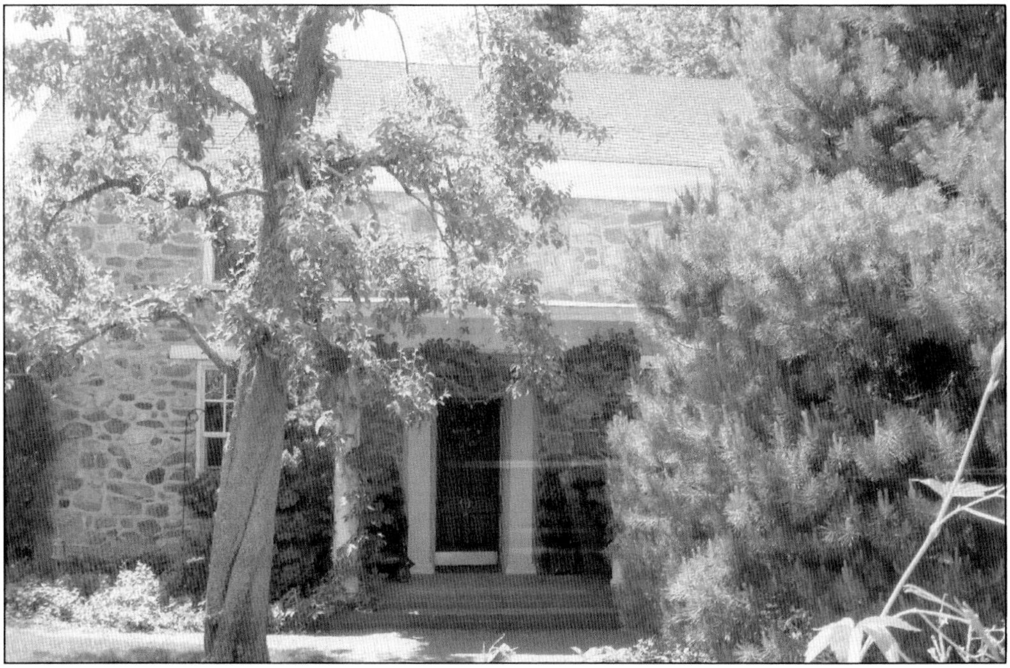

This home was built in 1875 for Melvin Harley Randall. He led a campaign in 1915 to incorporate the city, which would then allow an underground water system to be installed. The opposition refused to concede and become part of the incorporated city. Randall was elected as the first town board president of Centerville. The only candidate, he received 100 percent of the votes.

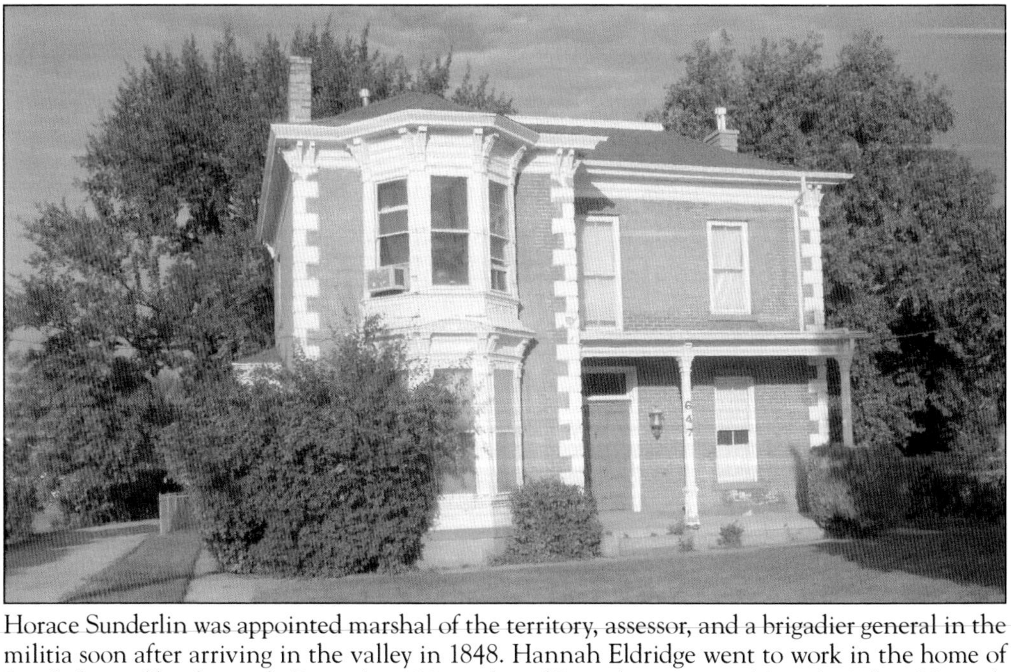

Horace Sunderlin was appointed marshal of the territory, assessor, and a brigadier general in the militia soon after arriving in the valley in 1848. Hannah Eldridge went to work in the home of Sunderlin and his first wife, Betsy Ann. Hannah and Betsy became good friends. When Hannah turned 22, she married Horace as well. In 1862, he built this home for her at 647 North 800 West in West Bountiful.

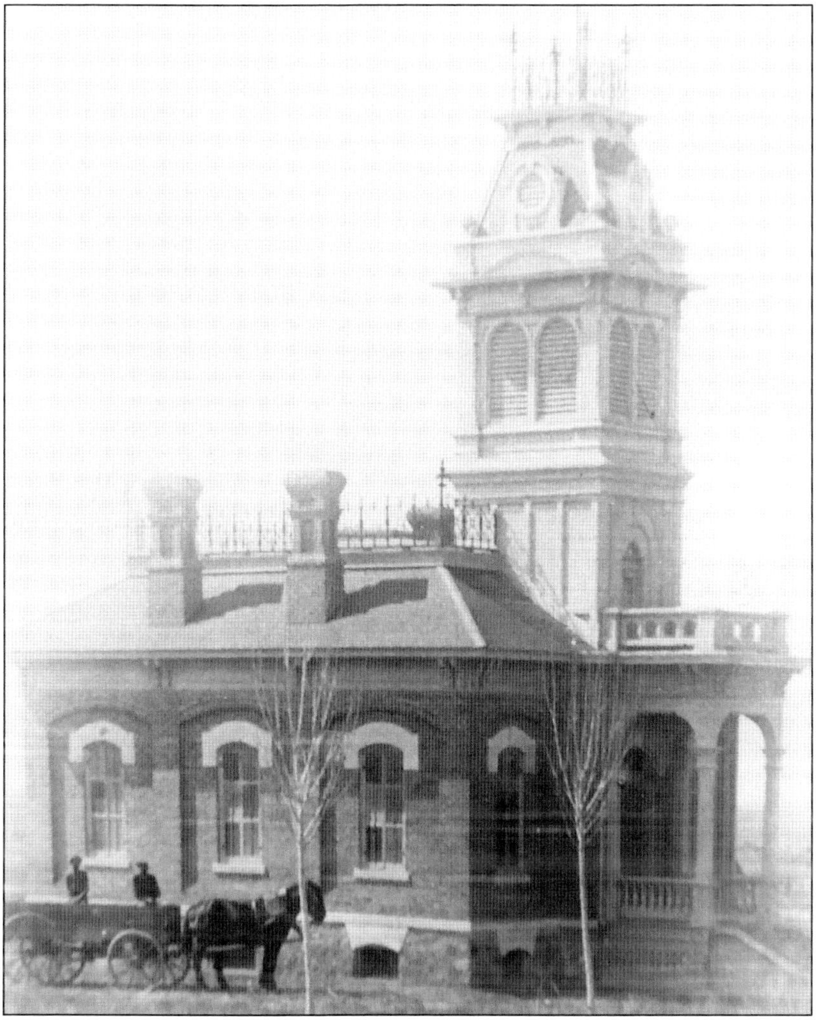

Just two miles north of Farmington, the first settlers arrived in what would become Kaysville in 1849. In 1851, it was organized as a ward of the Church of Jesus Christ of Latter-day Saints. William Kay was assigned as the first bishop of the ward, and the community became Kays Ward. After the fort wall was built as a protection from Indians, the name was changed to Kays Fort and, eventually, Kaysville. It was incorporated on March 15, 1868, becoming the first city to be incorporated in Davis County. The first city hall (above) was built at 363 North 300 West in 1889. The photograph below shows the Davis County sheriff and his deputies with their high-speed cars. (Above, courtesy Kaysville City Records; below, courtesy Farmington Historical Museum.)

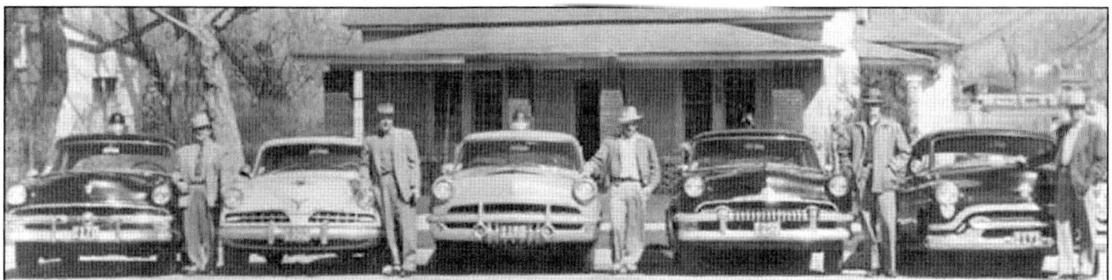

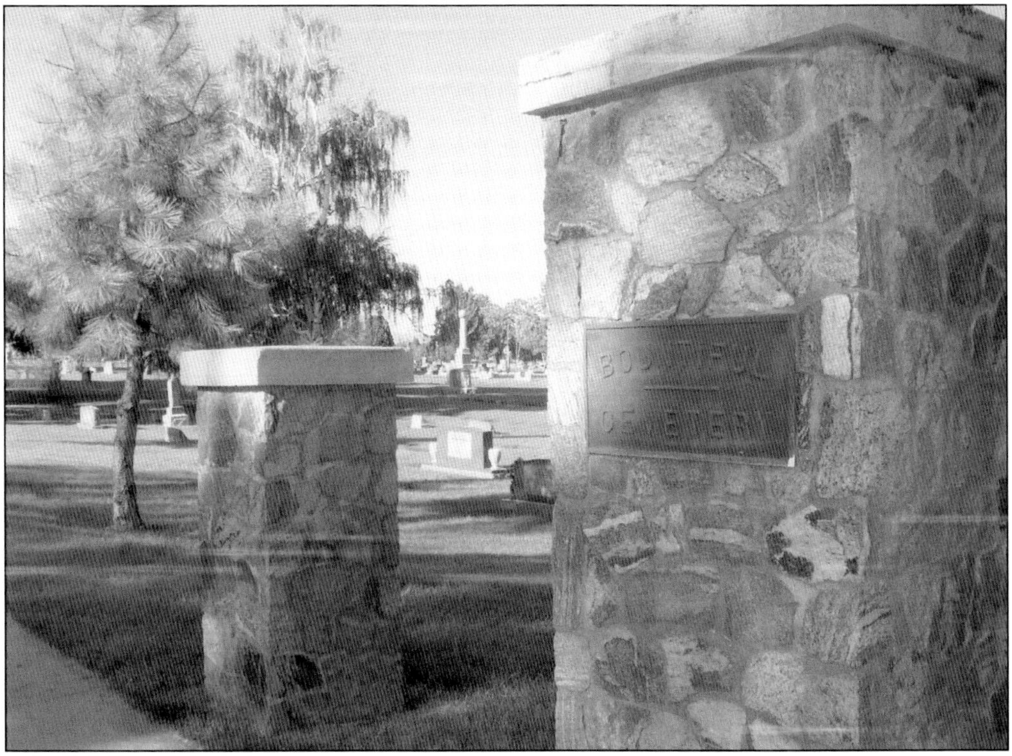

After subterranean water flooded the graves in the first Bountiful Cemetery in Woods Cross, another cemetery was established on 400 West. However, it was not a good location, and a new facility was established in 1855 at 2224 South 200 West, well south of the city. The cemetery contains 10 graves of individuals born in the 1770s, as well as many of the founders of Bountiful.

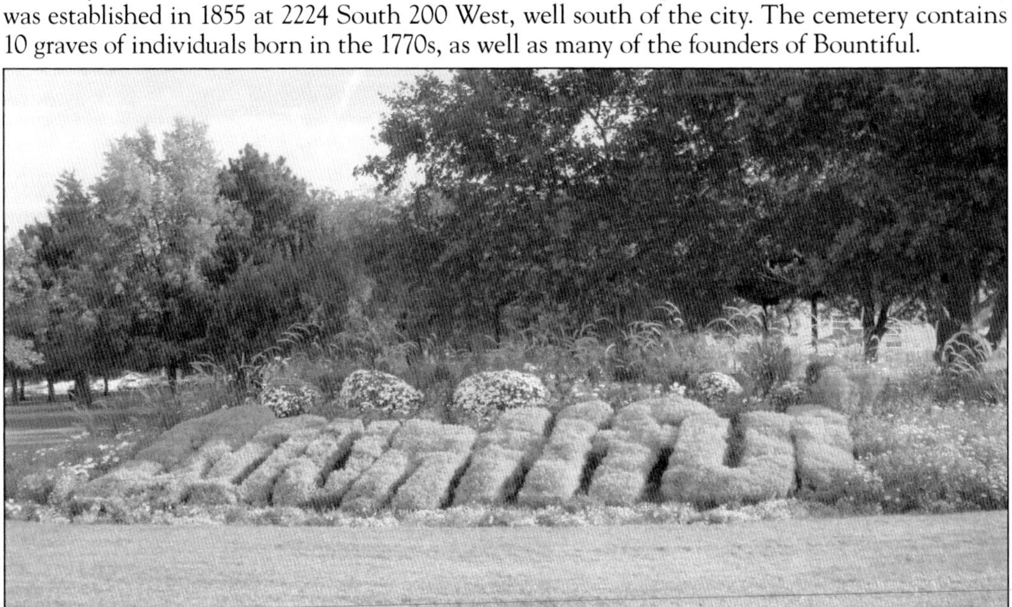

This "Bountiful" signage at the southwest corner of Bountiful City Park is located at 400 North 200 West. It is made from sculptured vegetation and surrounded by flowers. Each year, it shows off colorful annuals and perennial blooms and is a traditional photograph spot for visitors.

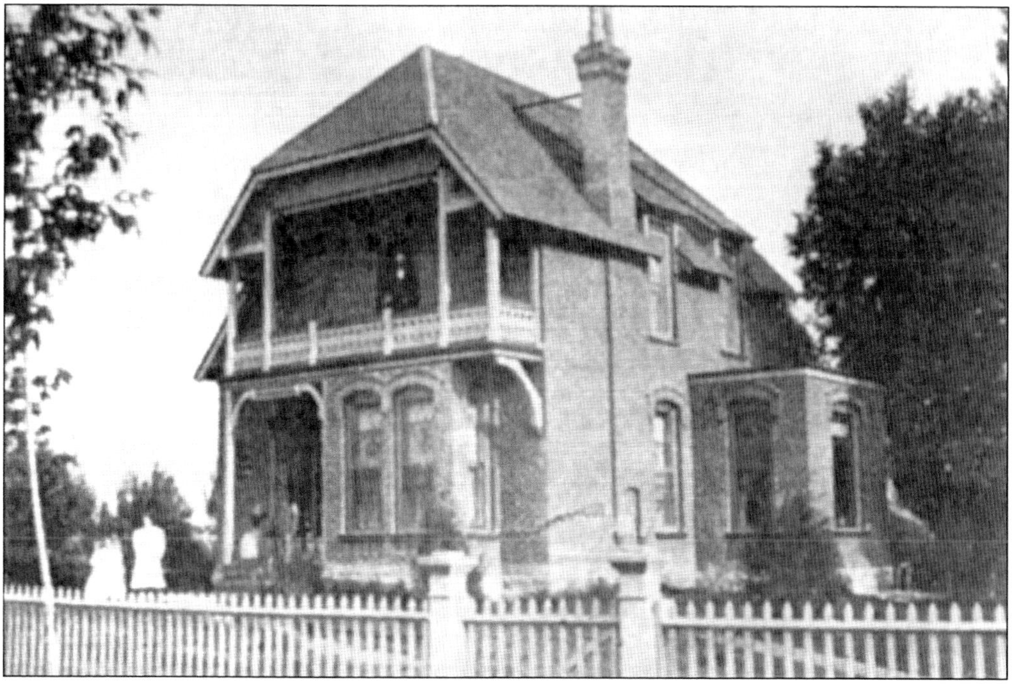

In 1892, Dr. Briant Stringham built a two-story redbrick-veneer home at 725 West 1000 North in West Bountiful (above). Dr. Stringham had attended the University of Deseret and graduated in 1876 in business, and he later attended the Eclectic Medical Institute in Ohio, receiving his Doctor of Medicine degree. He returned to West Bountiful as the first physician and surgeon in Davis County. He practiced medicine from his home, displaying a sign in front. In 1912, a two-story carriage house was added southwest of the home, with an upstairs room for a hired hand. One of these assistants, Charles R. Mabey, later became governor of Utah. In 1939, the house caught fire, and the second story was destroyed. When the home was rebuilt, the upper story was eliminated (below). (Both courtesy Bountiful History Museum.)

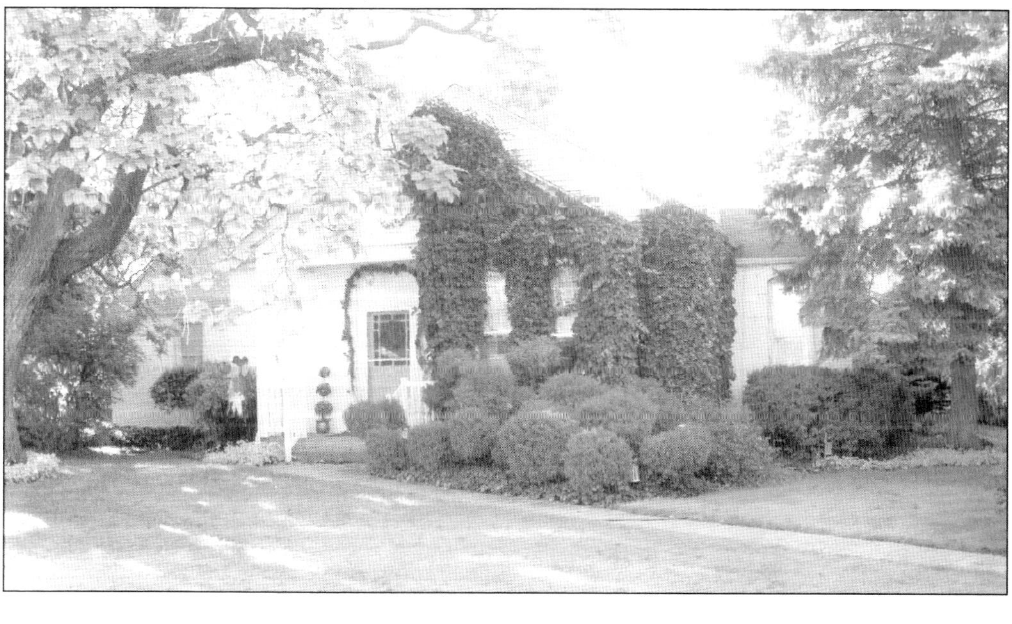

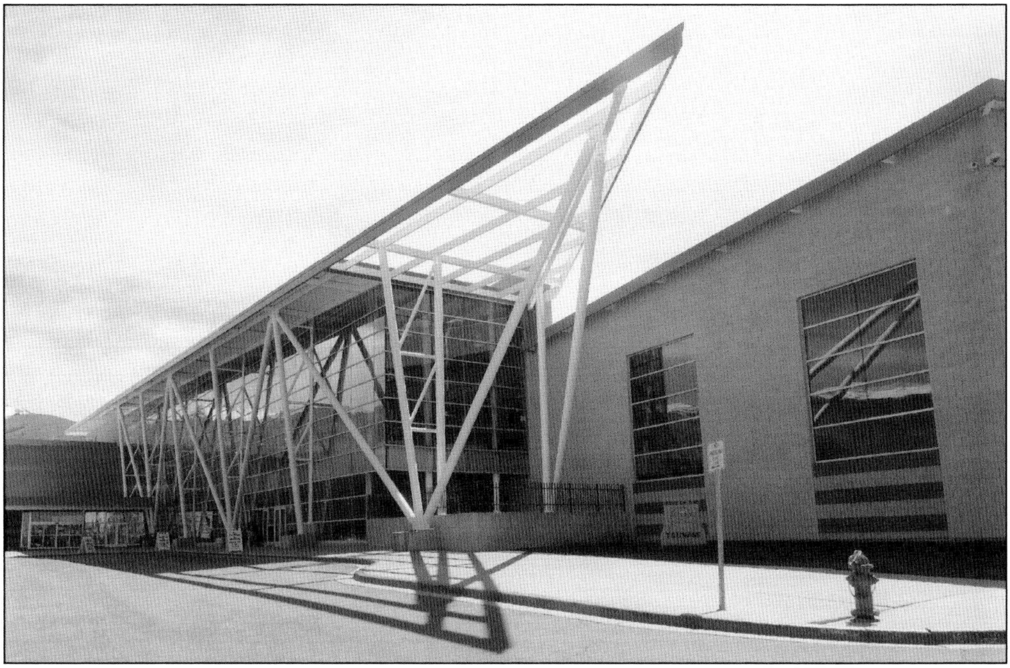

The two facilities shown here were built to serve all the citizens of South Davis County. Various recreation facilities and pools had been constructed at several sites over the years. Due to the growing population and aging facilities, they were replaced by a large multifunctional facility (above) at 400 North and about 100 West in Bountiful. Olympic pools, diving facilities, an ice rink, tracks, gyms, exercise equipment, and dance facilities are available. The center for the Davis County Performing Arts (below) is a modern facility with stages, storage, lift platforms, and more to meet the creative demands of modern theatrical productions. It includes a smaller studio and a black box theater for training and lesser productions.

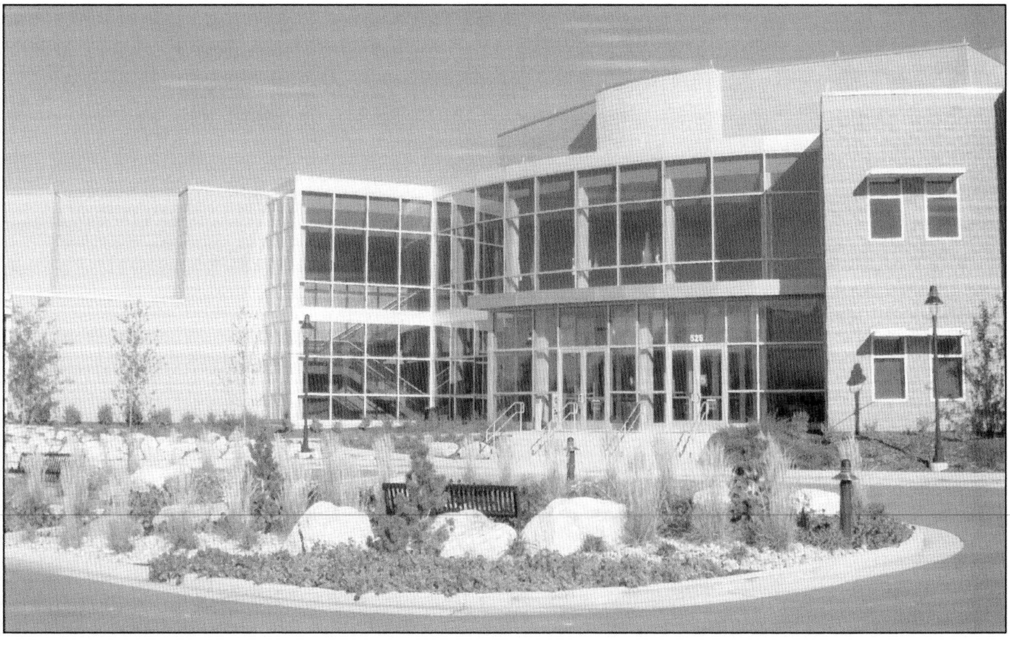

Six

Getting Connected

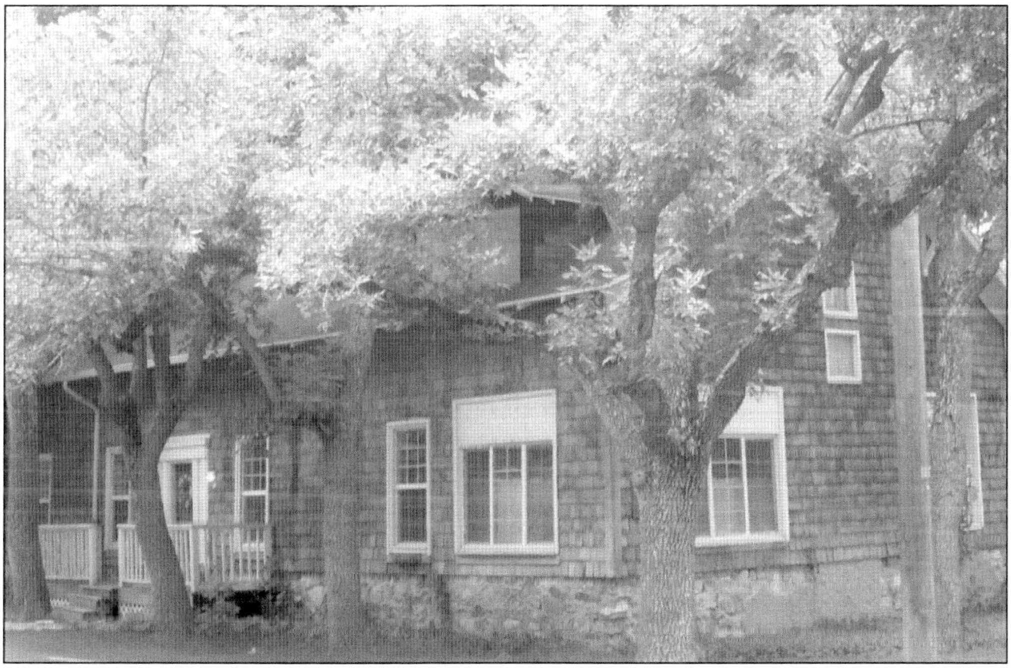

In 1866, the Wells Fargo Company, which provided control of the overland routes, built and operated a stagecoach service, including stations. This one is located in Centerville, at 16 South 200 East. William Reeves, the stationmaster, provided a comfortable stop for the passengers and water for the horses. Soon after the completion of the Utah Central Railroad in 1870, the stage service was discontinued.

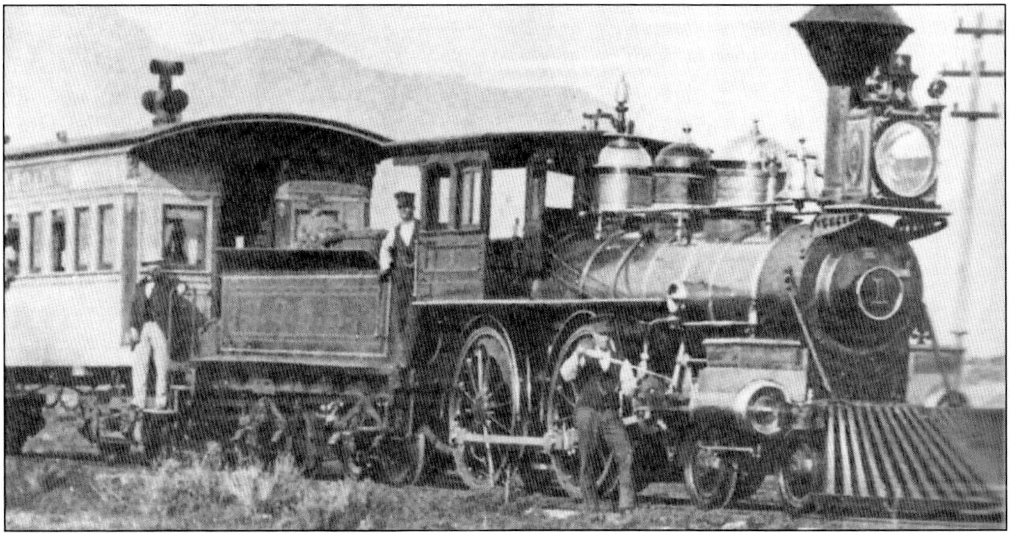

Brigham Young, leader of the Mormon settlers, encouraged the organization of the Utah Central Railroad, to provide rail service from the Ogden spur of the Transcontinental Railroad to Salt Lake City, 37 miles south. Local Mormons, without government subsidies, built the rail line under the direction of Mormon bishops. On June 10, 1870, an "Iron Spike" was driven into the rails at the southern endpoint in Salt Lake City, at North Temple Street and Third West. The first train to transit South Davis County paused for the historical photograph above at the Centerville station. Each town built its own station. For the full-distance run, which took place four times per day, the ride time was one hour and the fare was $2. An important stop was the auction yards (below), where farmers sold their livestock. (Above, courtesy Utah State Historical Society; below, courtesy Centerville City Historical Records.)

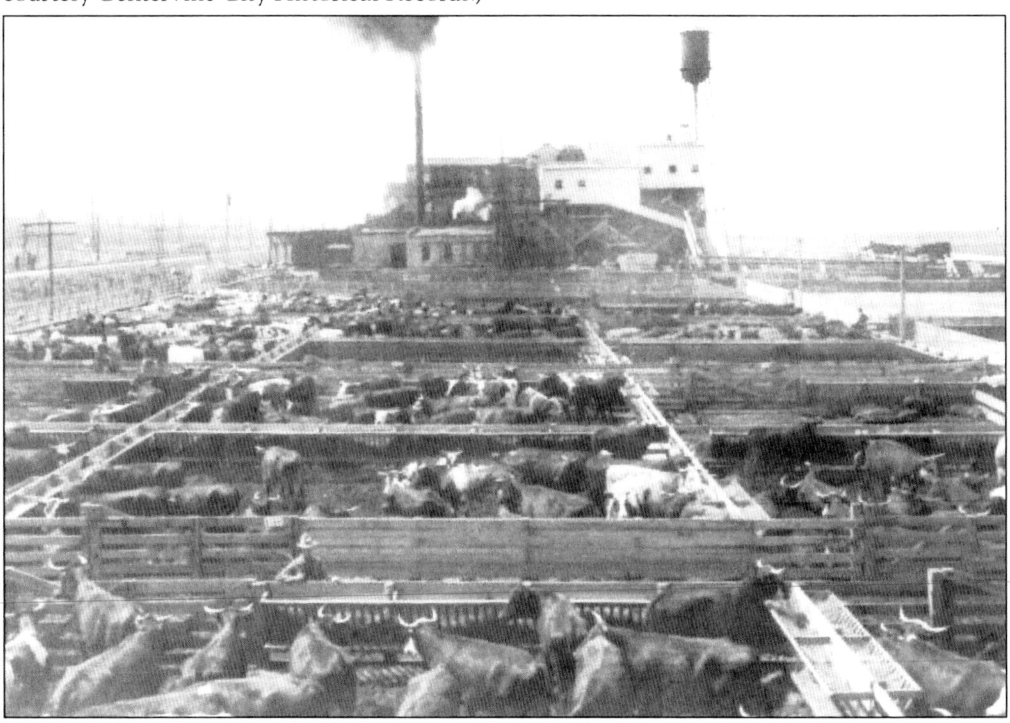

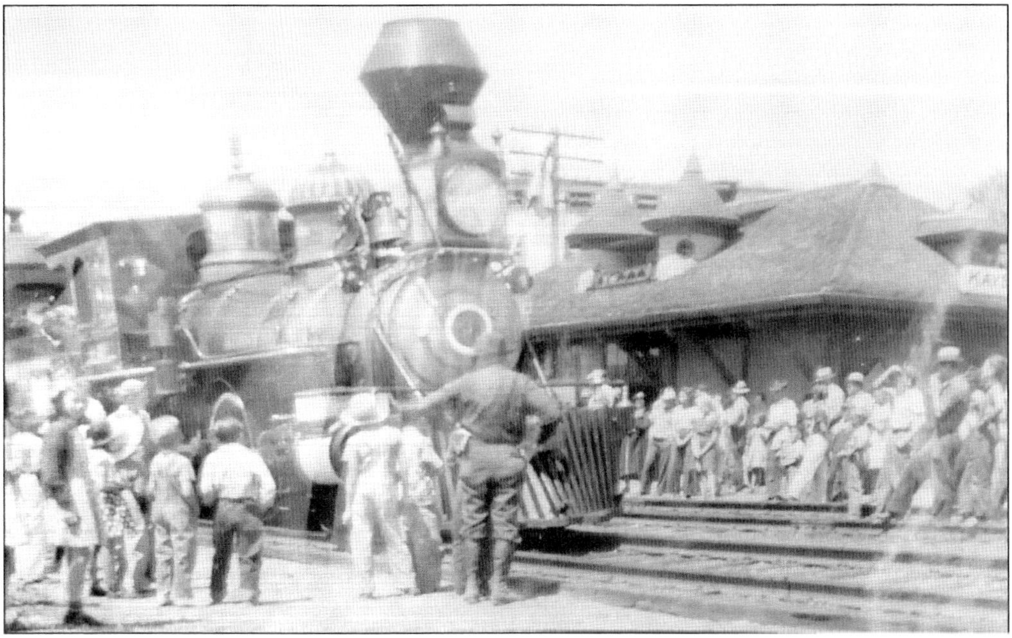

Other railroads were built. The Utah Northern Railroad, providing service through Brigham City and north to Logan, was completed in 1874. The Utah Southern Railroad, connecting Salt Lake City to Provo, and, later, to points farther south, began service in 1873. In 1890, these local railroads consolidated as subsidiaries of Union Pacific Railroad. Union Pacific had built the spur from Promontory Point to Ogden and now offered service throughout the territory and beyond. Mail service was now carried by trains. Couriers picked up the mail sacks at the depot and brought them to the local post office. The small steam engines were soon replaced with larger, more powerful engines, such as the one shown above, pulling into the station at Kaysville. Below, an old horse-drawn wagon sits abandoned. (Above, courtesy Utah State Historical Society.)

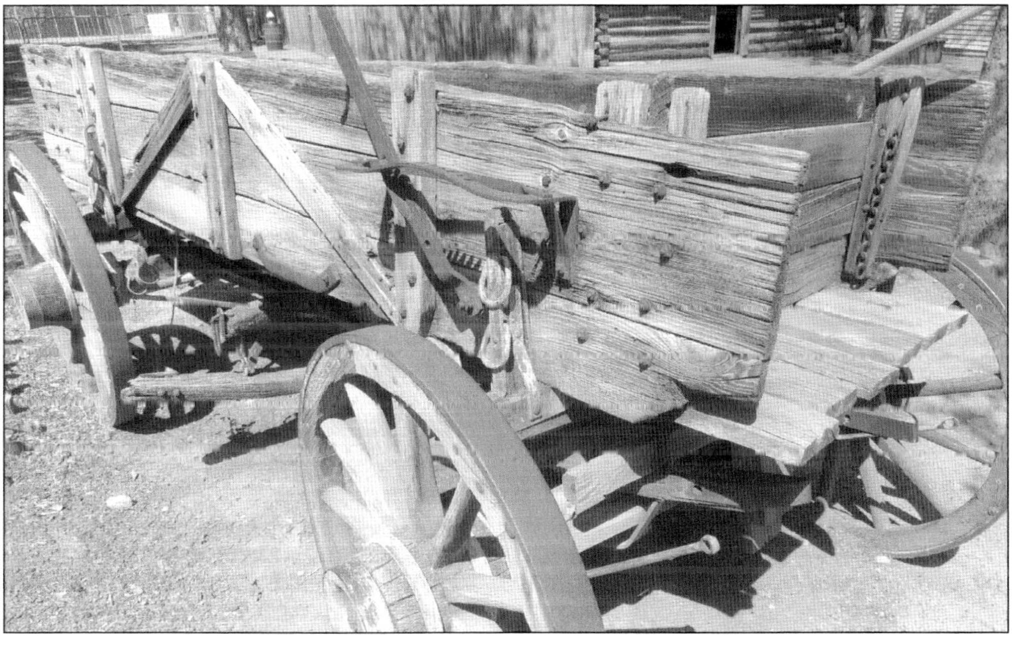

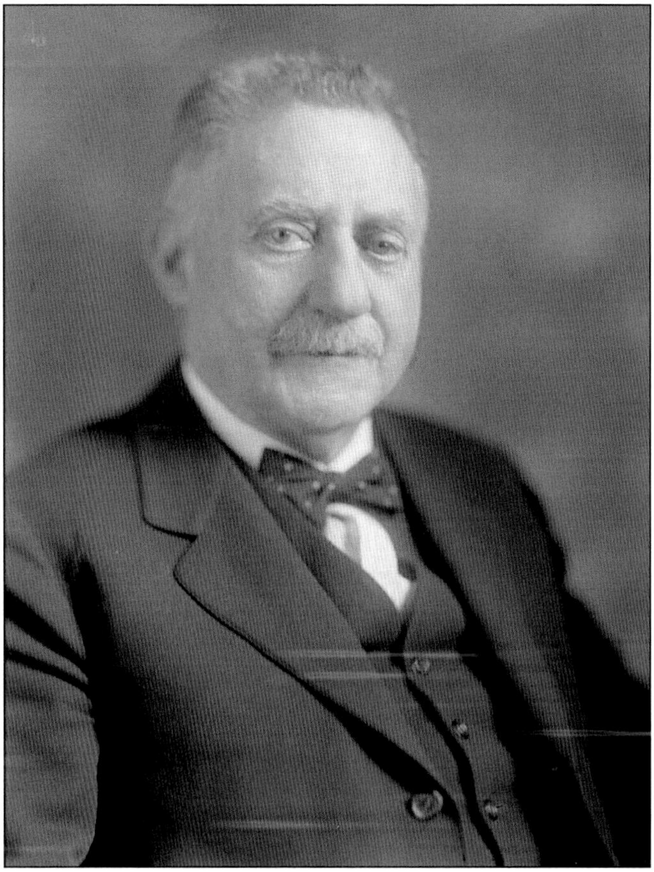

Simon Bamberger, born in 1846 in Germany, struck it rich in the Centennial Eureka mine in Juab County. When Lake Shore Resort closed, Bamberger dredged out a swampy lagoon of freshwater near Farmington and created a new resort, called Lagoon. He was elected the fourth governor of Utah in 1917, the first Democrat and the only Jew to hold that office. He supported public education and organized the Bamberger Electric Railroad, providing service from Salt Lake to Ogden by 1908. The Bountiful Bamberger train station (below) was located at 253 South 200 West. The photograph shows an early "dummy" steam-powered engine enclosed in a wooden body to resemble a train, before Bamberger converted his operation to electricity. (Both courtesy Bountiful History Museum.)

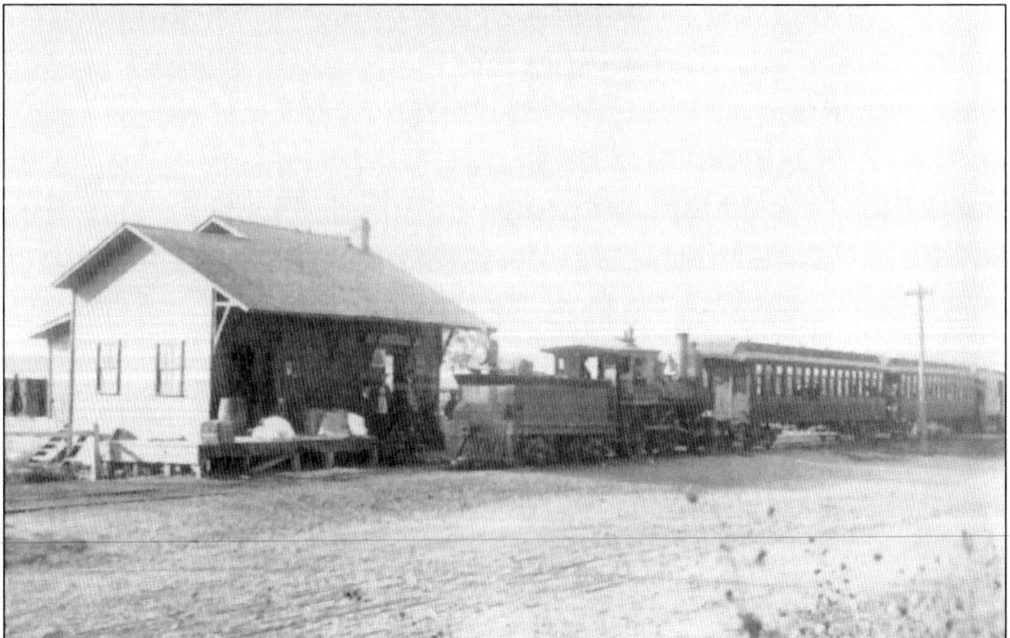

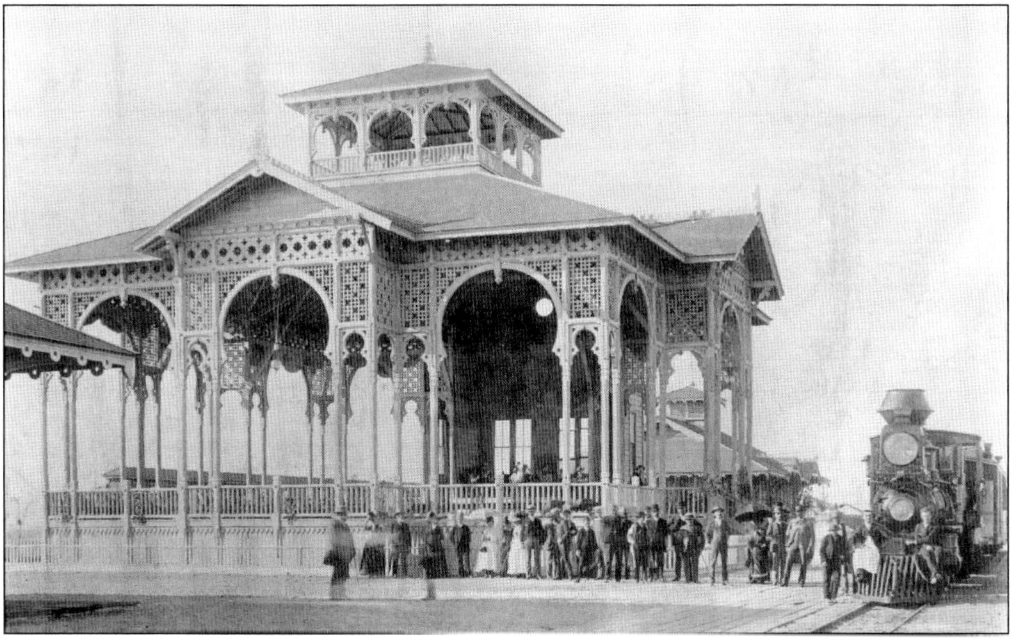

With the closing of Lake Shore Resort, Simon Bamberger moved the main pavilion to the new Lagoon facility. The building, seen above around 1900, was used as the station for the Bamberger Electric Train. It was located right on Bamberger's rail line and was the only access to Lagoon Park. Later, this structure was relocated near what is now the Maple Terrace and converted to a dance hall, where bands played on weekends. It was also used for performances of famous entertainers and for special events. A new train station was constructed near the Lagoon Lake (below). (Both courtesy Lagoon Corporation.)

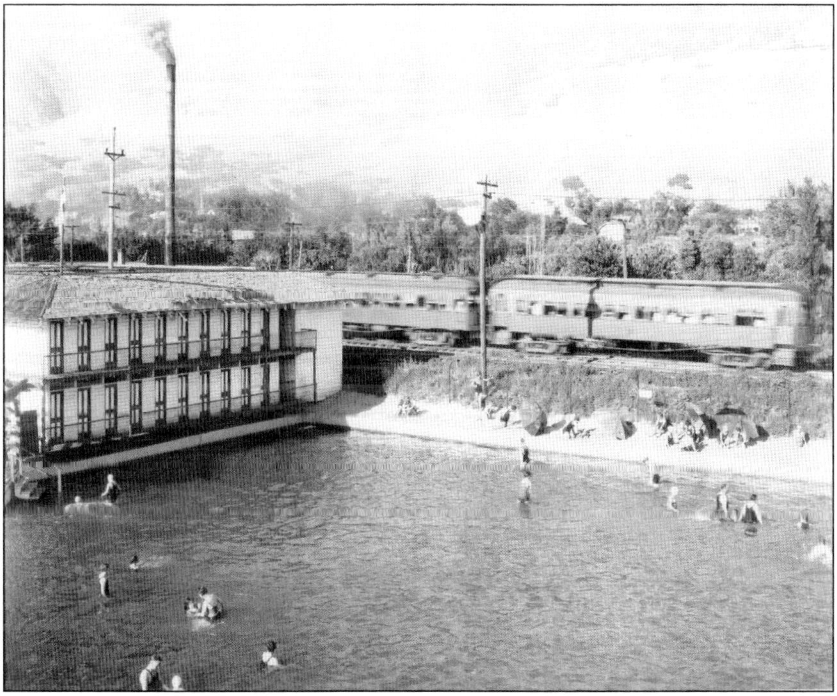

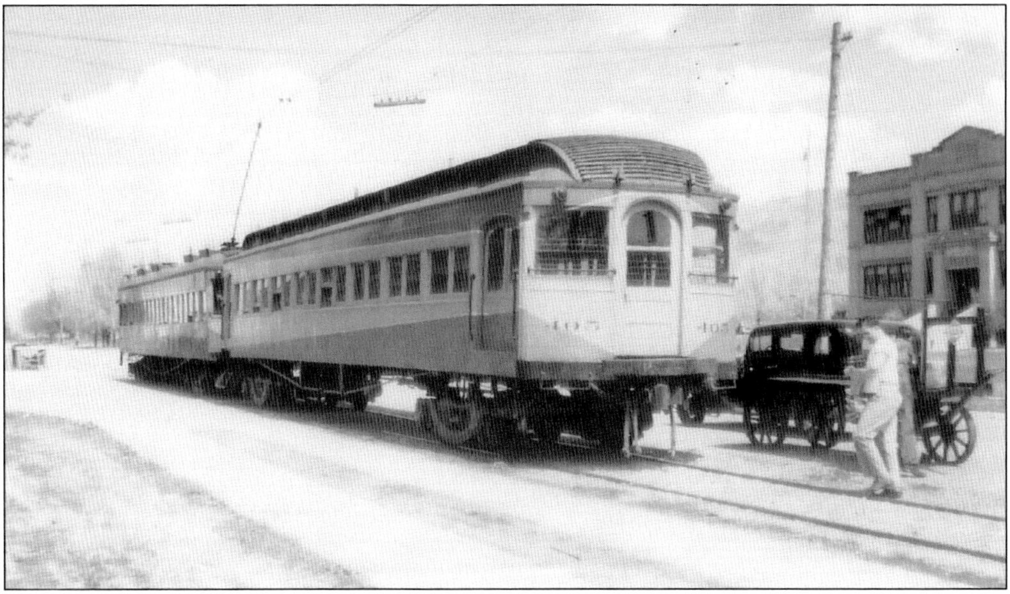

Comfortable coaches were soon available on the Bamberger Electric Railroad, making the ride from Salt Lake to Ogden an enjoyable journey. A passenger could catch the train in the morning in Salt Lake City, ride to Ogden, and return back in the evening. (Courtesy Centerville City Historical Records.)

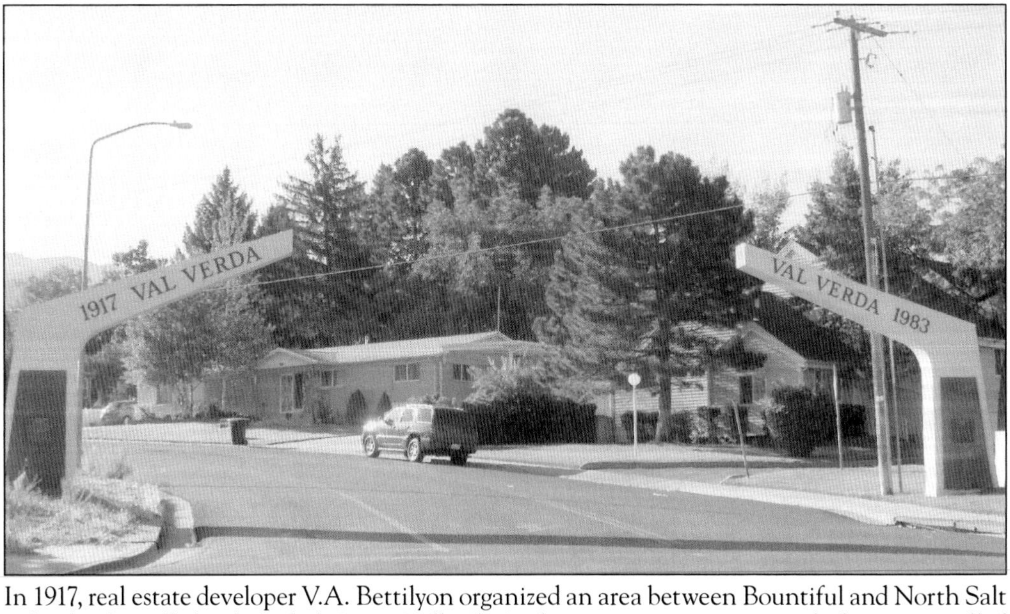

In 1917, real estate developer V.A. Bettilyon organized an area between Bountiful and North Salt Lake that he called Val Verda ("Green Valley"). At the entrance was a sign with the name spelled out. After the sign was knocked down twice by tall equipment, it was configured with an open top to permit high-profile rigs to pass through. Val Verda was a stop on the Bamberger line.

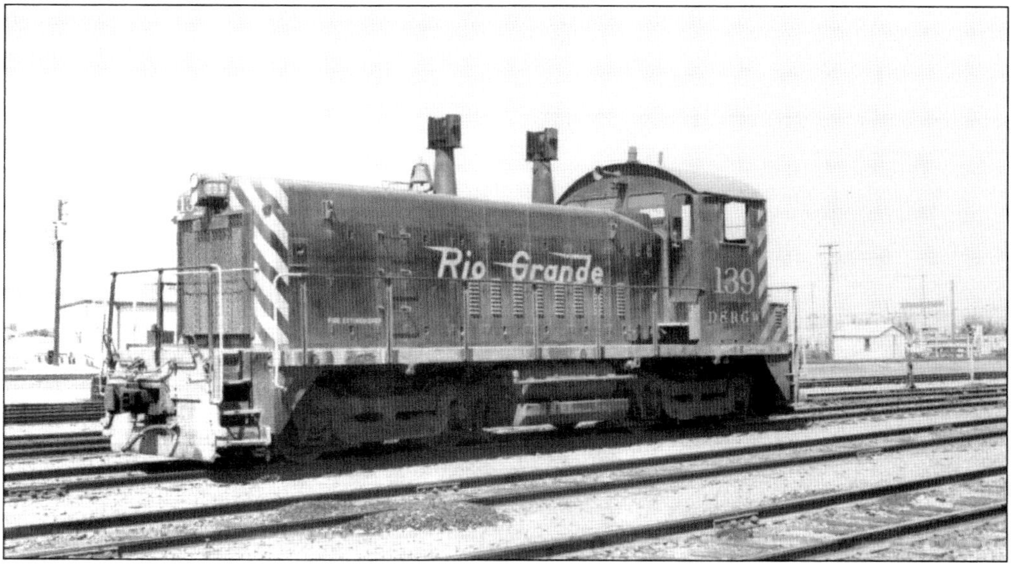

The Denver & Rio Grande Railroad built a connection from Colorado to Ogden and competed with the Union Pacific Railroad, forcing prices down. Passenger and freight fares were reduced by as much as 50 percent. (Courtesy Utah State Historical Society.)

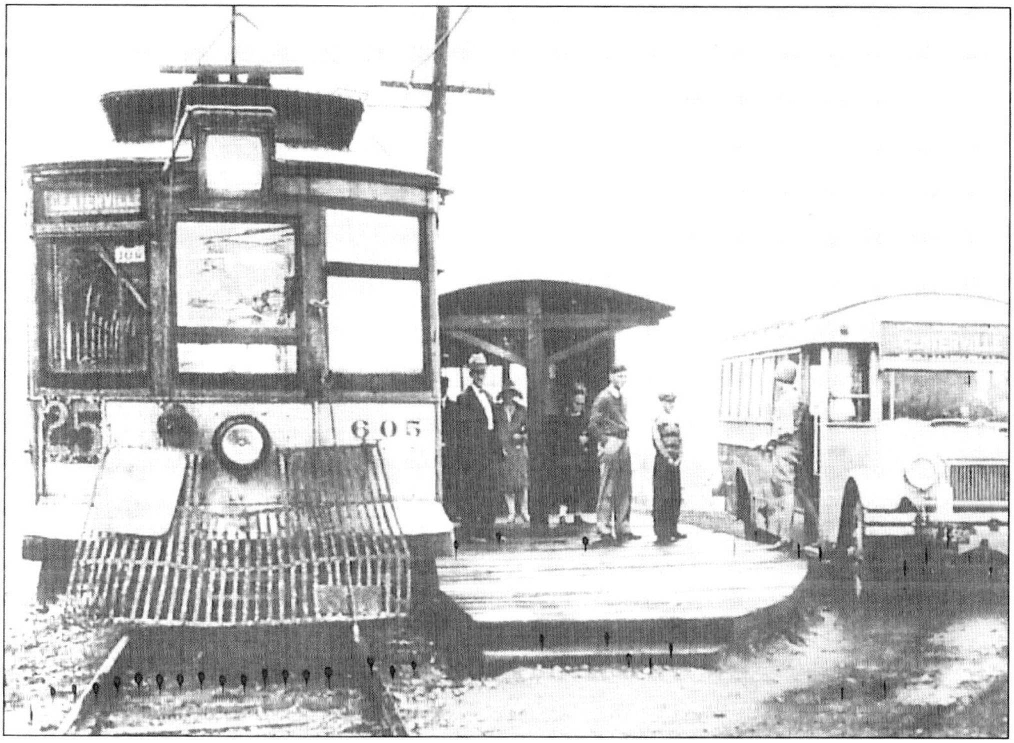

For the convenience of passengers, local bus service to and from the train stations was added. The train stations were located a short distance from town to reduce noise, meaning that returning train travelers often had to walk through snow and mud to their homes. Now, for a small additional fee, passengers could get off the train and ride to their homes on the bus. This photograph was taken around 1915. (Courtesy Centerville City Historical Records.)

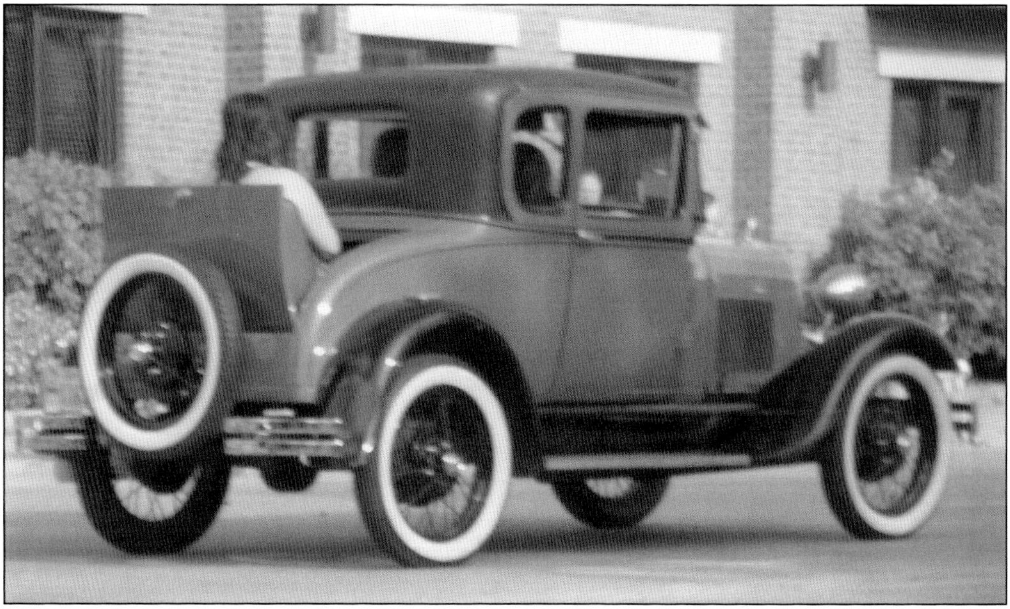

By the early 1900s, automobiles were being purchased by local citizens. Touring cars and trucks were quickly replacing horses, buggies, and wagons. Farmers still operated with horses through the Great Depression and during World War II, due to rubber and gasoline rationing. But gasoline stations, such as the one shown below, located north of Beck's Hot Springs, began to be established to provide service to car owners. The price of gas around 1948 was about 10¢ per gallon. The pumps were operated by the customer. Using the crank handle on the side, gasoline was pumped into the glass receptacle on the top, which had a graduated scale showing the number of gallons. The customer would then put the hose into the automobile and release the gas into the tank. (Below, courtesy Bountiful History Museum.)

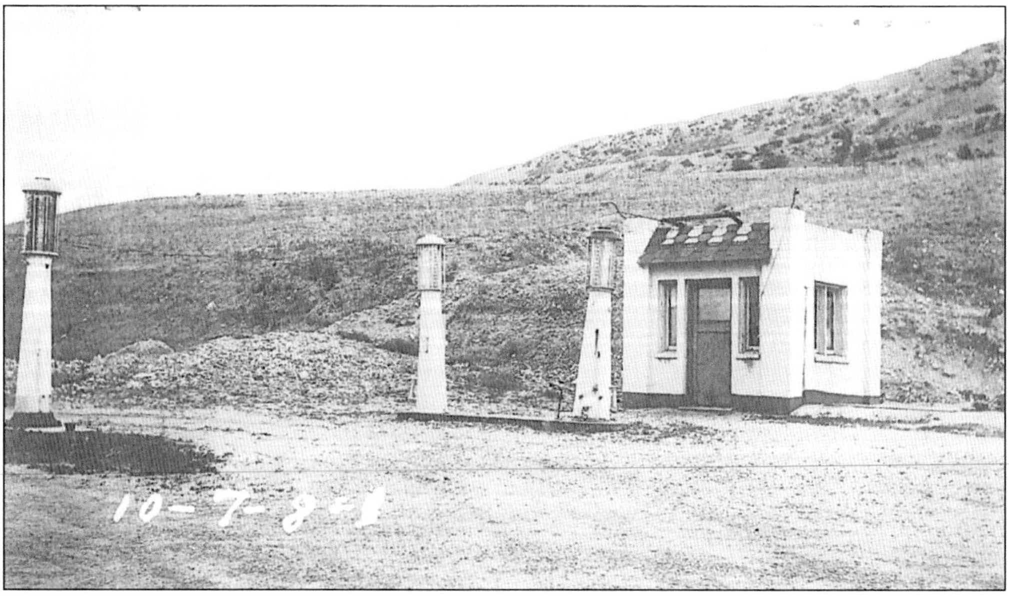

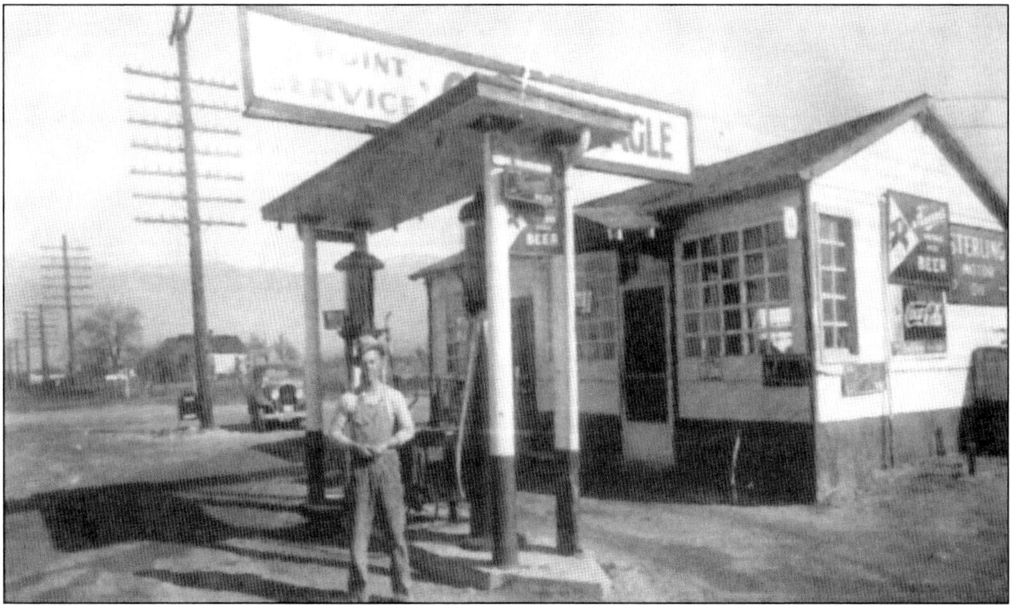

The photograph above, taken in 1941, shows an unidentified man standing in front of a Standard Oil service station on North Main Street in Farmington. Below, Jack and Chris Brown and an unidentified man stand in front of their Davis County Sinclair station around 1952. This is one of the earliest examples of a gasoline station with a covered pumping area. It was a great convenience for the customer, not only keeping them from filling their tank in the rain or snow, but also keeping the ground fairly dry, so that customers weren't walking in deep mud. (Both courtesy Farmington City Historical Museum.)

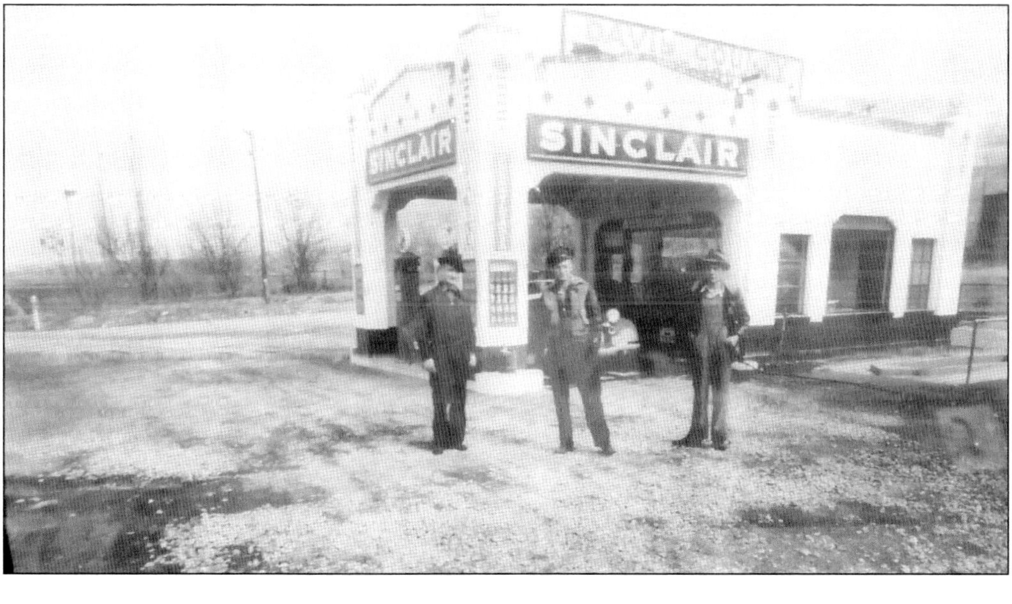

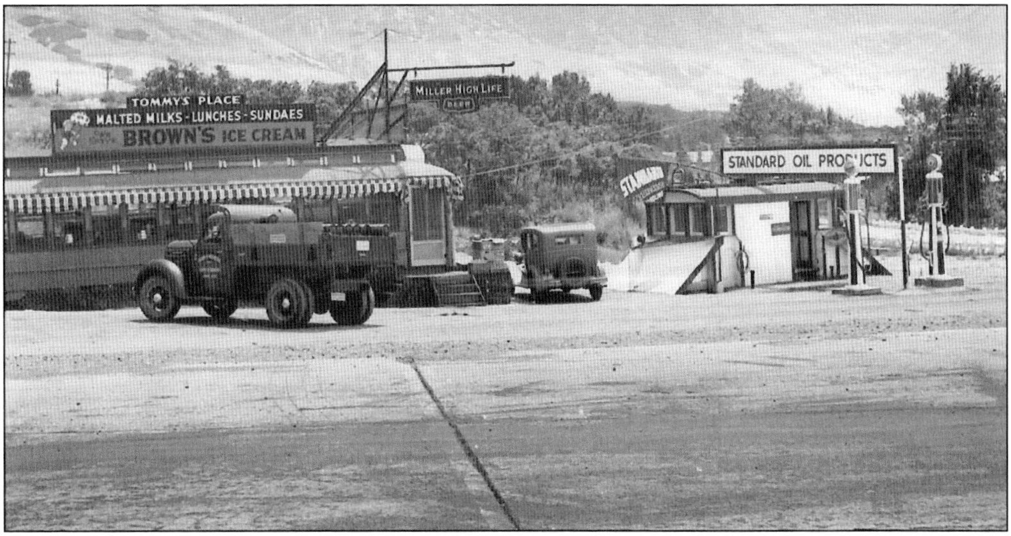

This Standard Oil station was located where Kaysville's Main Street intersects with Highway 89. It was one of the first stations to be combined with a restaurant. Brown's offered sandwiches, drinks, and ice cream, and it quickly became a favorite stop. (Courtesy Farmington City Historical Museum.)

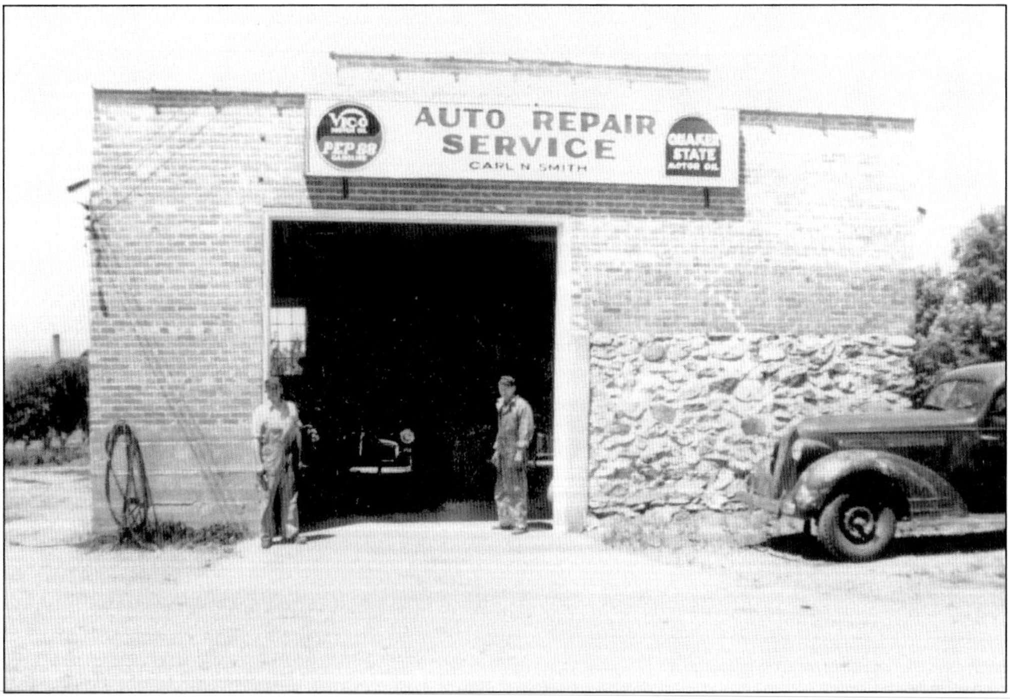

The Auto Repair Service, at 200 South 400 East in Centerville, was built around 1938 over the old Centerville fort wall. The rough stone section of the foundation is reported to be a remnant of the fort, built to protect settlers from Indian attacks. The towns outgrew the progress on the walls, and the construction efforts were abandoned. (Courtesy Centerville City Historical Records.)

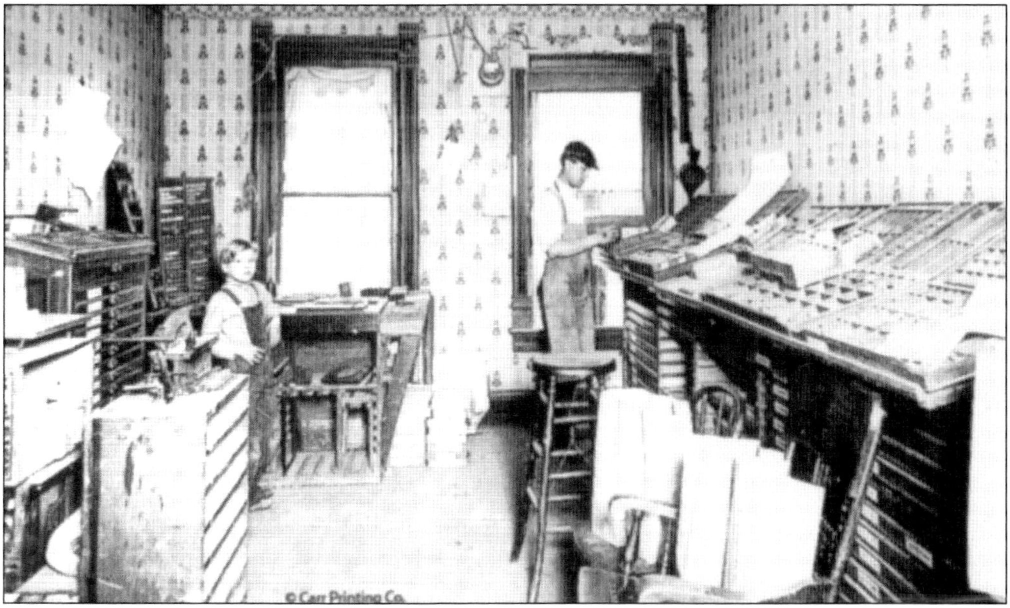

The *Davis County Clipper* was established by Lamonhi Call in 1890 in Bountiful. In the basement of his watch-repair shop, he produced an advertising sheet with a bit of news and called it *Ink Spot*. Adding a few clippings of news from other sources, Call then dubbed his paper the *Little Clipper*. Call and his grandson Willard Carr are shown here. (Courtesy Lloyd Carr/Carr Printing Co.)

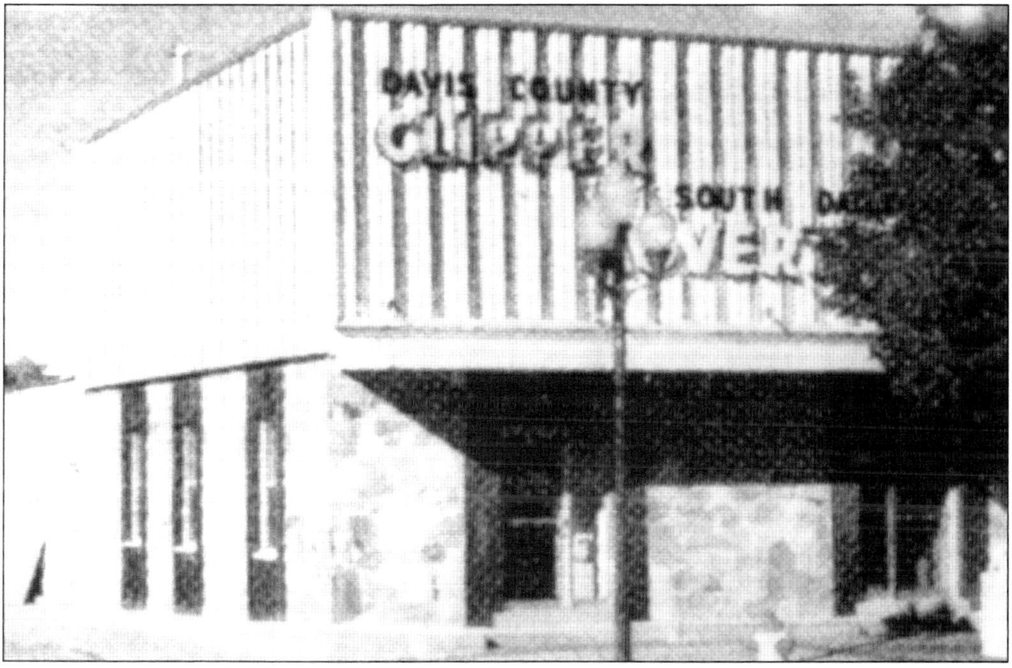

John Stahle Jr. became editor of the newspaper, changing the name to the *Davis County Clipper* in 1892, with deliveries made each Friday for $1.25 per year. Then, six years later, the operation was split, with Call taking the printing business and Stahle taking the newspaper. Call's son-in-law Willard G. Carr continued the business as Carr Printing. The *Clipper* office stood at 94 South Main Street in Bountiful until the building was demolished in 2006. (Courtesy Beverly Nowak.)

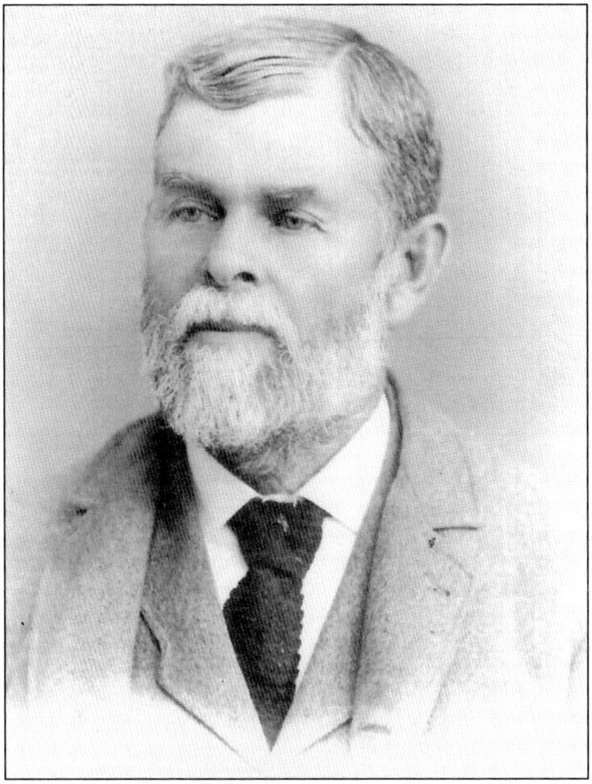

Richard and Sarah Ann Duerden came to Utah in 1868, and, in 1873, they were finally able to buy land and build a three-room adobe home. After digging a well, they were able to grow vegetables, which Richard sold in Salt Lake City. Making the trip twice weekly, he set up a small business in his kitchen. In 1878, he was able to build a storefront onto his house (below), where he sold vegetables and dry goods. The Duerdens are believed to be the people to the right of the house. Duerden obtained the first safe and installed it at the store, where people could deposit their valuables. Children coming into the store always received a piece of candy. On June 7, 1883, one of the first three telephones in South Davis County was installed at the Duerden store, at a cost of $18 per quarter or $72 per year. (Left, courtesy Beverly Nowak; below, courtesy Bountiful History Museum.)

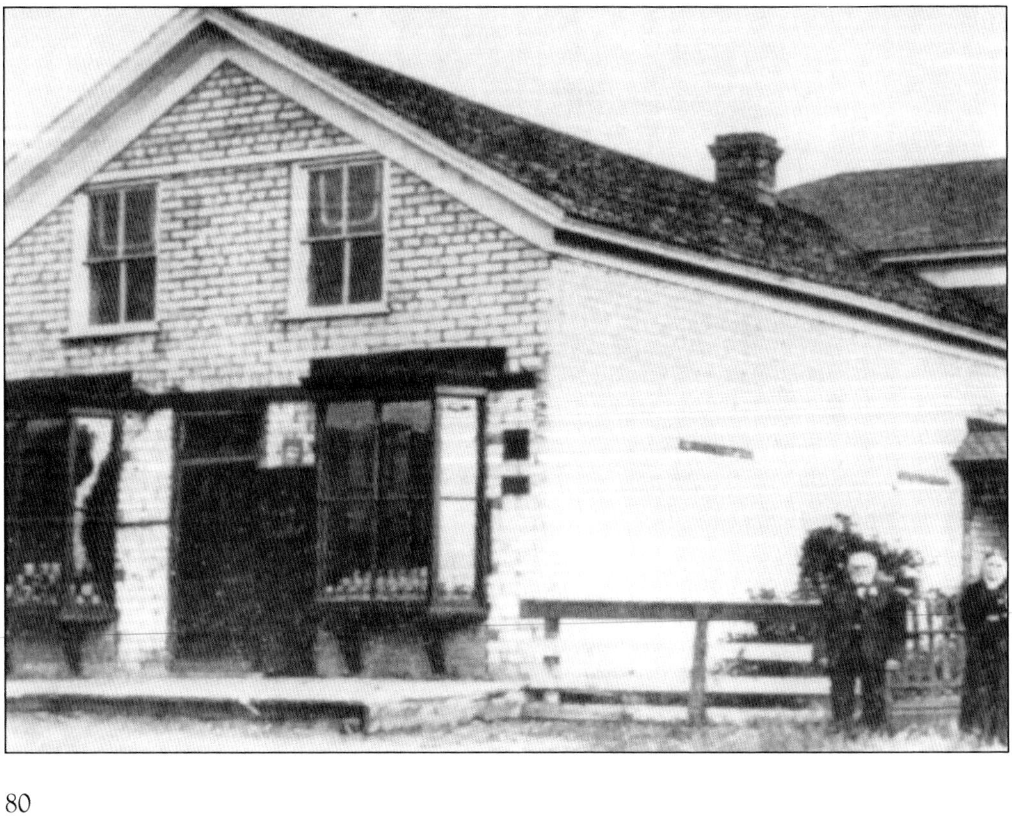

Seven

Education and Worship

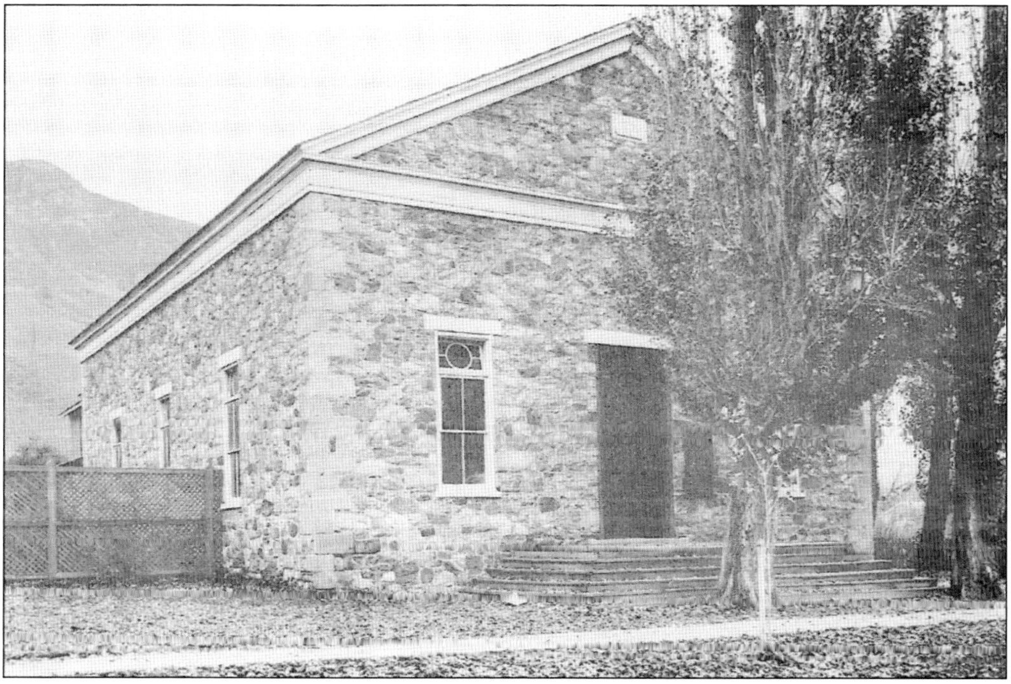

On Main Street in Farmington stands an old Mormon church, built around 1848. Here, in 1878, Aurelia Spencer Rogers organized a children's program called the Primary Association, enlisting 215 children. Her focus was on principles of honesty and faith—in short, to "keep the boys from stealing fruit from the orchards and the girls from sneaking rides on passing wagons." The organization now has a worldwide presence. (Courtesy Farmington Historical Museum.)

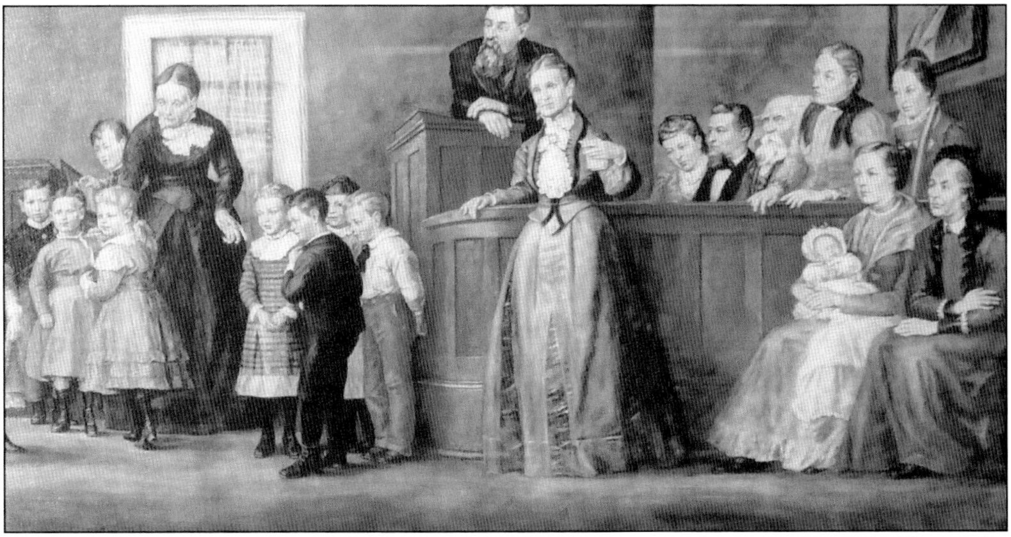

This is a portion of an artistic depiction of the first Mormon Primary meeting, held in 1878. Parents and leaders were concerned that children had too much free time. The organization published its own songbook and taught children to appreciate God's world around them. They received lessons in manners, grooming, and social behavior. The artist of this 25-foot mural in the old rock church was Kenneth R. Mays. (Courtesy Farmington Historical Museum.)

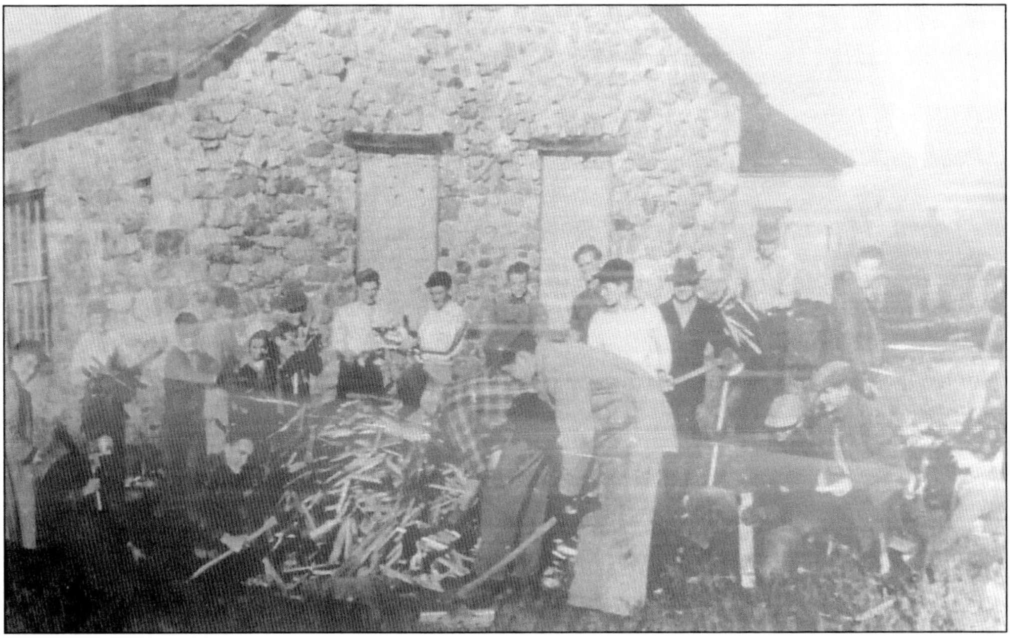

Here, boys and men cut firewood for distribution to widows and the needy through the harsh winter. Such service projects included planting gardens, participating in barn raisings, and helping to harvest crops. These programs taught the youth industry and how to serve others and to give of one's self. This group became the Young Men's Mutual Improvement Association. A similar program was established for young girls. (Courtesy Farmington Historical Museum.)

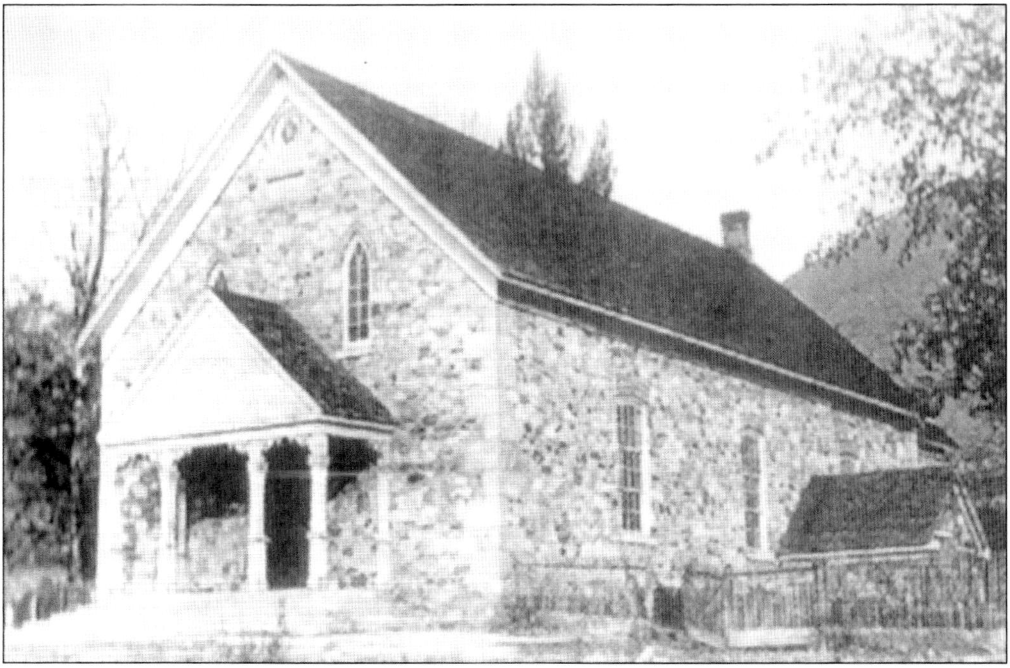

The first Mormon church in Centerville was completed in 1879. It featured a large assembly room, a vestry, and one small upstairs room. Nathan Cheney was bishop of the ward at this time, but he moved to Brigham City in 1888. He was replaced by Bishop Aaron B. Porter, the grandson of the first bishop in Centerville, Sanford Porter. (Courtesy Utah State Historical Society.)

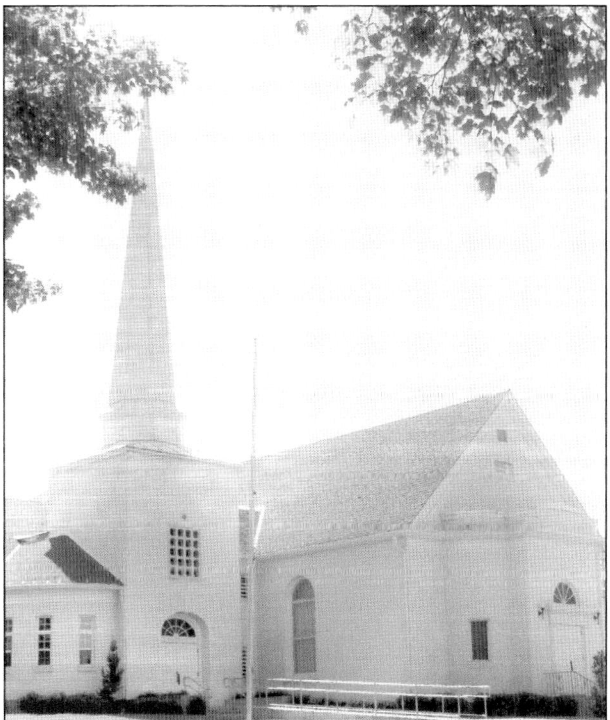

The historic church has undergone several renovations. A wing was added on the north side to house a gym, a stage, a kitchen, and Sunday school classrooms. Later, a two-story addition was erected on the south side to accommodate the Relief Society, the Boy Scouts, and the bishop's office. Although the interior has been updated, it still shows the charm and character of its pioneer roots. Unfortunately, the children's cry room was eliminated.

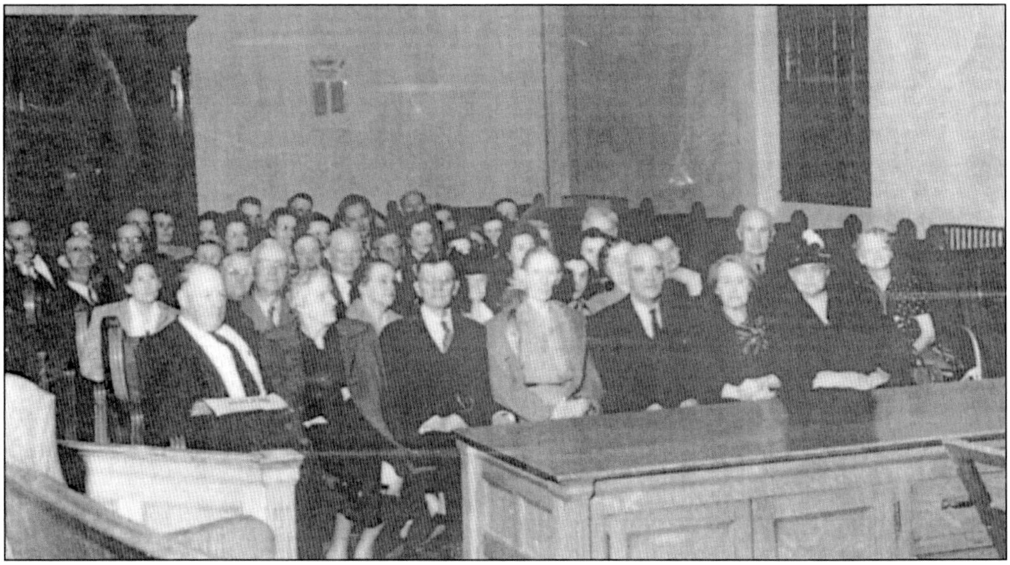

The interior of the Centerville First Ward Church has retained its warmth and charm. The benches and arching windows remain much as they were in the original church. The pulpit area now accommodates a choir and provides cushioned seating. A small anteroom to the north is now an overflow area, unique to this chapel. (Courtesy Kathleen Dalrymple.)

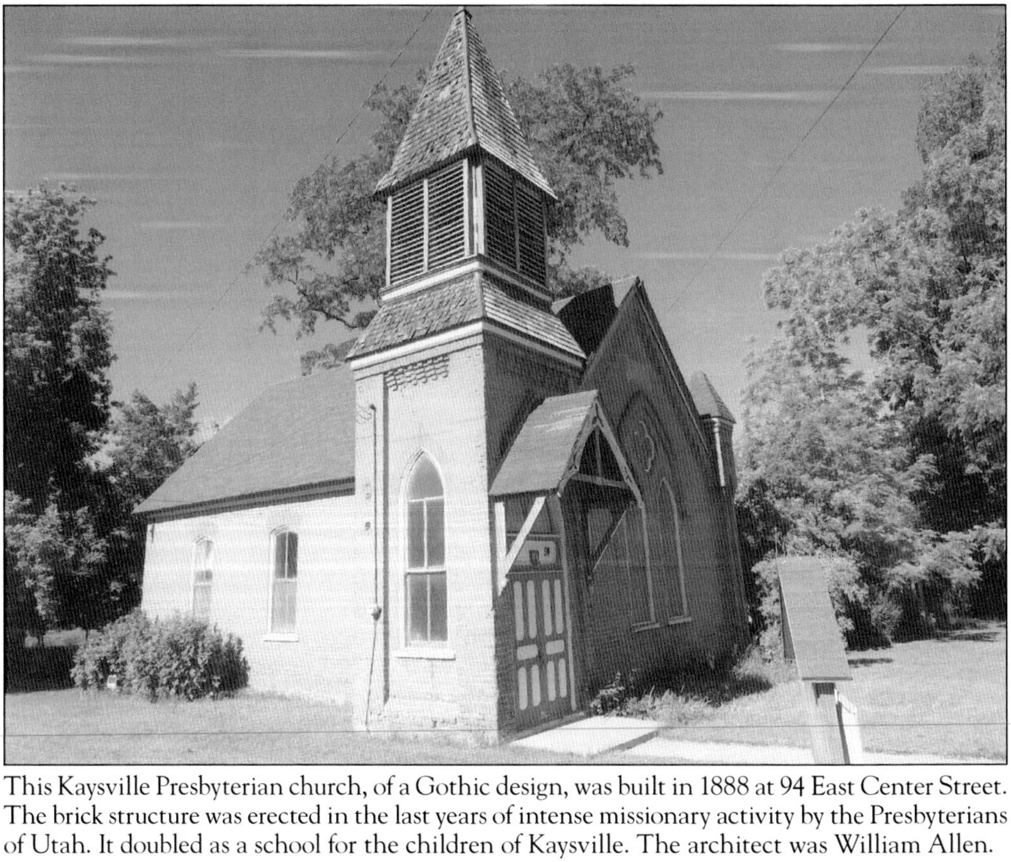

This Kaysville Presbyterian church, of a Gothic design, was built in 1888 at 94 East Center Street. The brick structure was erected in the last years of intense missionary activity by the Presbyterians of Utah. It doubled as a school for the children of Kaysville. The architect was William Allen.

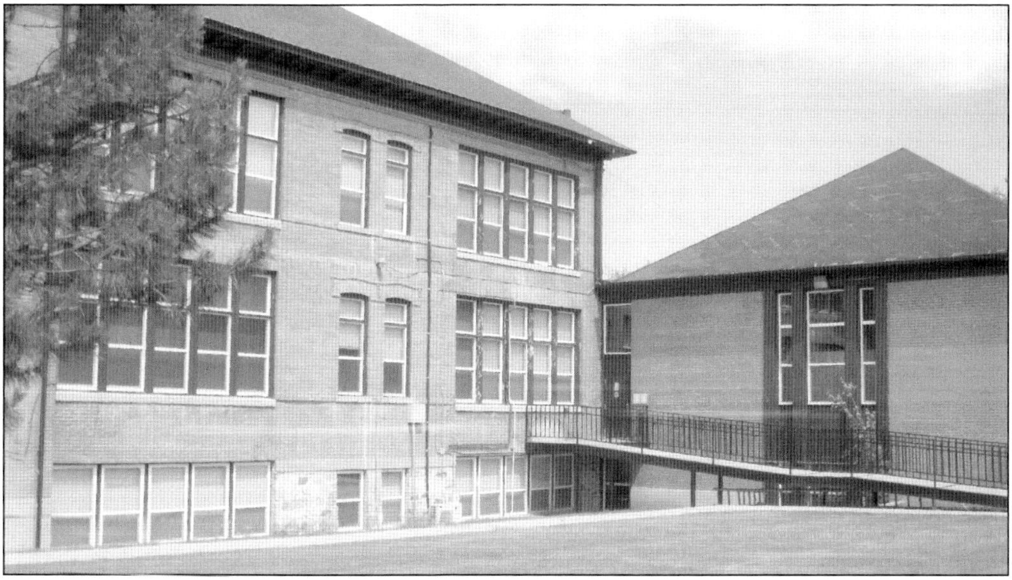

The Stoker School, at 75 East 200 South in Bountiful, was named after Bishop John Stoker. It was built over the foundation of the old Central School in 1904. Potbellied stoves heated each room until 1907, when a coal furnace was installed. Leo J. Muir was the first principal, serving until 1910. The new principal, David Tolman, was known for his school bell, tenor voice, and yardstick.

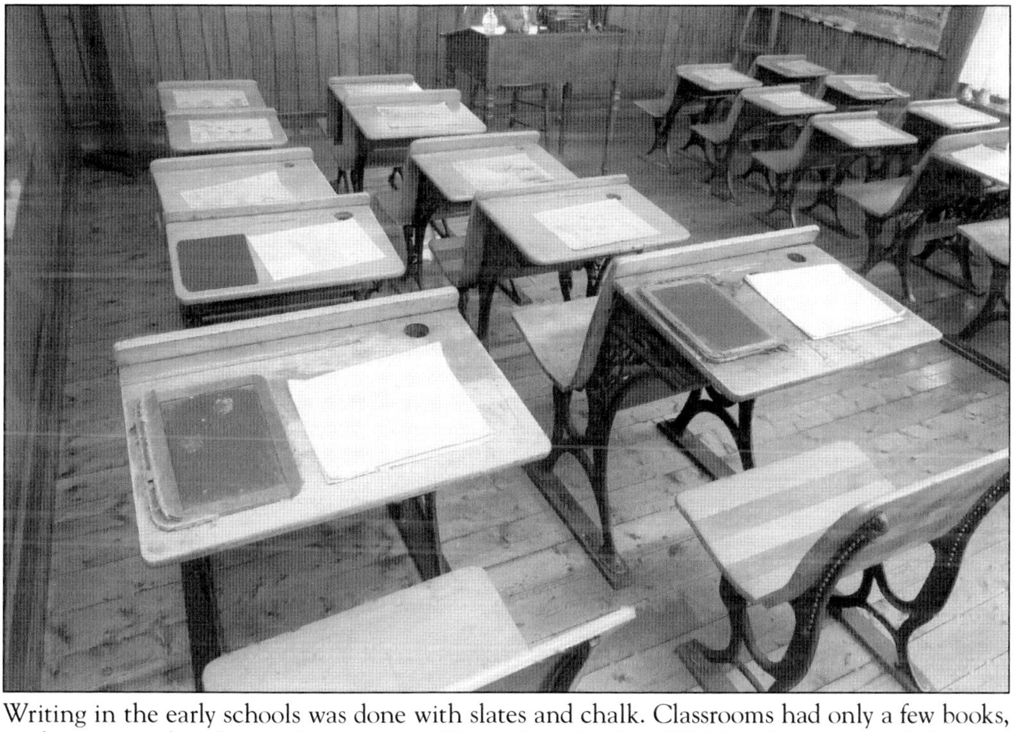

Writing in the early schools was done with slates and chalk. Classrooms had only a few books, students sat on benches, and paper was of limited availability. Within a few years, individual or two-student desks (shown here) were introduced, creating an improved, disciplined environment. Slates and chalk continued in use until the early 1900s. Note the inkwells on the desks, for use with quill pens.

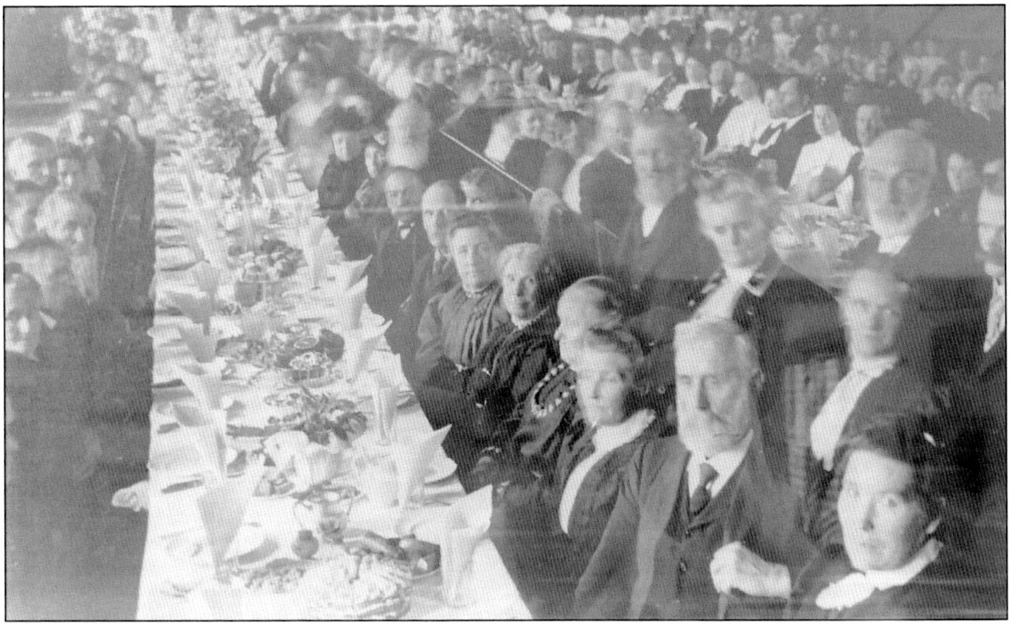

Shown here is a church dinner in Kaysville at the release of the beloved bishop of the ward in 1901. For the dinner, held in the basement of the church, three long tables were set up. Since many bishops served in leadership roles for 15 years or more, it was a special occasion when they were released and a new bishop was selected. (Courtesy Kaysville City Records.)

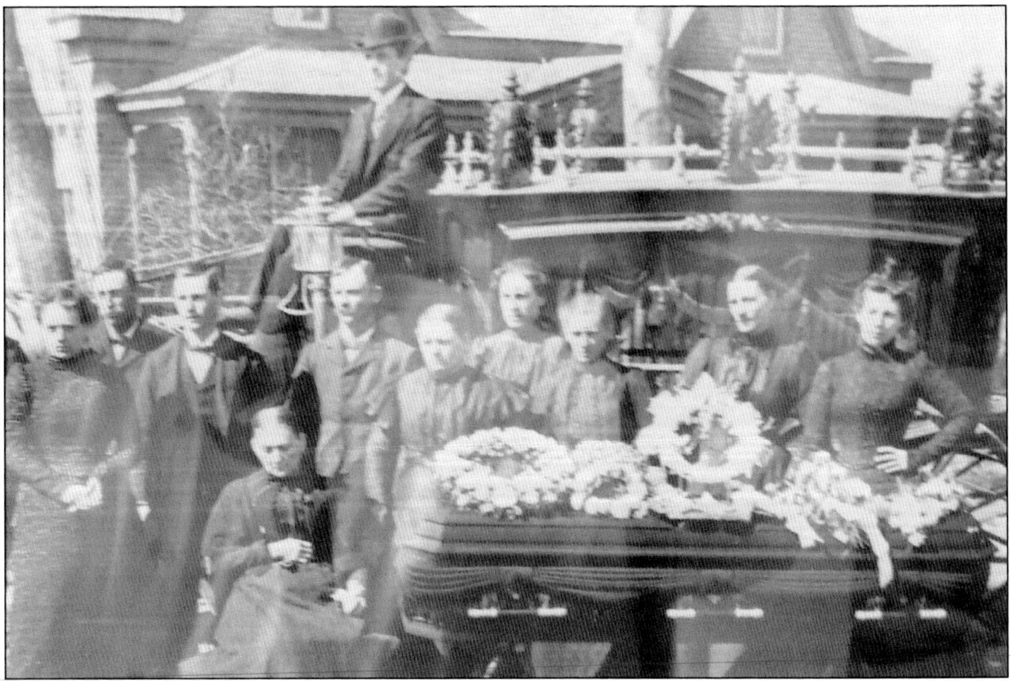

Seen here is the funeral of William Henry Bone, on March 12, 1900, in Kaysville. Bone, who came from England in 1861, suffered from injury as a result of a broken knee he acquired in a teeter-totter accident when he was eight years old. He became known as the "best cobbler in the county." In 1865, he built a home at 100 North Main Street with a small shop on the corner.

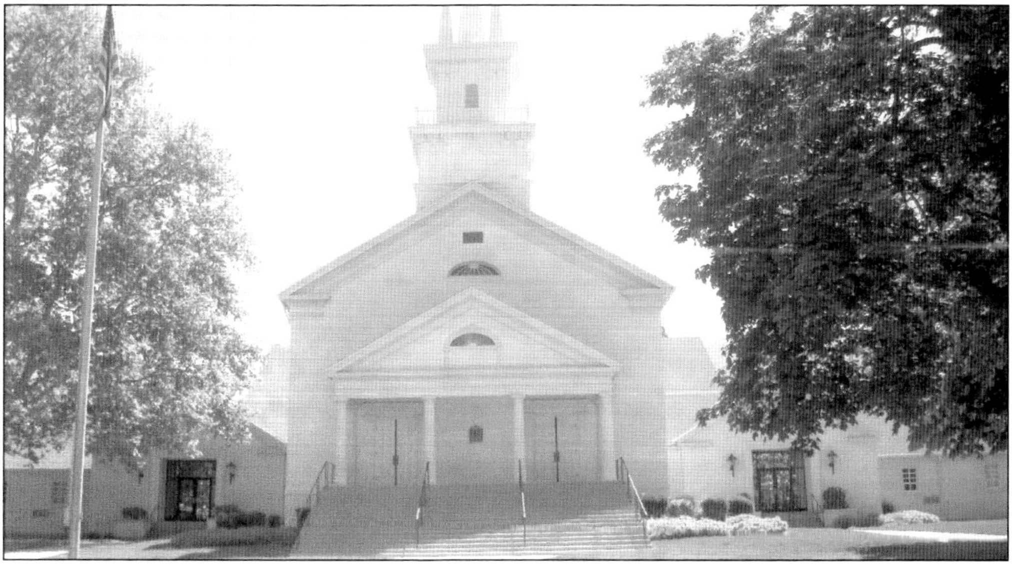

The Bountiful Tabernacle was the finest building owned by the Mormon Church when it was dedicated in 1863. It was designed by architect Augustus Farnham and built with adobe walls, roof timbers fastened by wooden pegs, and lumber harvested in Holbrook Canyon. The original tower had five spires, the center spire being a sundial. This building replaced an earlier, 20-foot-by-30-foot building made of logs at Fourth North and Second West.

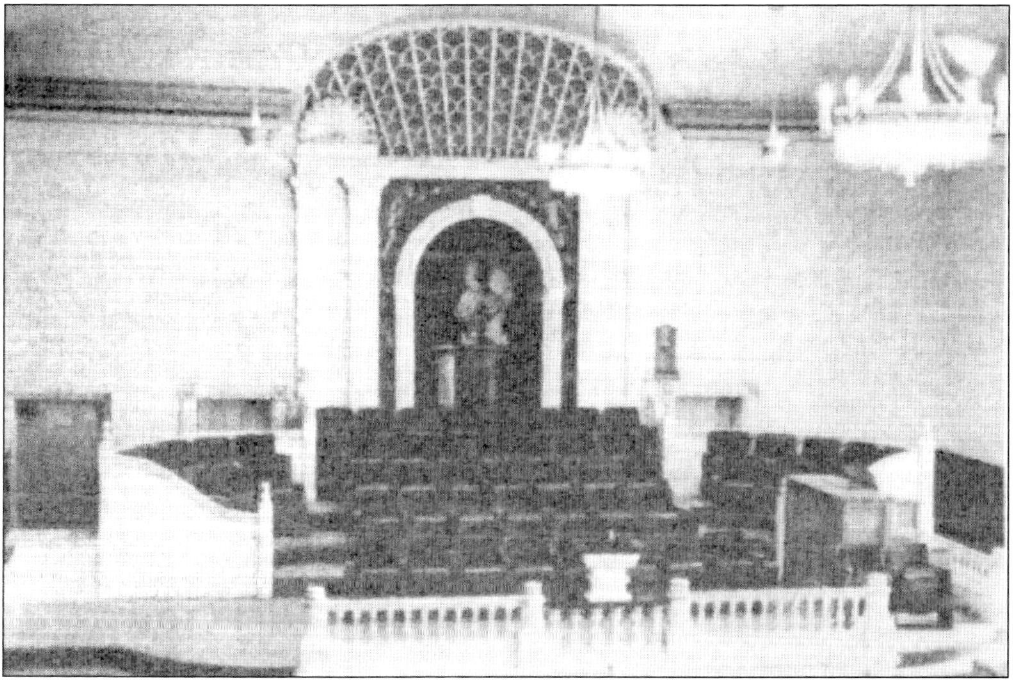

This is an early photograph of the interior of the tabernacle in Bountiful. The pulpit and choir seats were beautifully done by skilled workmen, some of whom had worked on the Mormon temple in Nauvoo, Illinois. The hanging light fixtures originally held candles. The fixtures could be lowered to allow the candles to be lit when light was needed for a meeting. (Courtesy Bountiful History Museum.)

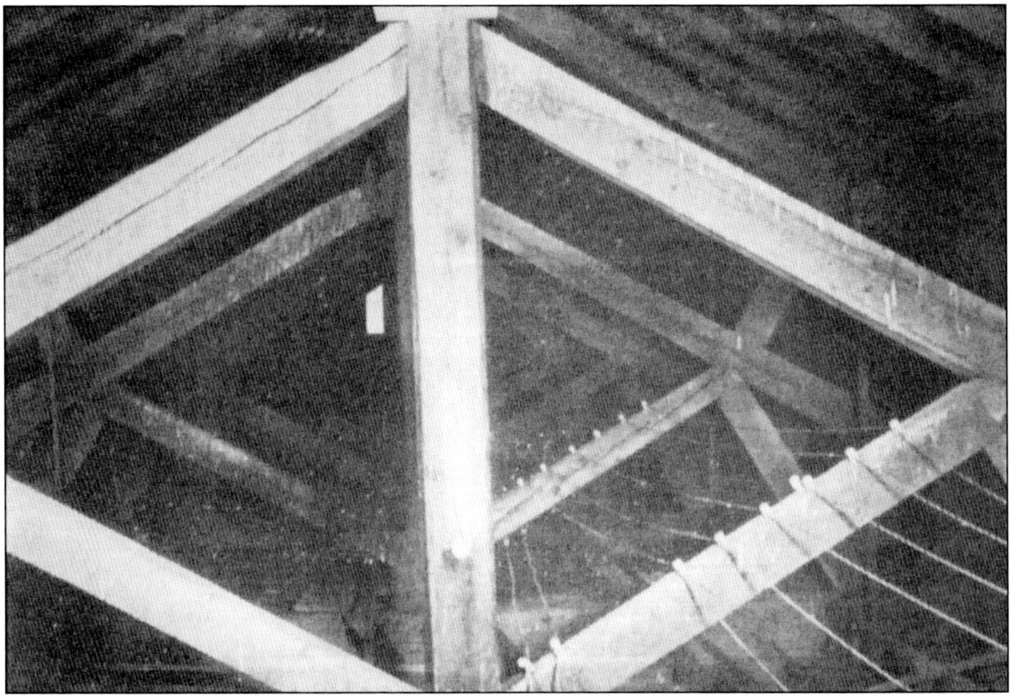

The foundation of the Bountiful tabernacle is six feet thick at the base and nine feet high, with stone pillars one and a half feet square supporting the floor. Adobe bricks formed three-foot-thick walls. This photograph of the attic provides a glimpse of the heavy red pine beams held with wooden pegs. The electrical wiring was completed later. (Courtesy Bountiful History Museum.)

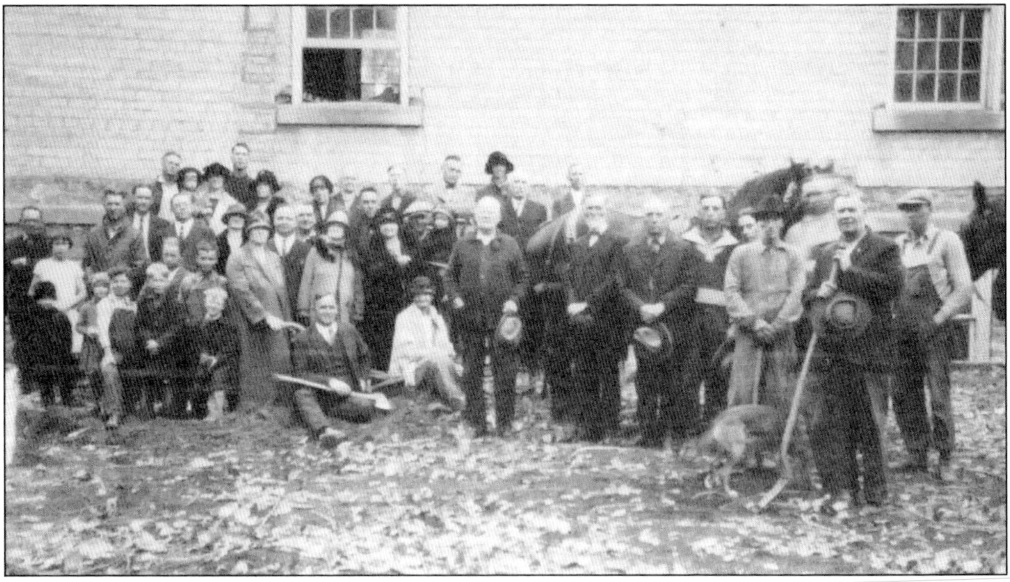

This photograph shows the ground-breaking ceremony for the remodel of the tabernacle and the addition of the north wing. A south wing was added later. In 1974, when a proposal was made to demolish the old building and construct a modern worship facility, the outcry from the populace led to many newspaper articles and columns. The public pressure saved this historic structure. (Courtesy Bountiful History Museum.)

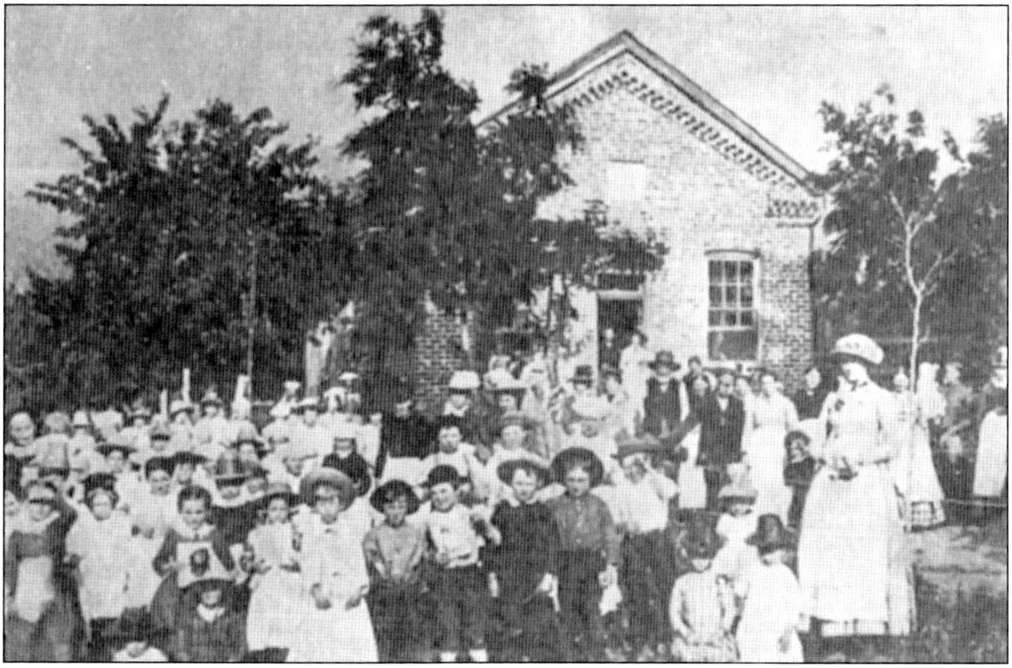

Located at 200 South and 200 West in Bountiful was the Patty Sessions Academy, built in 1884. It was created for the instruction of the children in Sessions' family and for the poor, but, as the public school overflowed, the trustees of the academy allowed extra students to attend. Sessions funded the academy by purchasing stock in Zions Cooperative Mercantile Institution (ZCMI) and applying the interest and dividends to the school. (Courtesy Bountiful History Museum.)

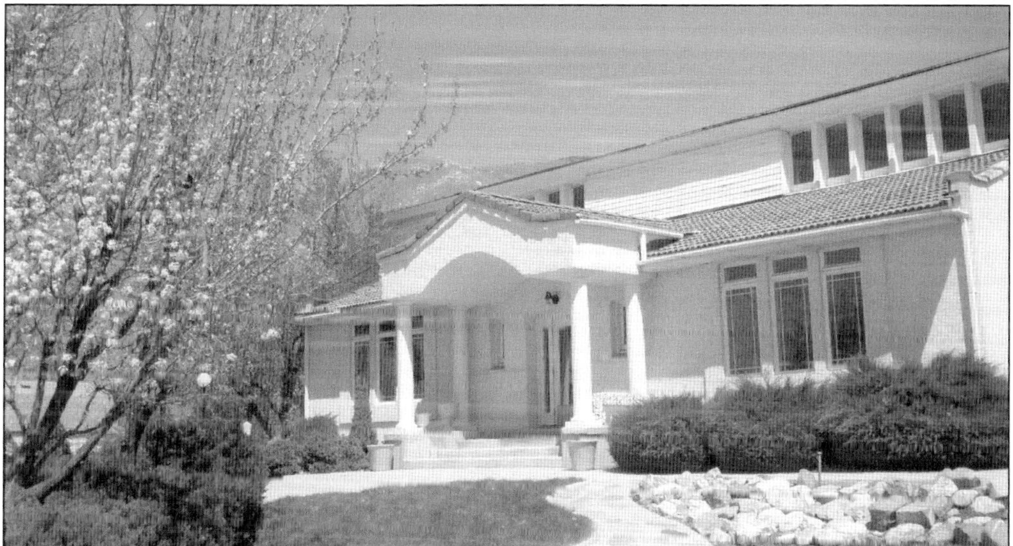

The Centerville Second Ward on North Main Street was organized in 1917, with Joseph Nelson Ford as the first bishop. For two years, the congregation met in a district school, before building this beautiful little chapel, dedicated in 1919. A baptismal font was installed in the basement, and it served both Bountiful and Centerville until 1961. Before the font's installation, baptisms were commonly done in the millponds.

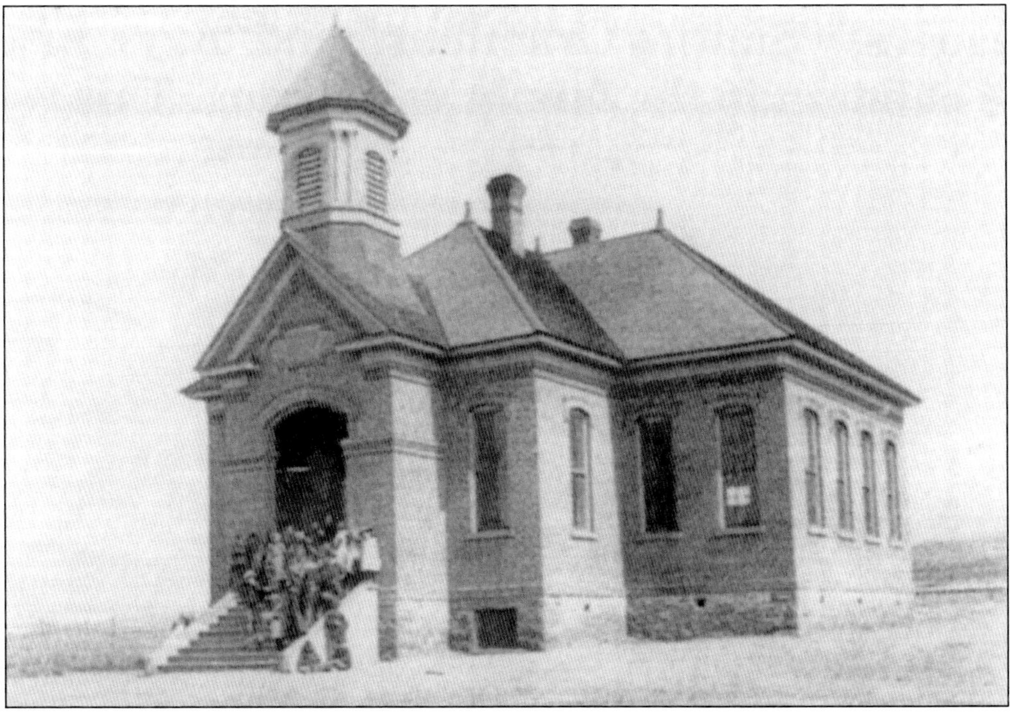

In 1878, a rock schoolhouse was built just north of the Hot Springs. The teacher was Mary Jane Winegar Mills. Her family lived in two rooms behind the school. About 1880, a one-room school was built at 700 North on Highway 89. In 1898, this larger two-room school was built out of brick. It had a potbellied stove, no water, and an outdoor toilet. (Courtesy City of North Salt Lake.)

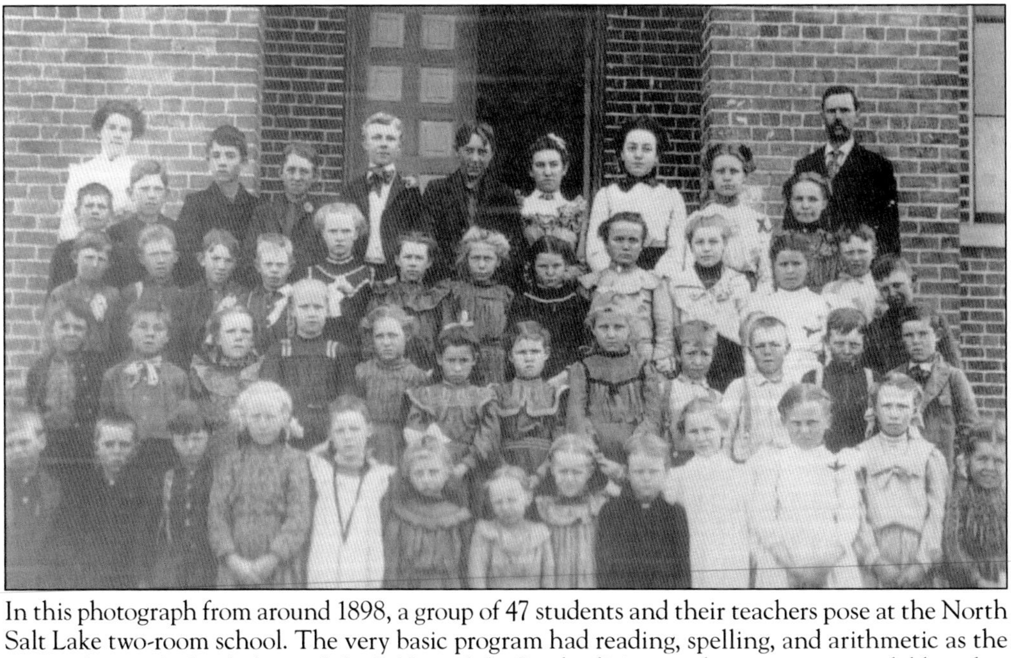

In this photograph from around 1898, a group of 47 students and their teachers pose at the North Salt Lake two-room school. The very basic program had reading, spelling, and arithmetic as the main subjects. As books beyond the Bible and the Book of Mormon became more available, other subjects were added. (Courtesy City of North Salt Lake.)

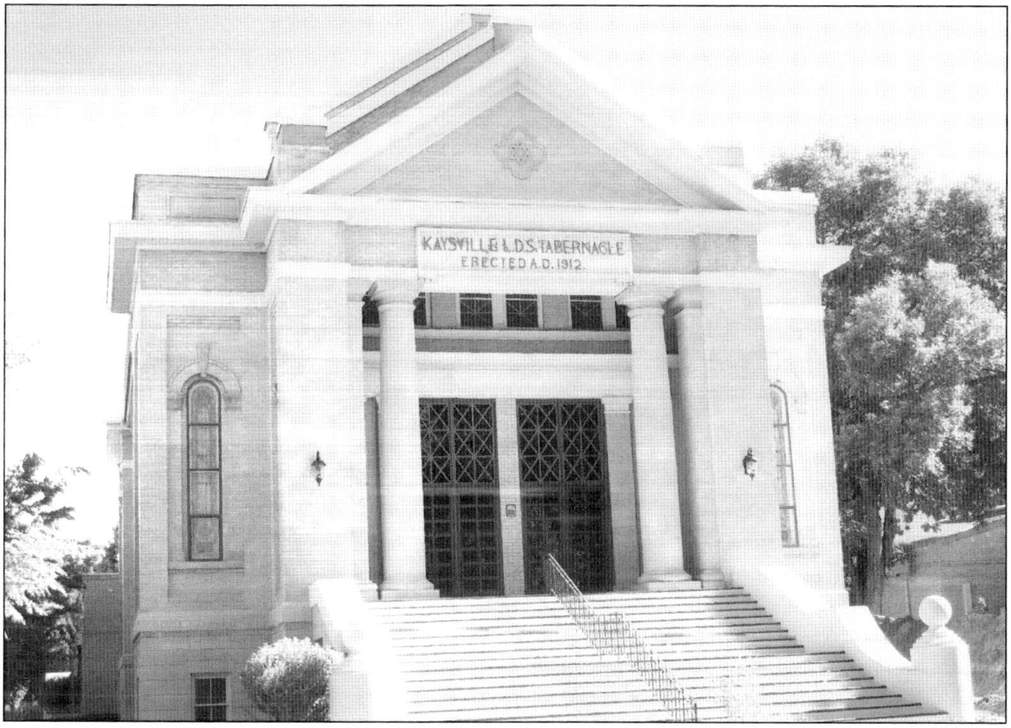

The Kaysville Tabernacle was completed by the Mormon Church in 1914. Located at 198 West Center Street, it is known for its beautiful stained-glass windows. It was constructed under the direction of Bishop Henry H. Blood, who later served as Utah's governor from 1933 to 1941. Previously, the congregation gathered in an adobe meetinghouse across the street, which had been built between 1855 and 1863.

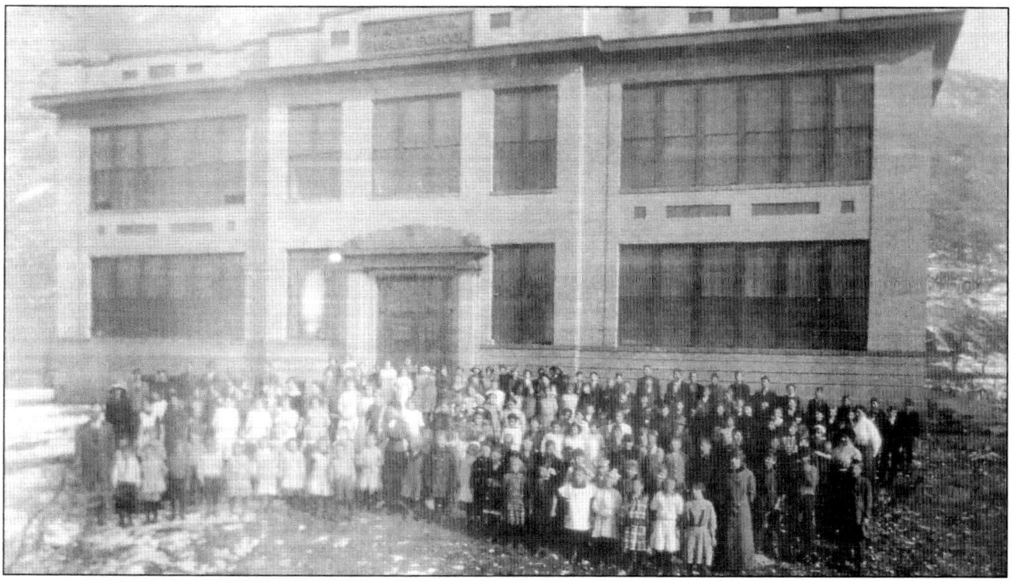

A new public school was constructed in Farmington in 1911. The two-story facility allowed in ample light from the many windows along the side of each classroom. Posing in this photograph is the first student body of the school. (Courtesy Farmington Historical Museum.)

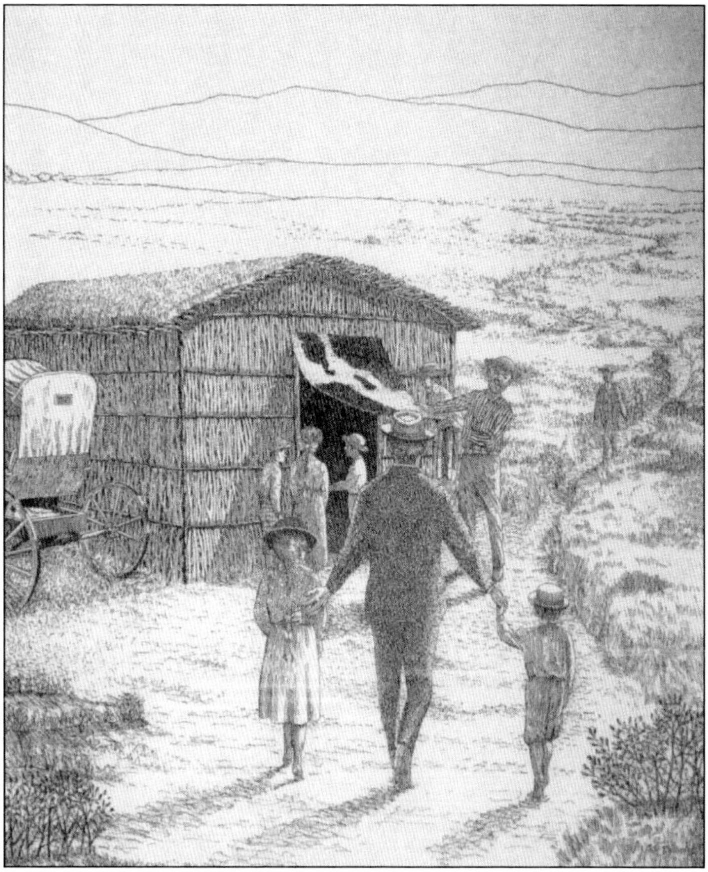

In the fall of 1848, Hanna Holbrook taught six children in their "wickiup" (wikihut) home on the banks of the Jordan River, located due west from 1500 South in West Bountiful, where they found ample grass and cane to feed their stock. The willow and mud shanty was recorded in this pencil sketch by artist G. Dowding. (Courtesy Bountiful History Museum.)

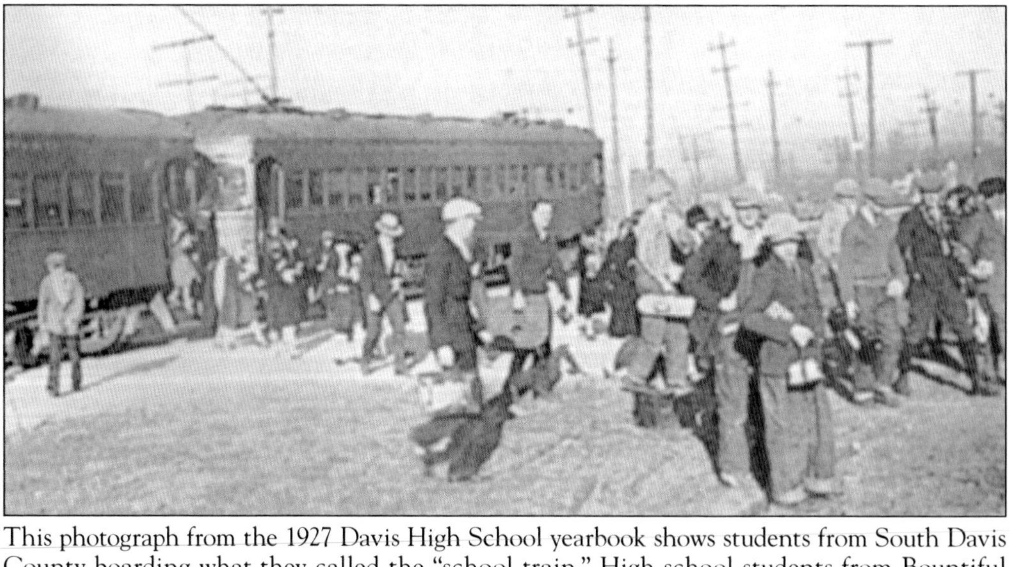

This photograph from the 1927 Davis High School yearbook shows students from South Davis County boarding what they called the "school train." High school students from Bountiful and Centerville would board the Bamberger train in the morning, attend classes through the day, and return home at night. Davis High School was located in Kaysville. (Courtesy Nola Tingey Hatch.)

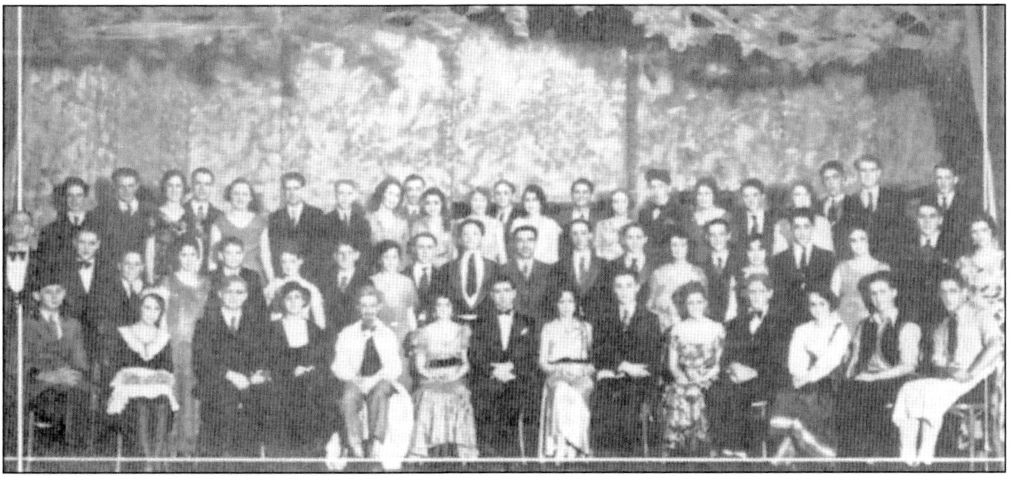

The 1932 senior class of Davis High School poses for a photograph. Until the new high schools were built—Viewmont and Bountiful High Schools in Bountiful, and Woods Cross High School in Woods Cross—all the students in South Davis County attended Davis High School. The high school built in 1914 has been replaced by a large, modern facility.

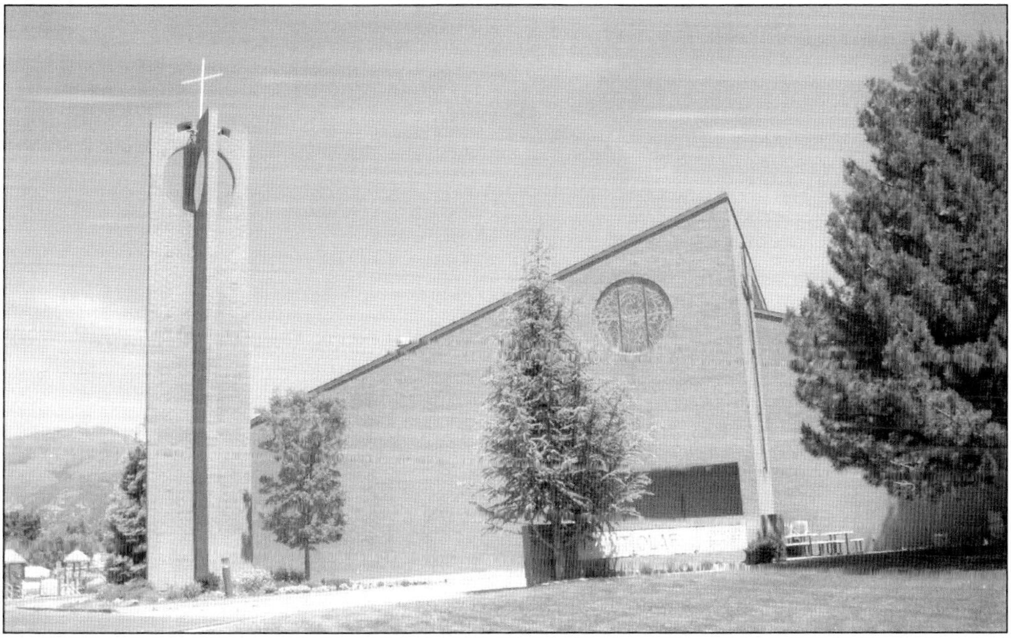

For 100 years after the pioneers arrived in the valley, there was no Catholic church between Salt Lake City and Ogden. St. Olaf Parrish, established in 1943, was named after the Viking king and patron saint in recognition of the many Scandinavian settlers. It is located at 1800 South Orchard Drive in Bountiful. The church was constructed in 1979 by architects Brotherton & Gillies.

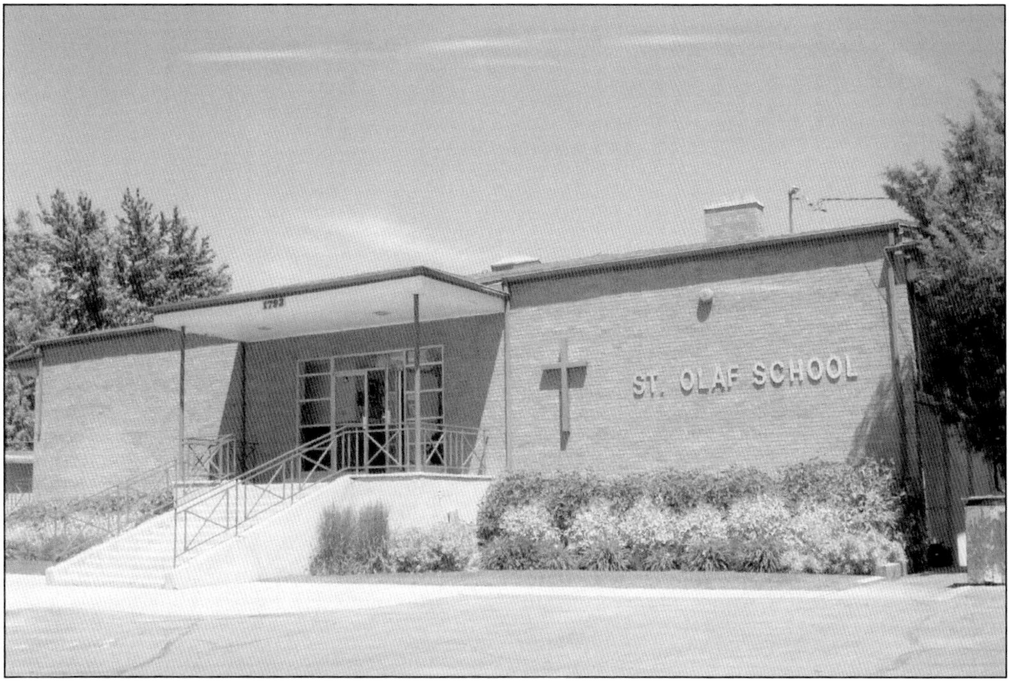

This school was added to the St. Olaf's Church facility in 1959. Three nuns arrived to teach at the school, but they soon returned to their order to serve the materially needy. They were replaced with lay teachers. Preschool through eighth grade are now taught at the school.

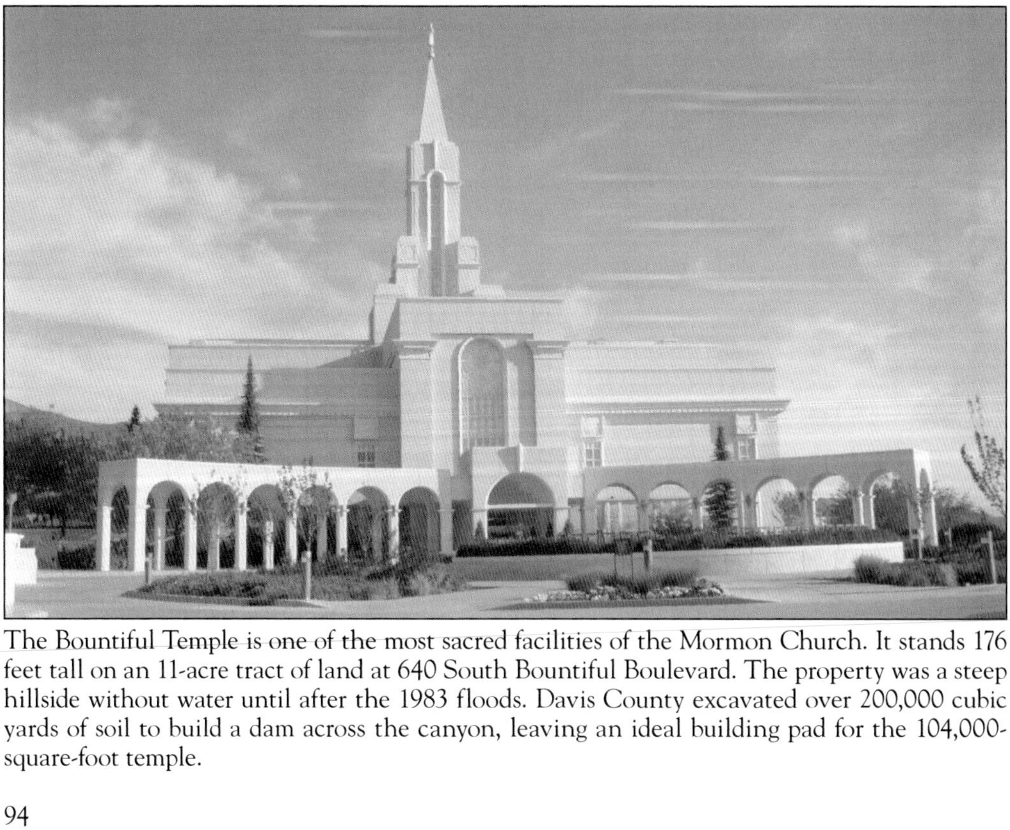

The Bountiful Temple is one of the most sacred facilities of the Mormon Church. It stands 176 feet tall on an 11-acre tract of land at 640 South Bountiful Boulevard. The property was a steep hillside without water until after the 1983 floods. Davis County excavated over 200,000 cubic yards of soil to build a dam across the canyon, leaving an ideal building pad for the 104,000-square-foot temple.

Eight

Fun Is Big Business

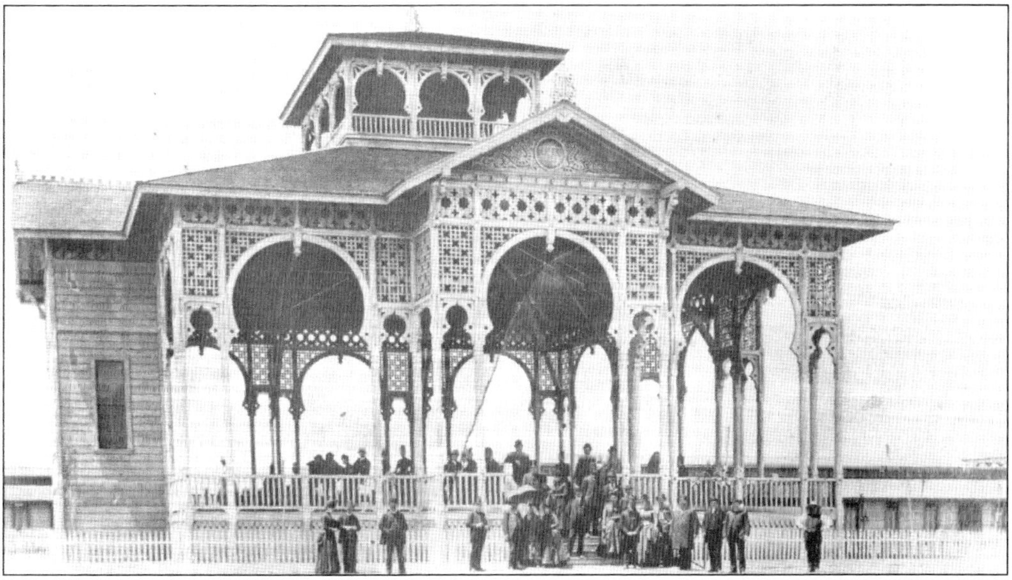

Constructed with wooden pegs in 1886, this pavilion welcomed visitors to Lake Shore Resort on the Great Salt Lake, southwest of Farmington. Thousands came to enjoy a swim in the salty lake or a cruise to the islands. The train dropped off passengers right at the park, into the colorful pavilion. (Courtesy Utah State Historical Society.)

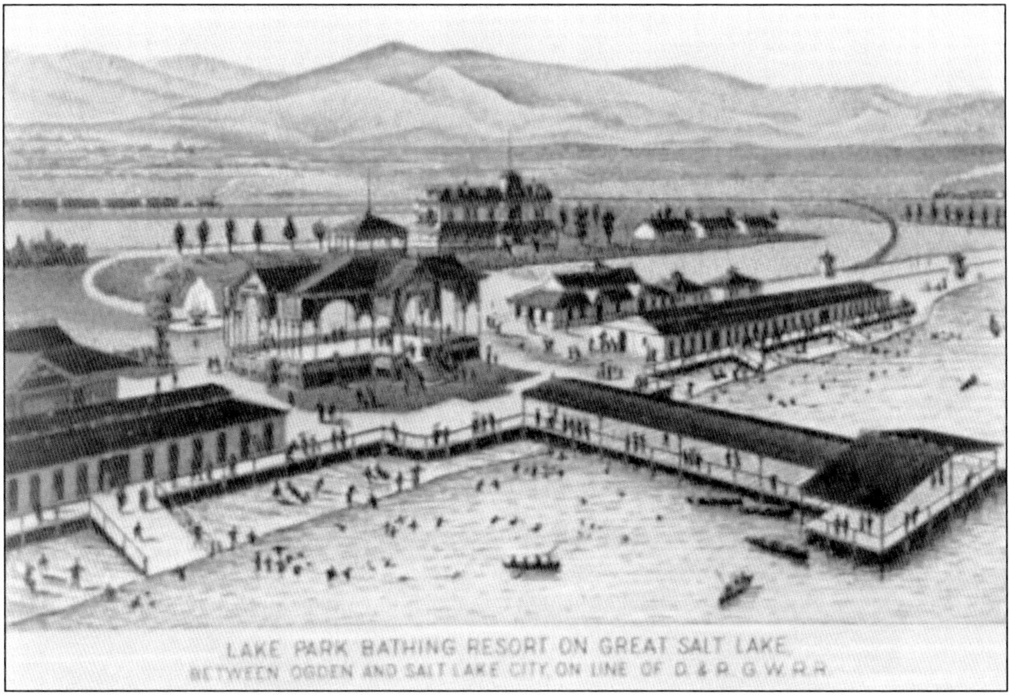

The Lake Park Resort, located on 215 acres of shoreline, opened in 1886, attracting 50,000 visitors per year. It offered swimming, bathhouses, picnic kiosks, a shooting gallery, and rowboats. The salty brine of the lake allowed a person to easily float in the water. The large open-air pavilion hosted bands and featured dancing. Visitors coming by train were dropped off right at the resort. (Courtesy Utah State Historical Society.)

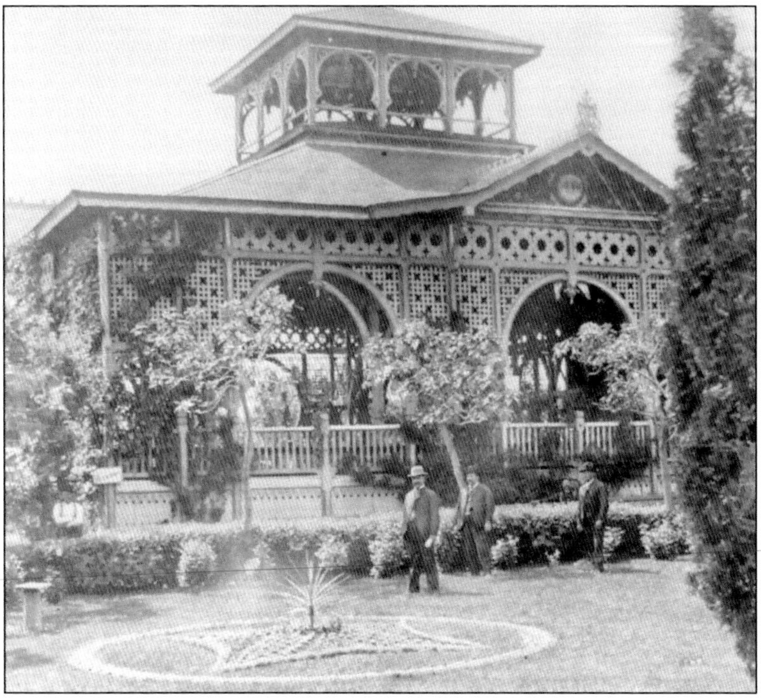

With the opening of a new lakeside resort in Syracuse and the Black Rock Resort on the south shore, Lake Park Resort began to fail. Built in shallow water over a muddy bottom, the water remained cloudy. Simon Bamberger, a Lake Park investor, purchased most of the assets and relocated the resort to a site farther east. (Courtesy Lagoon Corporation.)

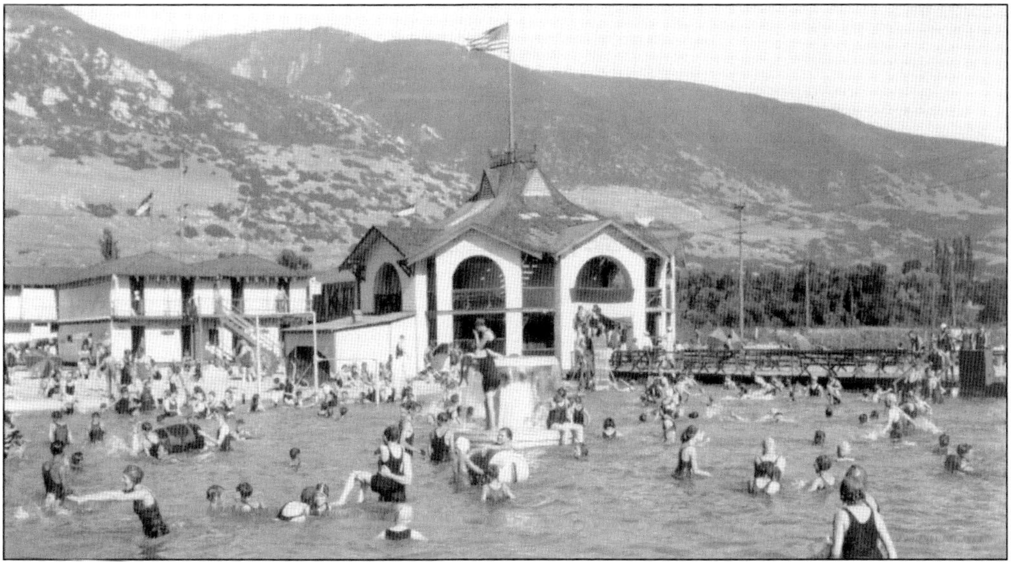

Simon Bamberger cleared a pond area closer to Farmington and built a 5,000-square-foot freshwater lake and park called Lagoon. The stench of decaying brine shrimp, muddy bottoms, murky water, and the biting "no-see-ums" of the lake were replaced with refreshing, clear water. Bamberger moved the dance pavilion and many of the old facilities to the new site. (Courtesy Lagoon Corporation.)

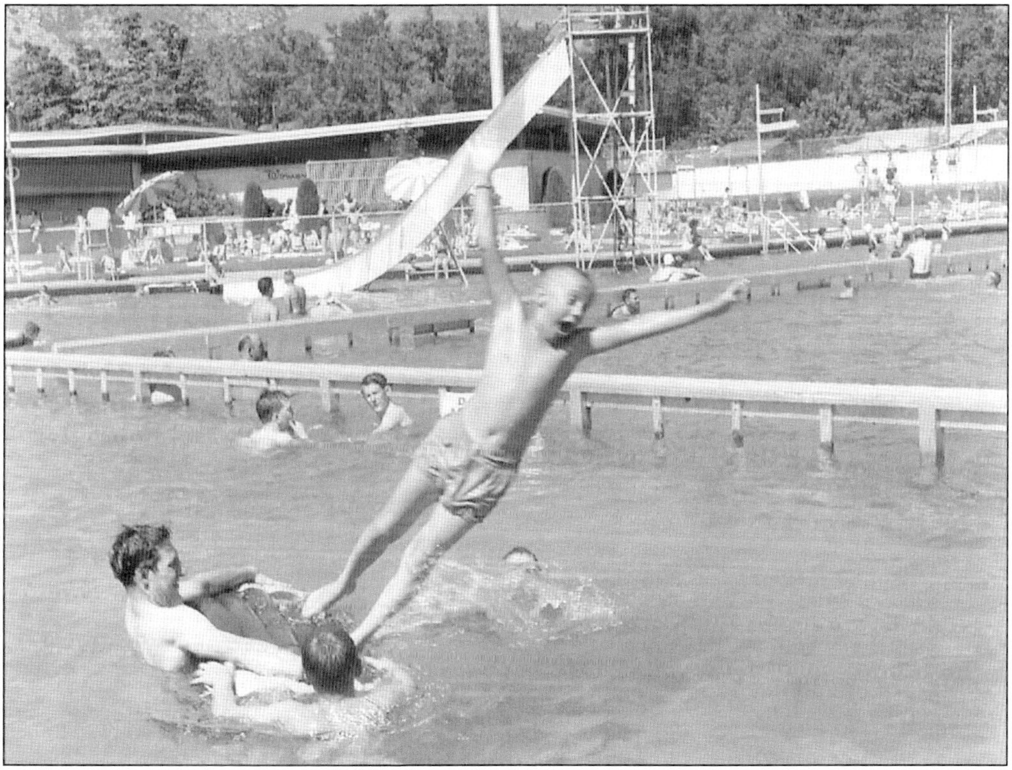

The Lagoon added new equipment to the pool each year. Slides of various heights, platforms barely under the water, and a variety of flotation devices were added, along with items for young and older swimmers. On a hot summer day, the water was refreshing and inviting. (Courtesy Lagoon Corporation.)

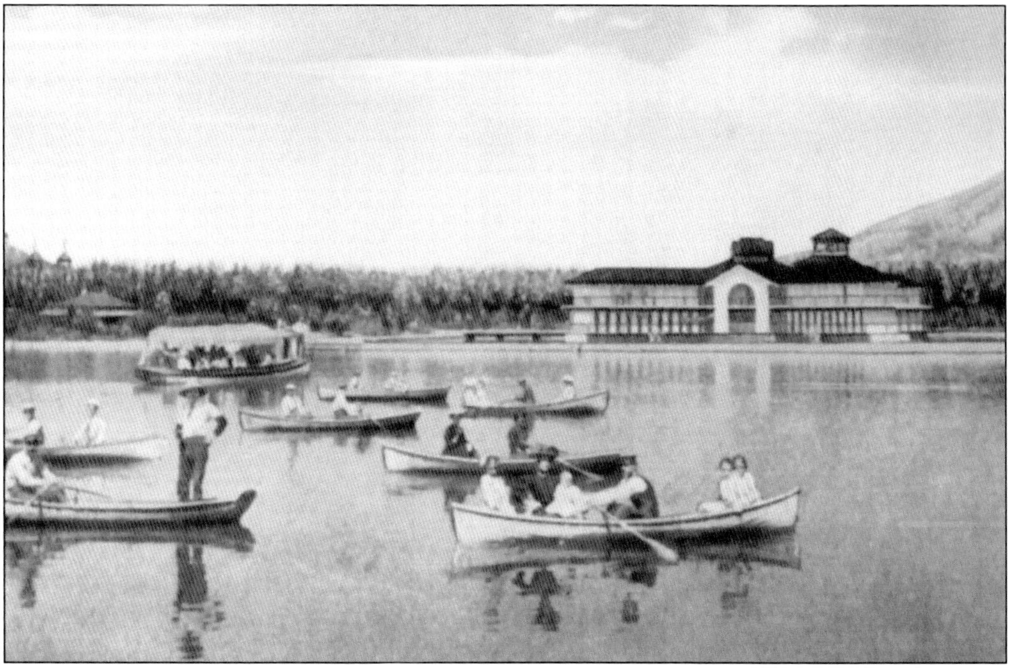

The man-made freshwater lake at Lagoon Resort offered boating, excursion rides, swimming, and canoeing. The popular attraction was a great alternative to the saltwater lakeshore resort. Bamberger planted flowers, beautiful shrubs, and trees, which provided a pleasant fragrance of fresh, green vegetation. (Courtesy Lagoon Corporation.)

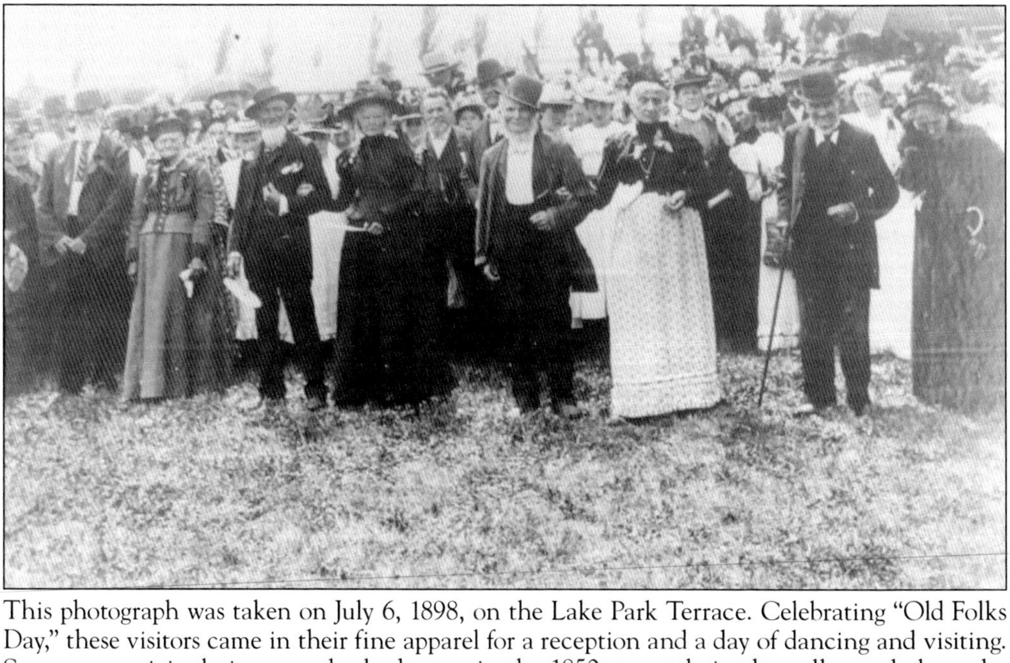

This photograph was taken on July 6, 1898, on the Lake Park Terrace. Celebrating "Old Folks Day," these visitors came in their fine apparel for a reception and a day of dancing and visiting. Some were original pioneers who had come in the 1850s to settle in the valley and along the lakeshore. (Courtesy Lagoon Corporation.)

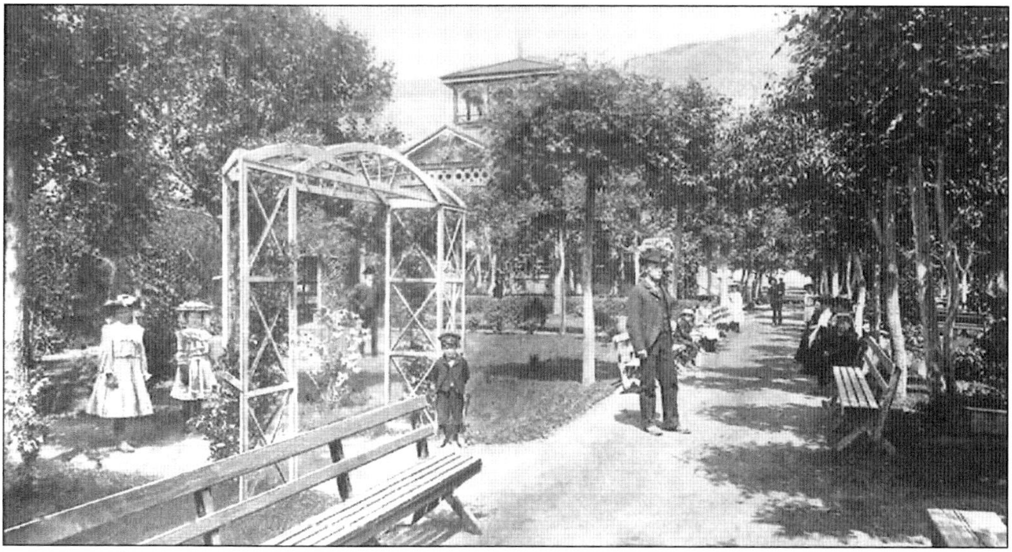

Terrace Park attracted many visitors, who would come to relax or stroll, as seen in this photograph from around 1900. In particular, they came to the park on Sunday afternoons to enjoy the gardens, read in the shade of a lofty tree, or perhaps show off a new bonnet. It was a place of social exchange. (Courtesy Lagoon Corporation.)

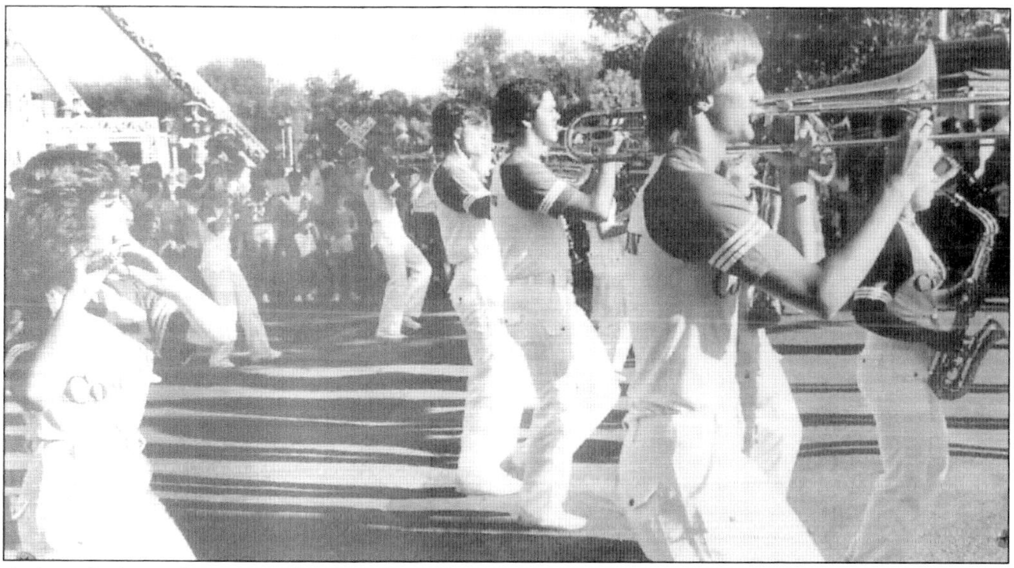

A dignified march was totally abandoned by the Lagoon marching band, initiated in the 1960s. The Lagoon band roved the grounds of the resort, playfully spinning, taking giant steps, or swaggering along while waving their instruments. This totally nonconformist behavior was a delight to the crowds, as the band members rollicked and played carnival music to cheers and applause. (Courtesy Lagoon Corporation.)

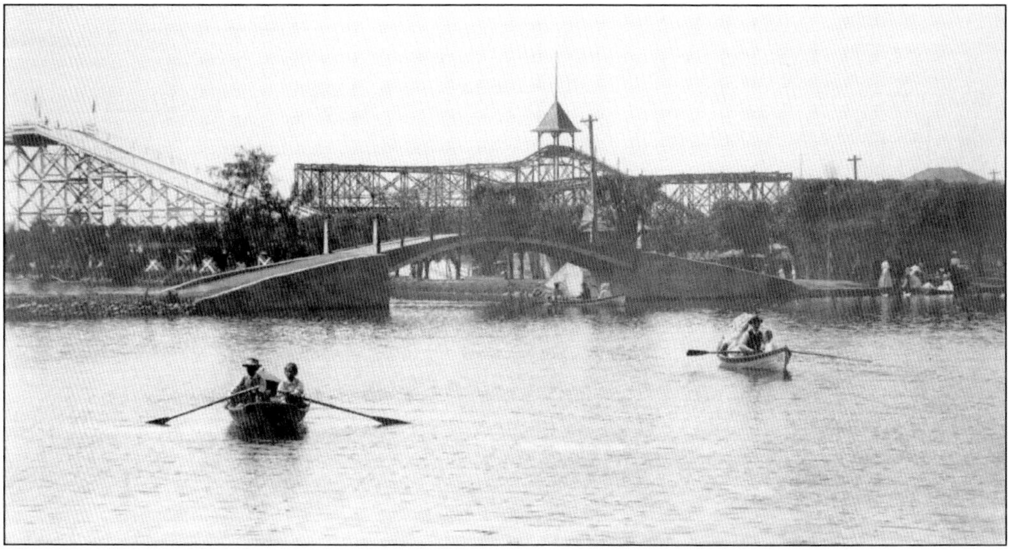

The best ride in the park for thrill-seekers was the wood-constructed roller coaster. This facility was unique for its time, and it remains in operation today. Although many new rides and concessions have been added, the roller coaster continues to reign as the granddaddy of them all. In the photograph above from around 1898, the structure spreads across the park and forms a backdrop to Lagoon Lake. The photograph below was taken around 1950. As with many coasters, the cars leave the station and climb a tall section of the tracks. The train then seems to pause momentarily before throwing the riders furiously downhill at heart-stopping speeds. (Both courtesy Lagoon Corporation.)

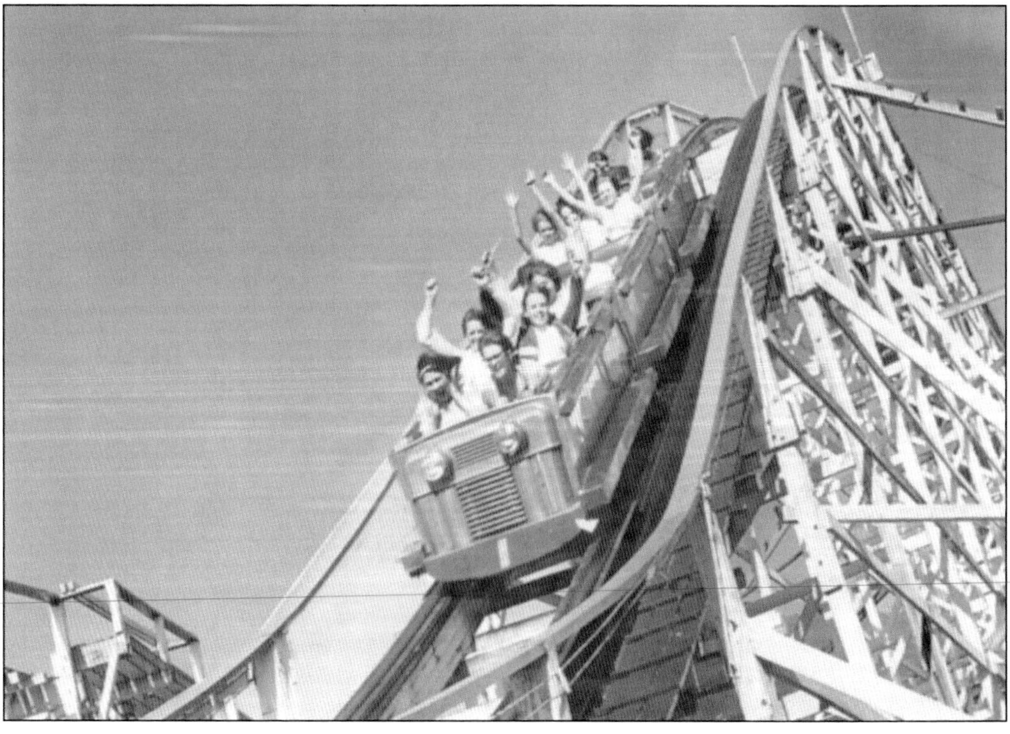

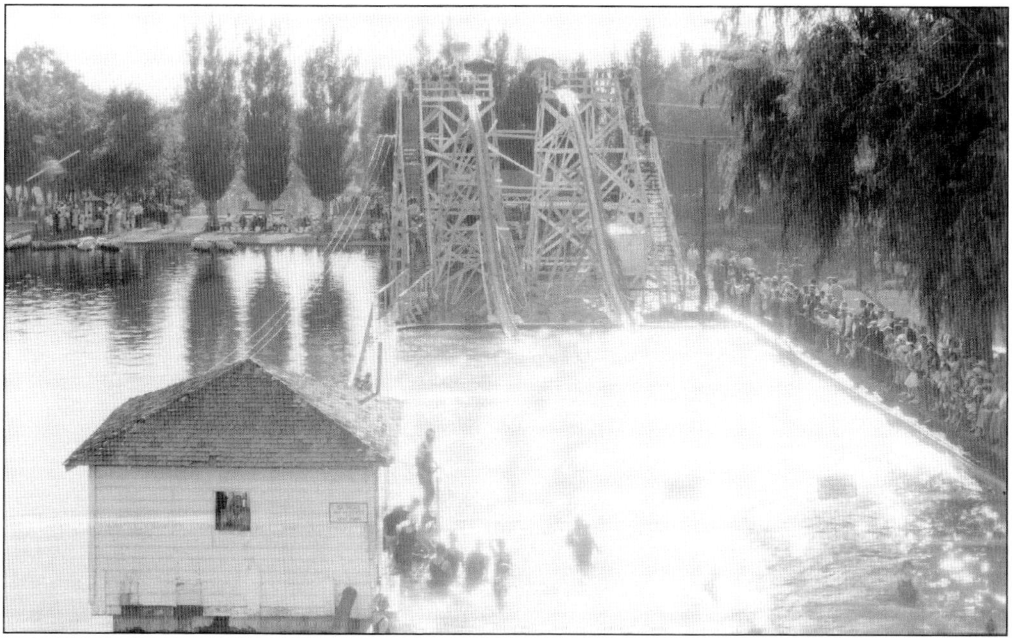

Ask any of the "old-timers" about the best rides at Lagoon, and they will recall the roller coaster. But they will quickly add the water slides, the fun house, and the spinning wheel. As riders climbed the walkway to the top of the slides (above), their hearts pounded harder and harder, anticipating the drop. Reaching the top, they would have second thoughts. Then, they peered down as their turn came up, anticipating a high-speed launch into the water below. Riders of a different kind experienced excitement while sitting at the center of the spinning wheel (below). They gripped their hands and braced their feet against the centrifugal force that would soon cast them from the center of the platform, sliding or tumbling to the side. Ouch, the scraped elbows! (Both courtesy Lagoon Corporation.)

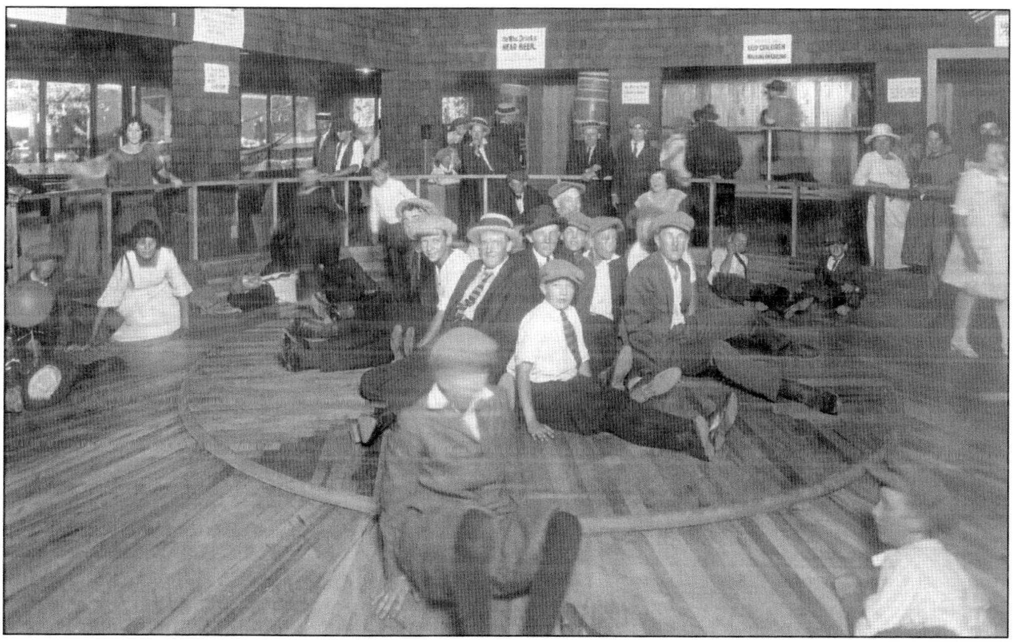

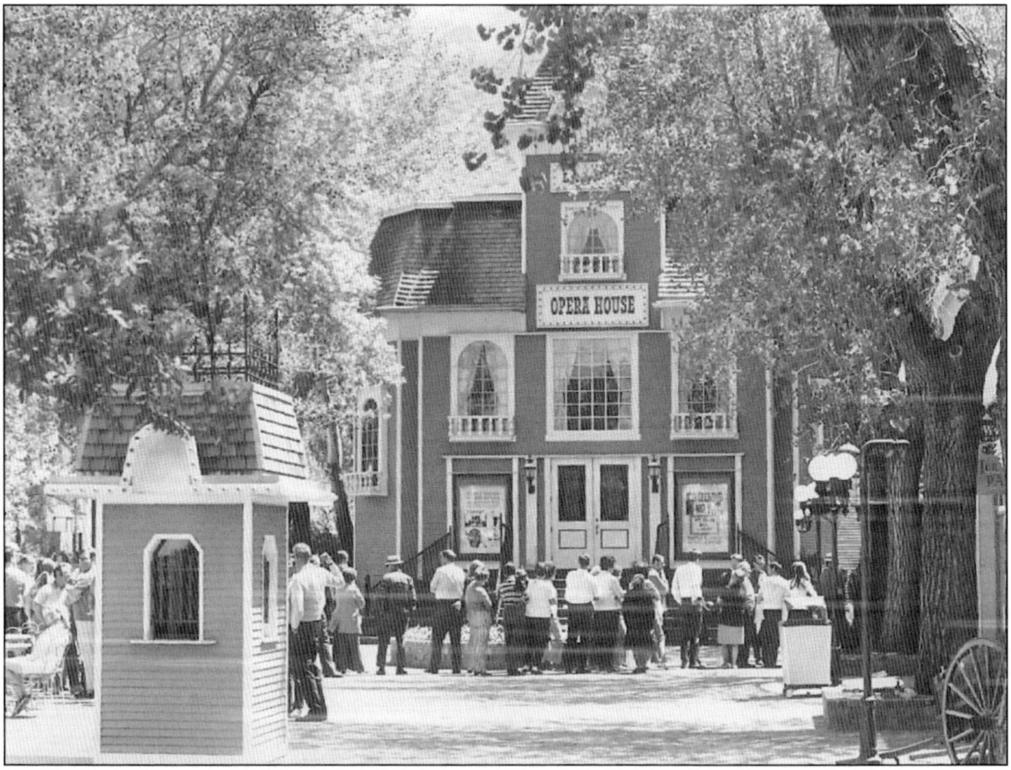

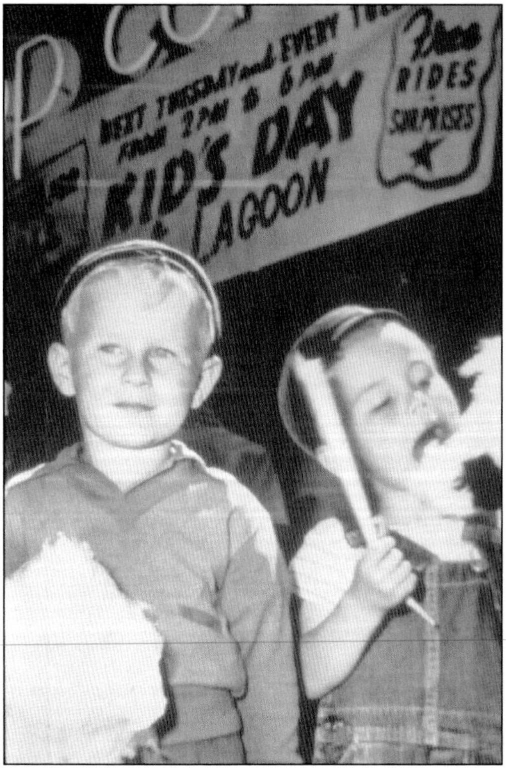

The Opera House (above) offered old-time vaudeville acts and theater performances that thrilled the crowds and tickled their funny bones. Often, traveling shows came to the area and requested to perform at the Opera House. It was a popular place, and a good act could realize a better-than-usual crowd to help pay their way. The venue also hosted more famous performers, who were well advertised to bring in the crowds. For many visitors, a day at Lagoon meant a swim in the warm sparkling waters of the pool. Small children would ride the merry-go-round and the airplanes, or perhaps travel around the lake in the small train. A day would not be complete without a cotton candy or a caramel apple, offered at one of the various concession stands (left). Young or old, Lagoon Park offered a fun-filled day for everyone. (Both courtesy Lagoon Corporation.)

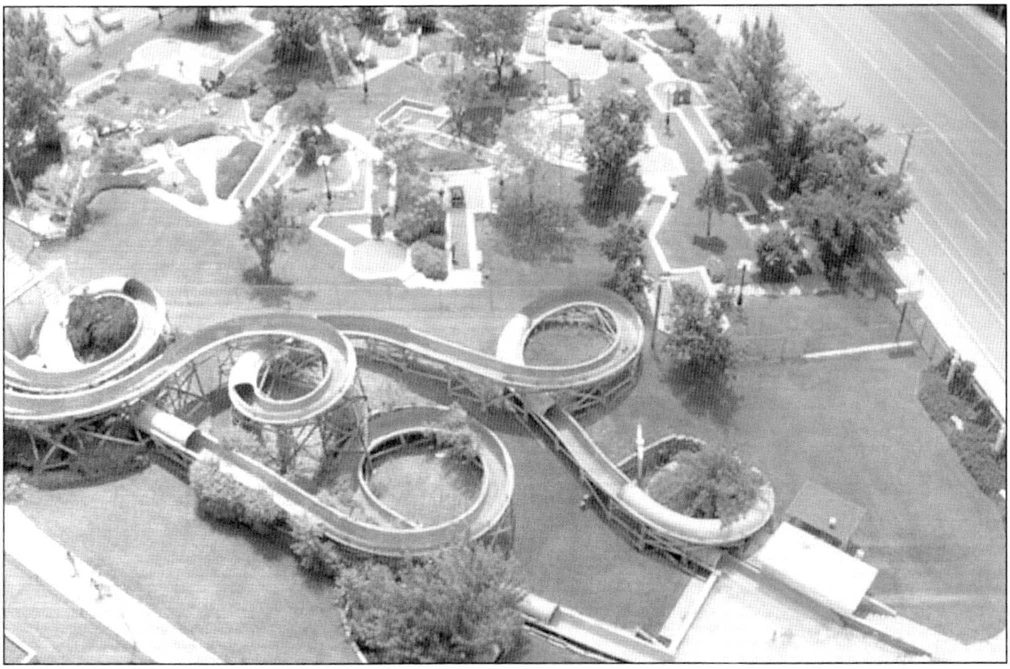

Grant S. Lloyd and his brother were both farm-raised youth. On their father's death, each inherited half of their father's cherry orchards. When approached by the state, Grant Lloyd agreed to sell two acres for highway construction. With easy access to the new freeway, he knew it would increase the value of his property. Lloyd created the Crossroads Campgrounds, which opened on June 4, 1967. The facility tried to appeal to motorists and the increasing number of campers and trailers. Lloyd teamed with Chevron, restaurants, and others to build and lease his property. After adding some water features, miniature golf, and a pie shop, Lloyd decided to expand and focus on the water features, creating the Cherry Hill Resort. This 20-acre park, located at 1325 South Main Street in Kaysville, now attracts thousands of visitors each summer with waterslides, a raging river, a children's cove, and more. (Both courtesy Cherry Hill Resort Management.)

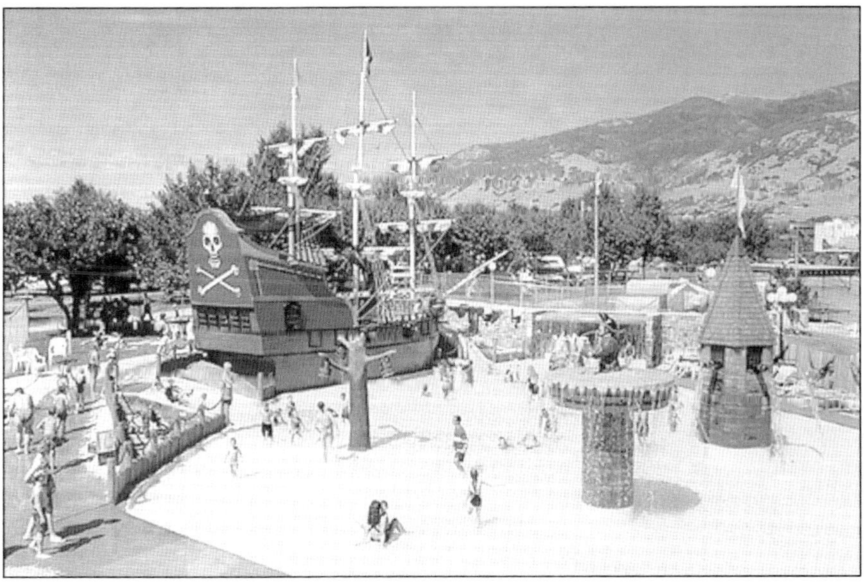

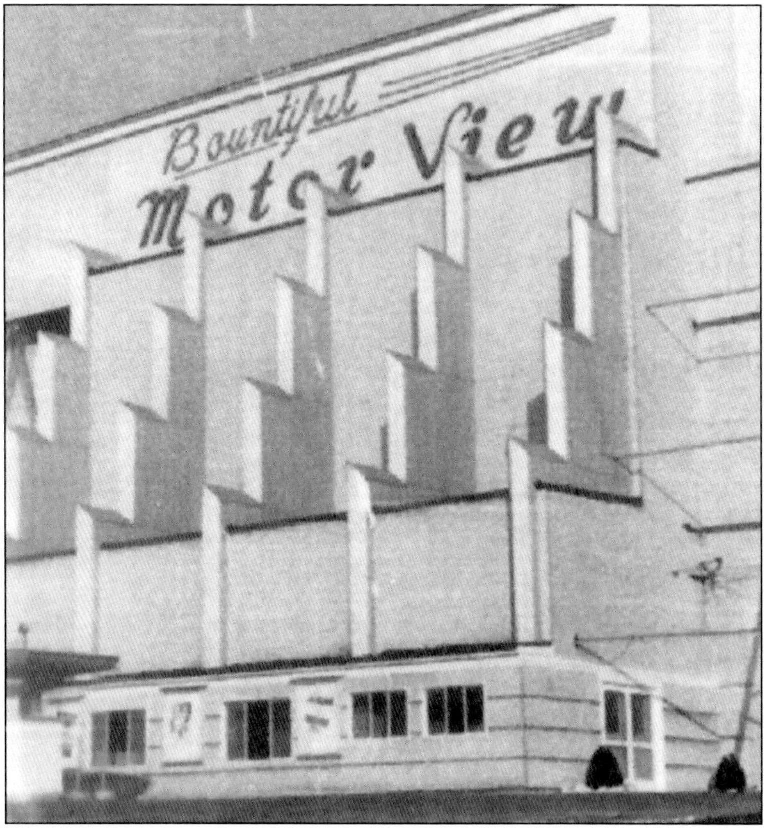

The Bountiful Motor View outdoor theater was part of an exciting era. On "Dollar Nights," one could take a whole carload of friends to the theater, all for a buck. A summer night with a date, the car windows down, a warm breeze, and a bag of popcorn was about as good as it got. (Courtesy Bountiful History Museum.)

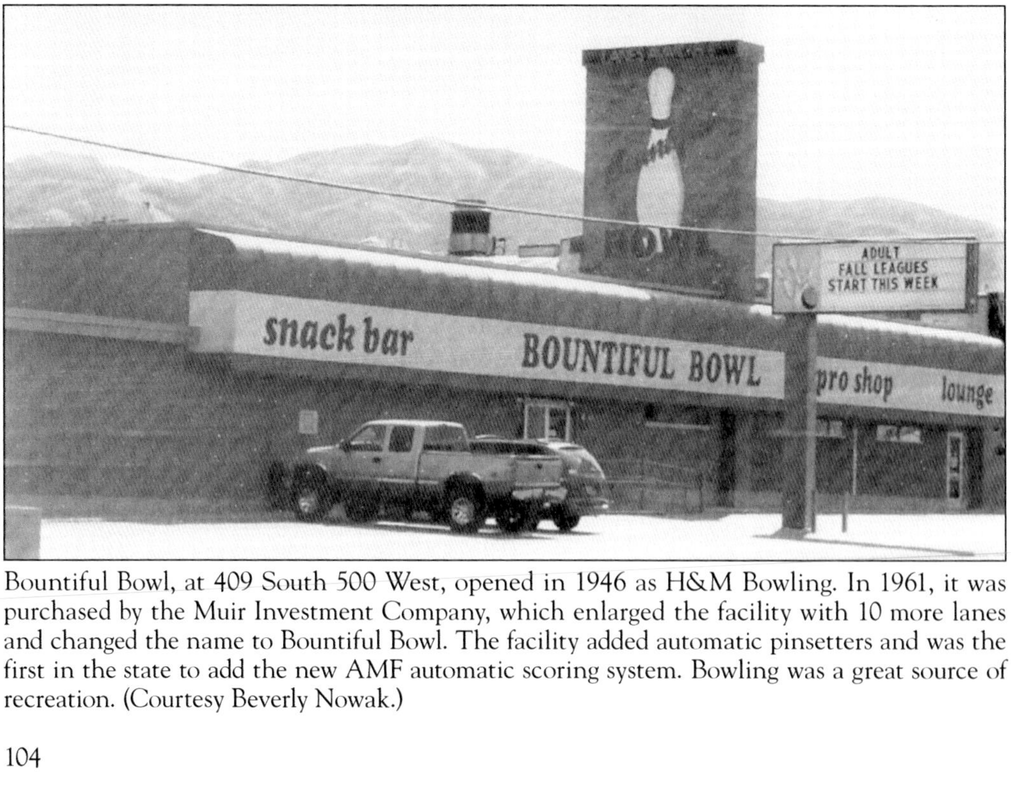

Bountiful Bowl, at 409 South 500 West, opened in 1946 as H&M Bowling. In 1961, it was purchased by the Muir Investment Company, which enlarged the facility with 10 more lanes and changed the name to Bountiful Bowl. The facility added automatic pinsetters and was the first in the state to add the new AMF automatic scoring system. Bowling was a great source of recreation. (Courtesy Beverly Nowak.)

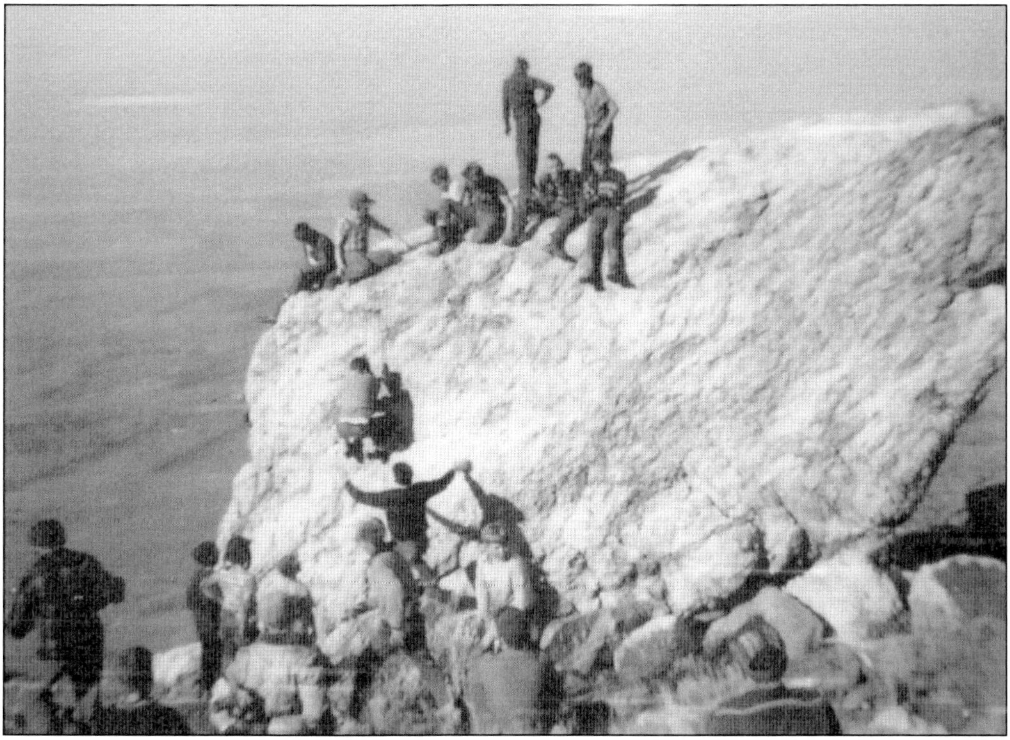

The adjacent Wasatch Mountains offer a variety of activities and sites for those seeking outdoor recreation. In the 1953 photograph above, Vern Goudy leads a group of local Scouts up the mountain to Sheeprock, the largest freestanding monolithic rock on the face of the mountains of South Davis County. It stands 30 feet long and rises 38 feet above the Centerville hillside. A marriage proposal was once made by a local couple after they climbed to the top. It can be readily spotted from the valley, standing white above 1800 North. An alternative is to hike a canyon trail to locate beautiful waterfalls. In all, 13 canyons bring rambling mountain streams to the valley floor. Rising over 5,000 feet above the lake, the steep canyons can be a challenge to hike, but the many beautiful falls and sites make it worthwhile. An 80-foot falls in Ford Canyon is shown at right. Framed in broken granite and brown gneiss, it is well worth the 30-minute hike. (Above, courtesy Clara Goudy.)

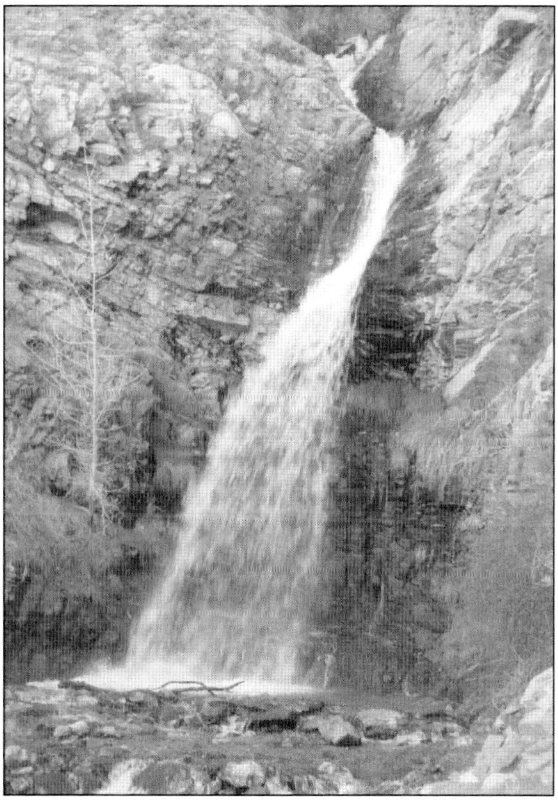

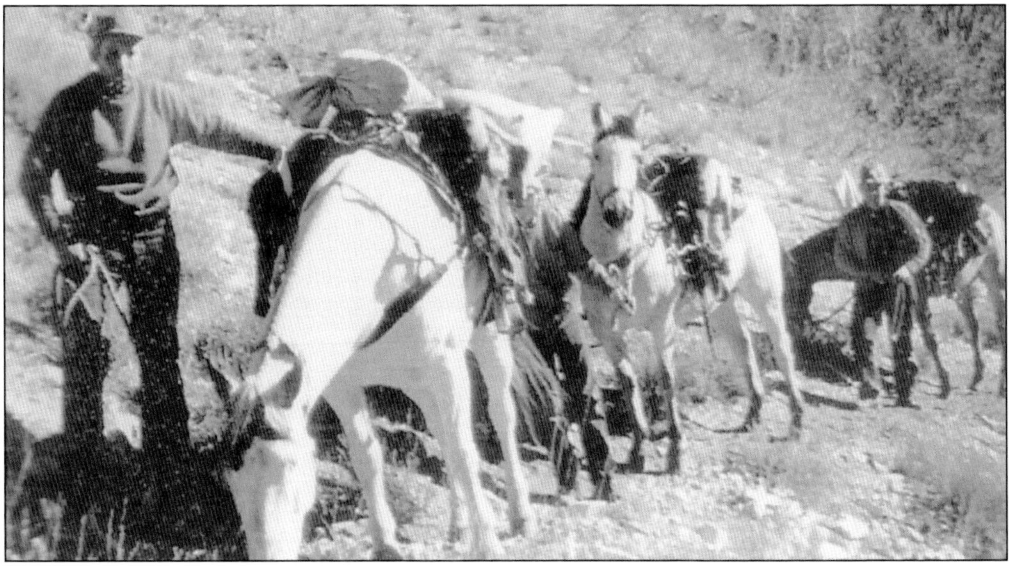

Hunting in the Wasatch Mountains dates to the first pioneers in 1847, when they went to find venison or rabbits to meet their needs. Taking horses and hunting deer has been a family tradition for many in South Davis County. The Tingey family dates back in this area to 1847, with pioneer ancestors Josiah and Anson Call. This photograph shows their horses loaded with venison around 1955. (Courtesy Nola Tingey Hatch.)

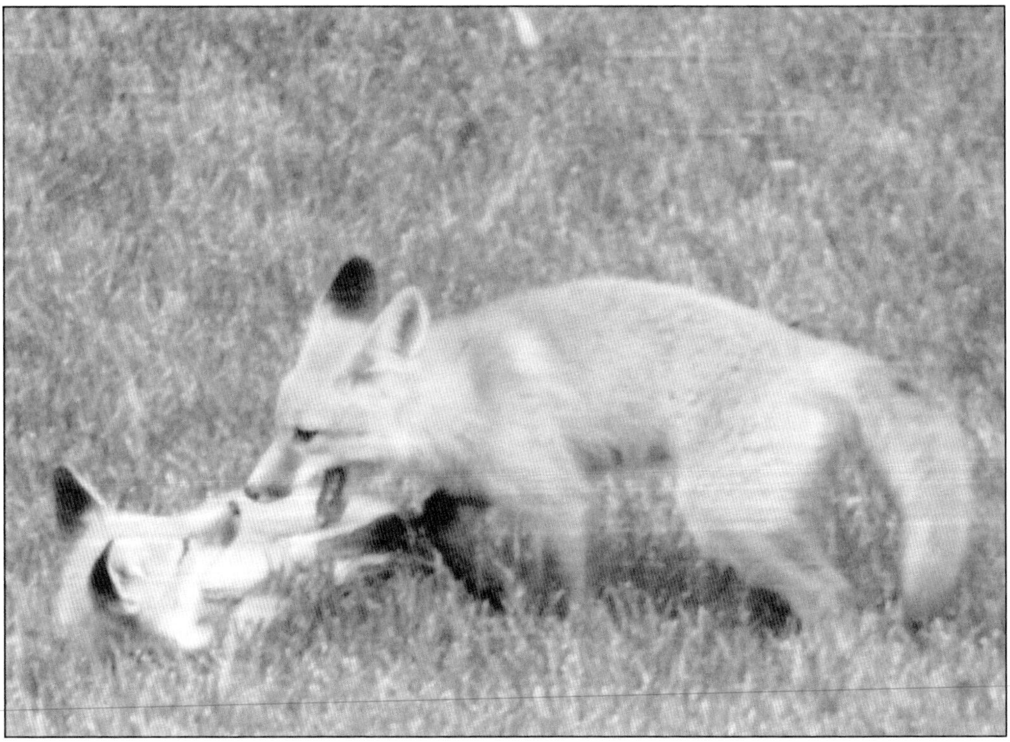

A pair of red fox kits romp in the foothills below Parrish Canyon. It is also possible to see bobcats, mountain lions, elk, and moose in the mountains. During the early summer, coyotes can often be heard hunting along the foothills.

Parasailing off the top of the mountains above South Davis County is a popular sport. The warm air from the valley rises as cold air drops down to replace it, causing "thermals"—upward columns of air. These columns lift the parasail to new heights, extending the ride until the participant eventually lands at one of the sports fields.

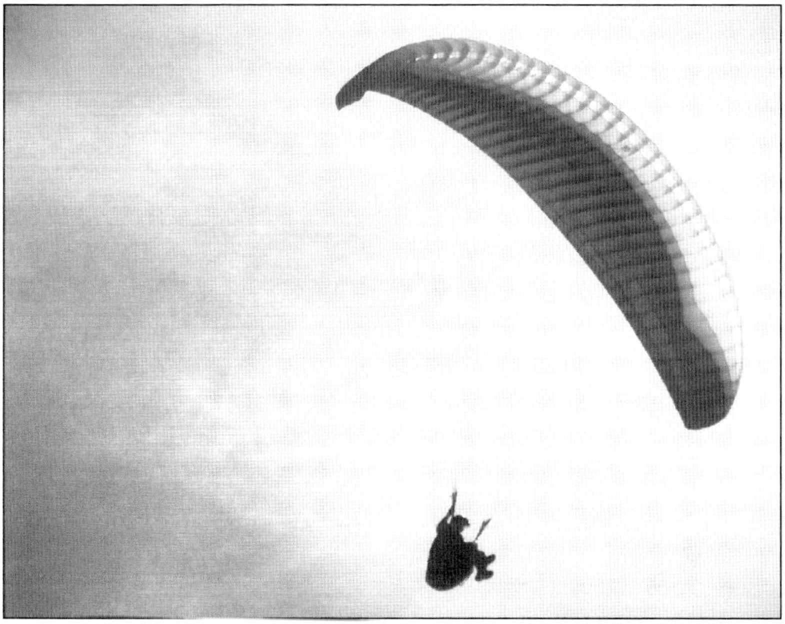

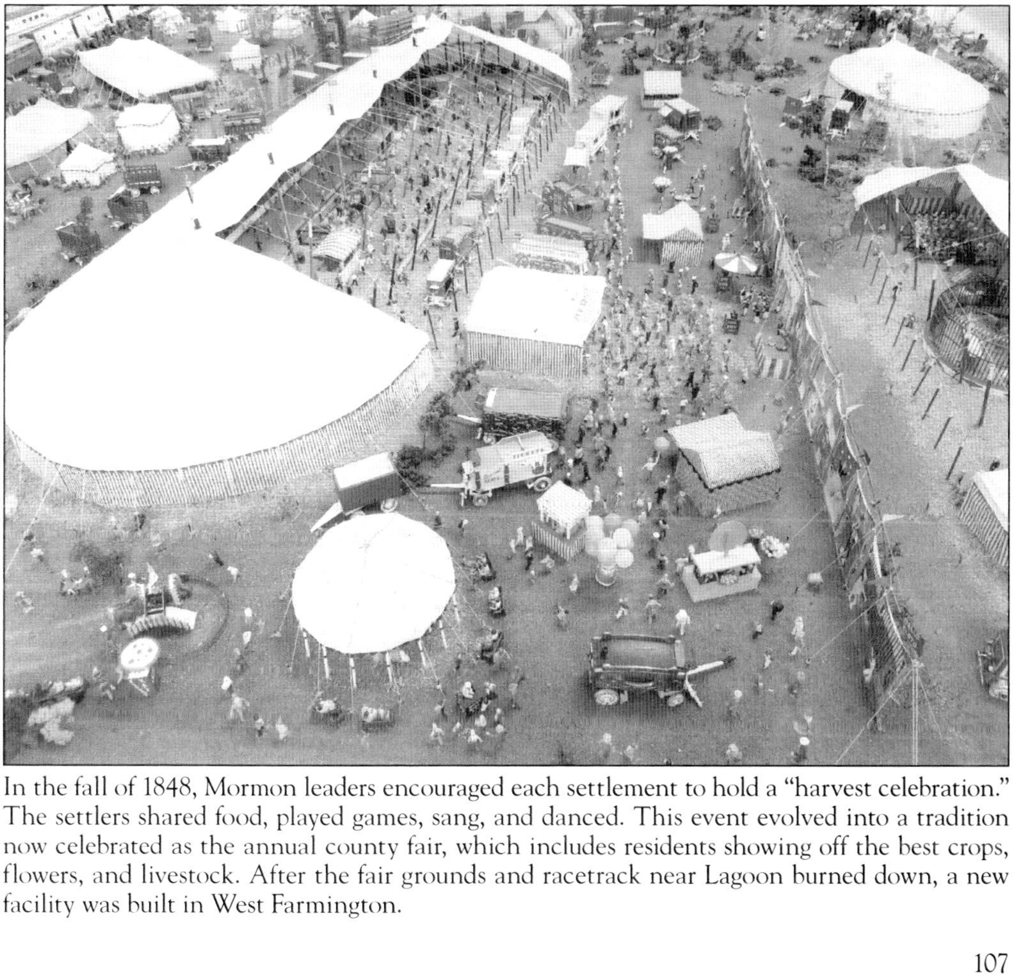

In the fall of 1848, Mormon leaders encouraged each settlement to hold a "harvest celebration." The settlers shared food, played games, sang, and danced. This event evolved into a tradition now celebrated as the annual county fair, which includes residents showing off the best crops, flowers, and livestock. After the fair grounds and racetrack near Lagoon burned down, a new facility was built in West Farmington.

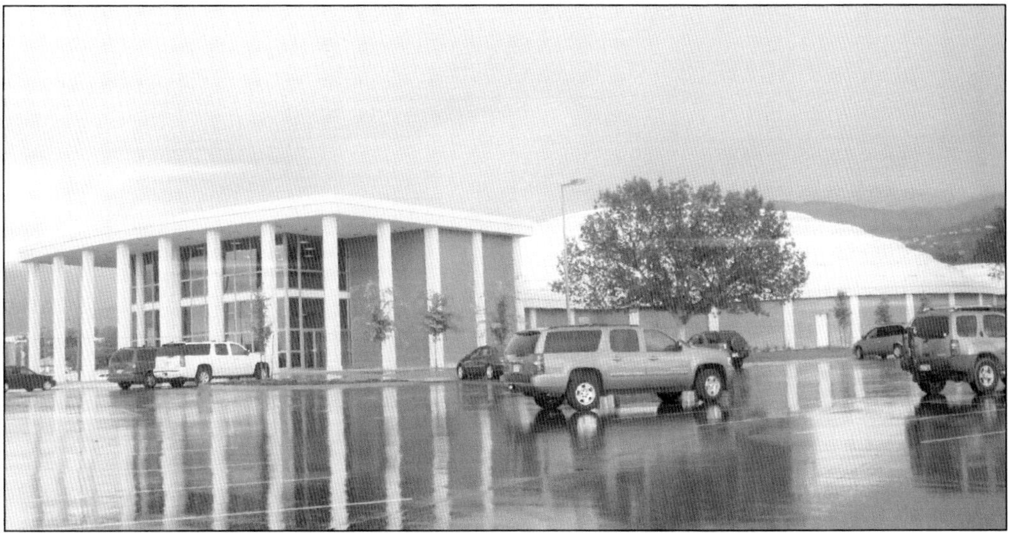

This facility, at 835 North 400 East in North Salt Lake, nicknamed the "turtle," was built about 1960 for theater-in-the-round. It was financed by television host Art Linkletter and a group of investors. The dome roof was constructed over a large mound of earth. Productions included a performance by pianist Liberace in 1966. The theater venture failed after a fire destroyed the interior. The building was later purchased by the Mormon Church.

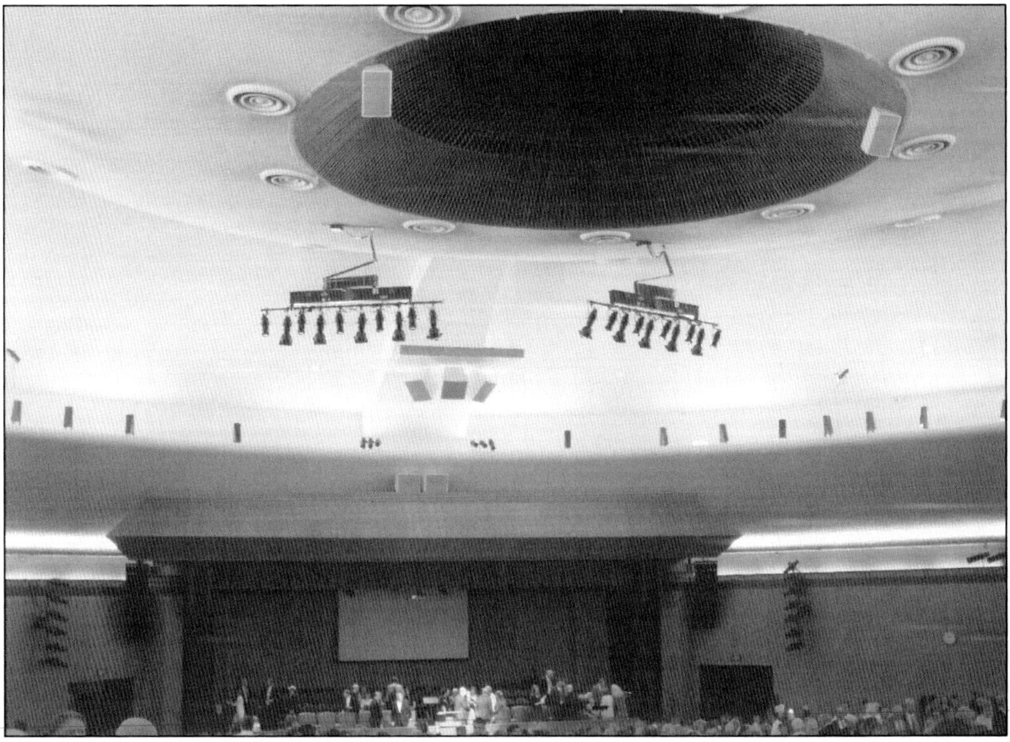

This is an interior view of the domed ceiling. Under the ownership of the Mormon Church, the building was converted from a theater-in-the-round configuration to a plush auditorium, with a stage on the west side. Additional lighting and acoustics were completed, and the building is now called the Bountiful Regional Center.

Nine

Antelope Island

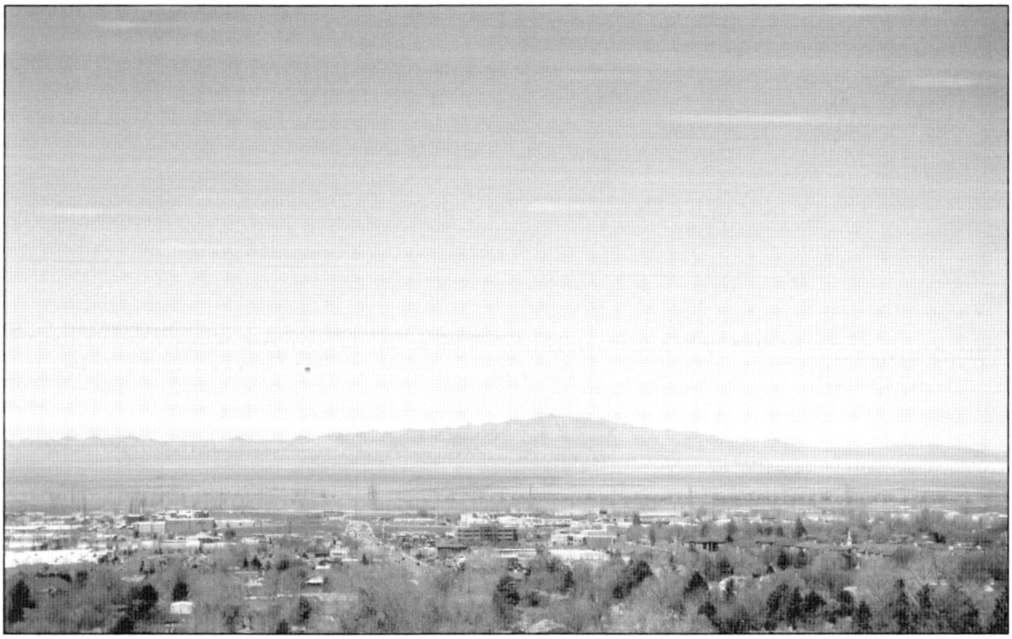

The largest island in the Great Salt Lake was named by explorer John C. Fremont in 1845, after his expedition hunted and killed an antelope there for camp meat. Antelope Island is 15.5 miles in length, 5.5 miles in width, and rises to 6,596 feet in elevation—1,396 feet above the lake. As seen from the South Davis County bench, it seems to form the western shore of the lake.

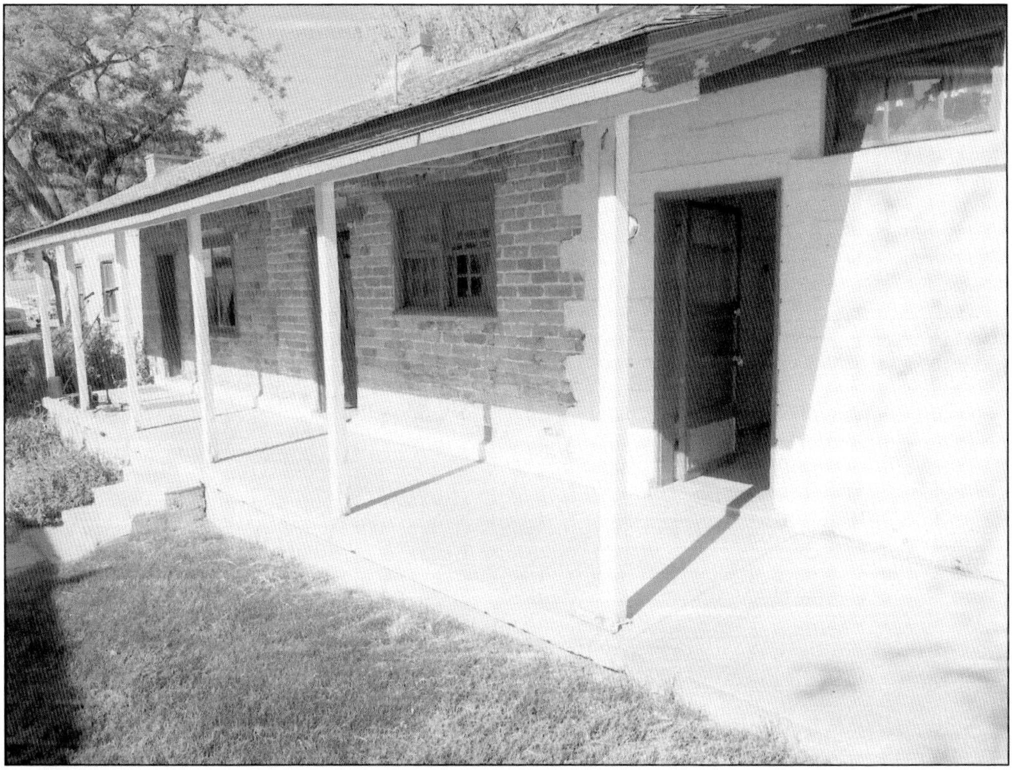

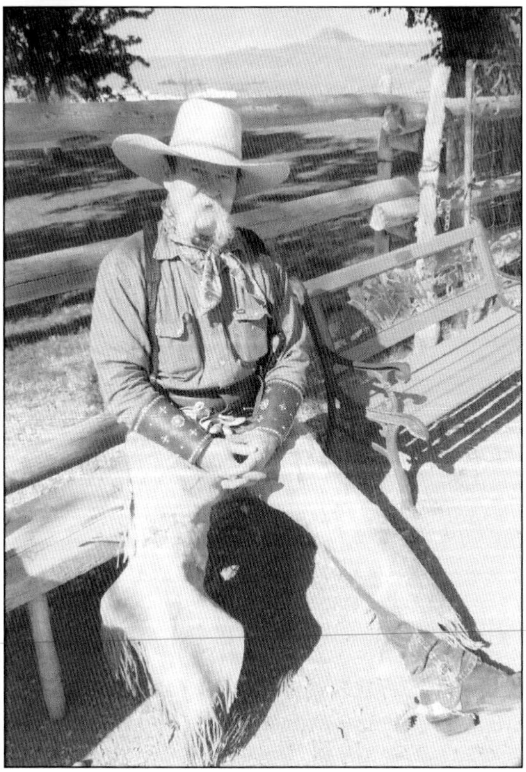

In 1848, a 52-year-old widower named Fielding Garr was sent to Antelope Island by Mormon Church leaders to establish a ranch. Garr, a large man at 225 pounds, was a bonded herdsman and an excellent stonemason. He was instructed to build a ranch house with extra rooms for visitors. Locating a site in the foothills adjacent to a freshwater spring, Garr built a large adobe cabin (above) and moved his family of eight children to the island the next year. His 26-year-old daughter, Nancy, who had a daughter of her own, ran the home and helped rear the younger children. Outbuildings were constructed, including a storage shed, a barn for horses, and other facilities. At left, a cowboy poses at the ranch.

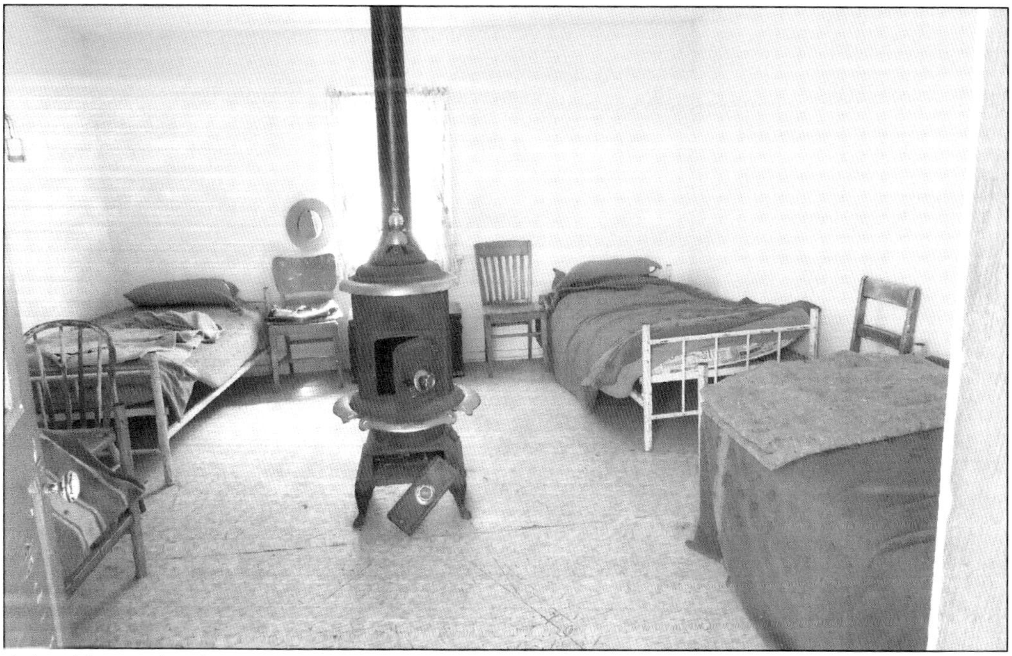

A bunkhouse for the Garr ranch hands is shown in the photograph above. A small washroom was built on the north end, with the floor level below the remainder of the house. The family and ranch hands could enter the house, remove their parkas and chaps, and wash off their boots before going farther into the house. The old washtub (below) in the anteroom is typical of what would have been available. It was likely left outside most of the year, as indoor space was limited. The washing was hung to dry on an outside clothesline. A fireplace was built into the main room of the house, but a small stove, seen above, was needed in the bunk area to take off the chill in the winter.

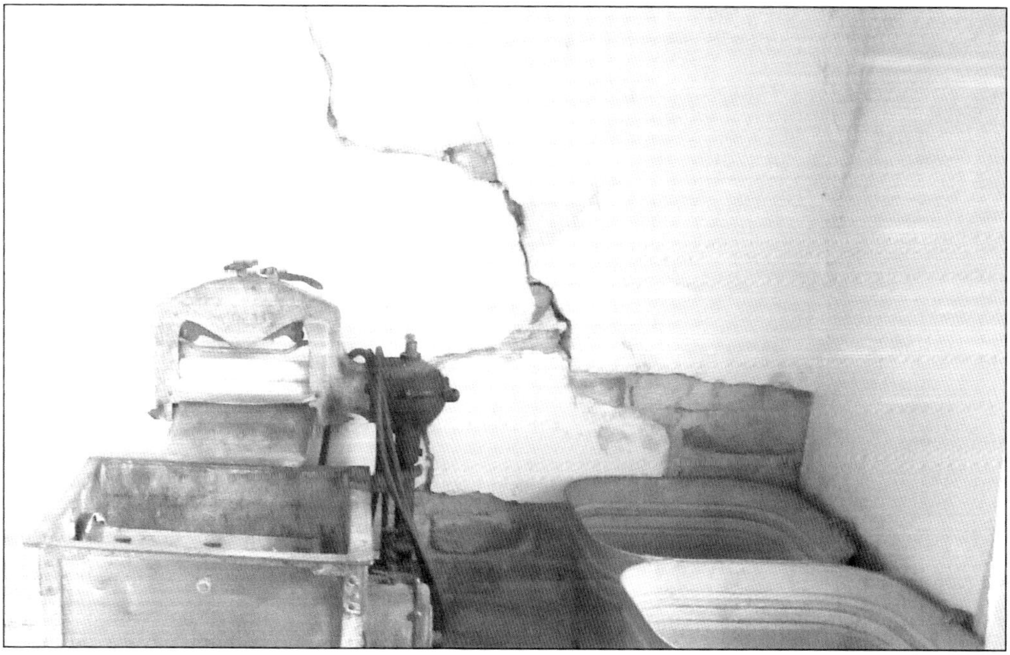

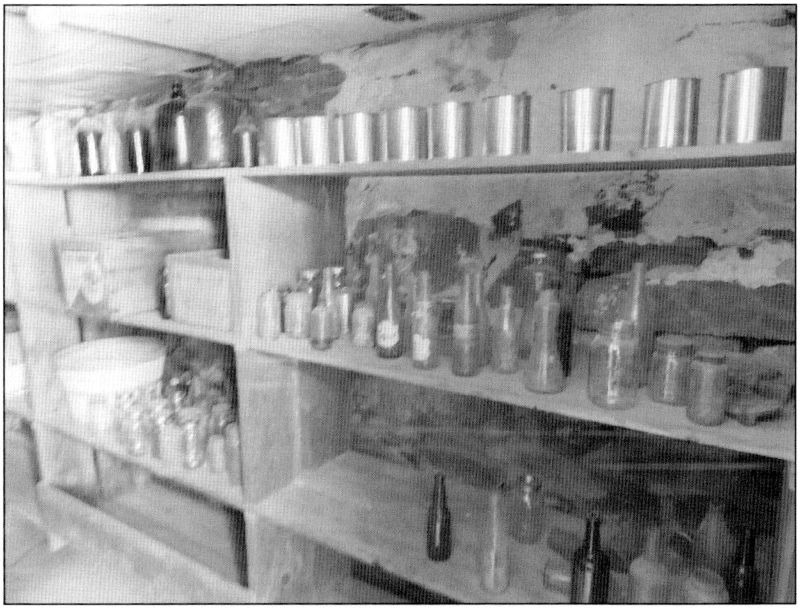

Fielding Garr planted a garden at the ranch and built a small cellar for food storage. There are also shelves found in the ranch house with stored fruit and foodstuffs. Antelope and deer were available on the island for meat, and Garr raised beef of his own for food and income.

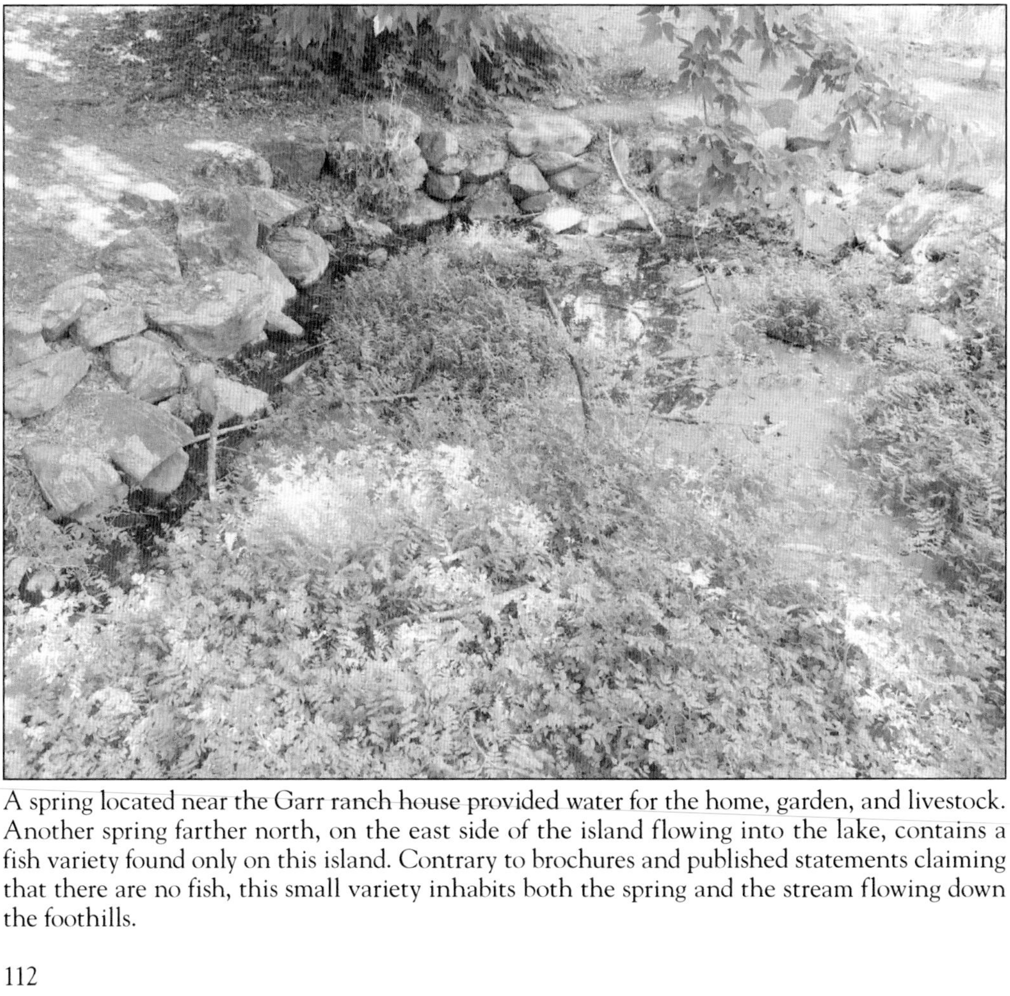

A spring located near the Garr ranch house provided water for the home, garden, and livestock. Another spring farther north, on the east side of the island flowing into the lake, contains a fish variety found only on this island. Contrary to brochures and published statements claiming that there are no fish, this small variety inhabits both the spring and the stream flowing down the foothills.

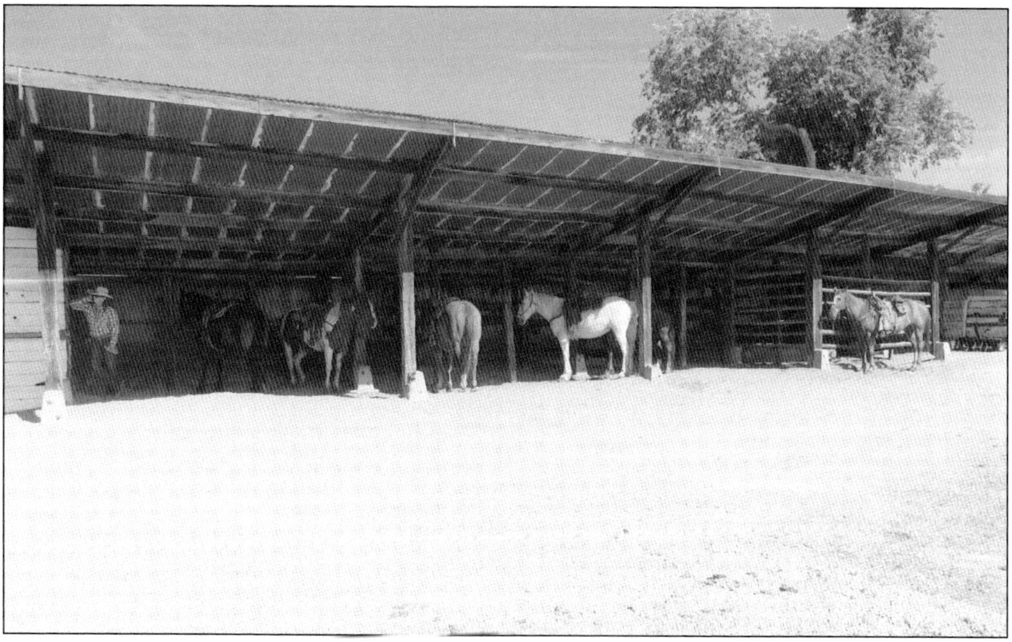

The first cattle were driven to the island in 1848, and, in 1850, the legislature designated the island for the sole use of the Perpetual Emigration Company stock. Over 10,000 Europeans received loaned funds to help them relocate to Utah. Their debt payments were often made in livestock, creating what was referred to as the "Bank with Hooves."

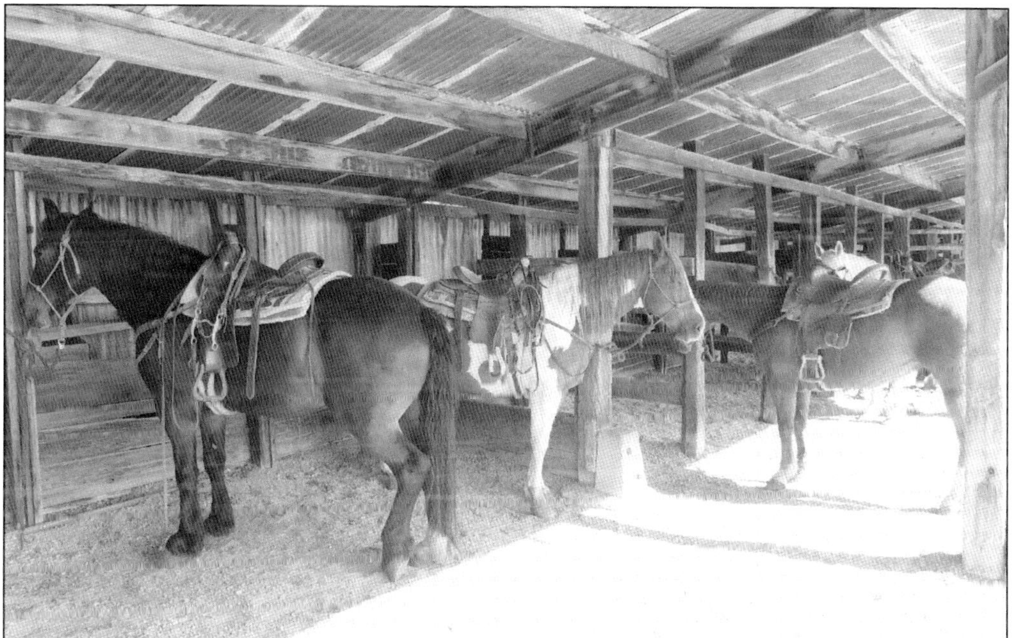

Saddled horses stand in the shade of the large barn. A tack room was built into the end of the barn to store harnesses, saddles, and bridles when not in use. A haystack was located nearby, and wagons and farm equipment were stored just outside the corrals. Although now owned by the state, this is still a working ranch.

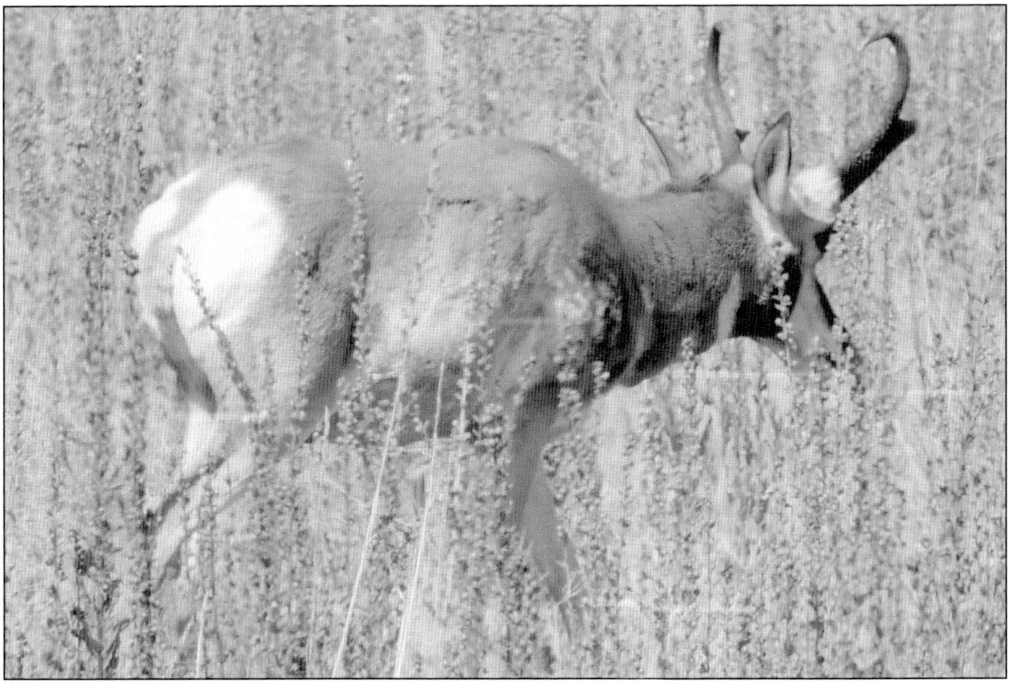

Known as pronghorns, the wild antelope roam the island, surviving and flourishing. They can be seen congregating in small herds, and a lone buck can sometimes be spotted. The antelope are swift and graceful as they dart through the tall grass and brush along the foothills. They were a key food source for the early ranchers.

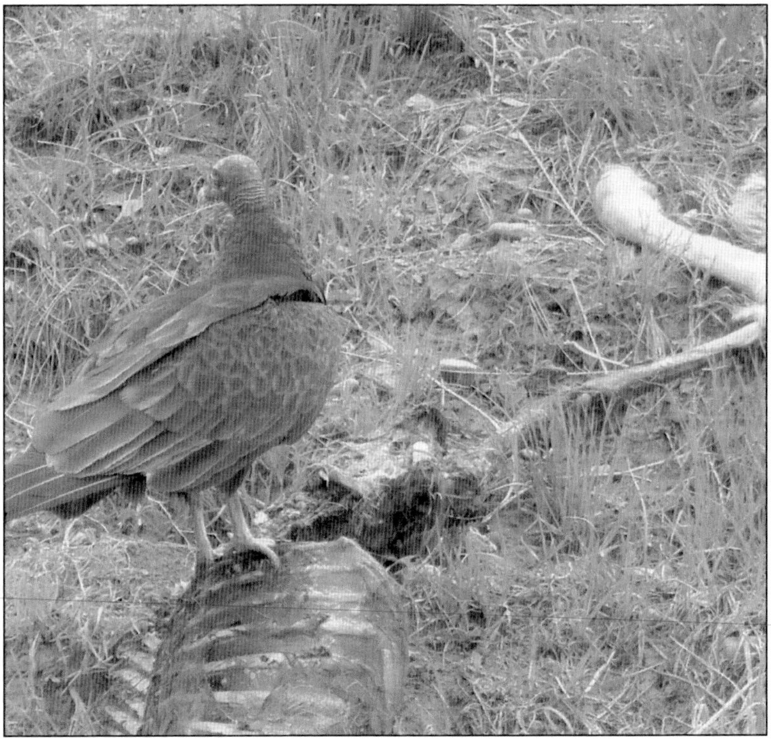

Other families moved to the island, some to homestead, others to prospect. A few men worked as cowboys. The church sold the ranch in 1884, and the island became overgrazed. In the hands of Anschutz Oil & Cattle Company, conservation efforts were put into place, and even the natural predators of coyotes, bobcats, and buzzards returned.

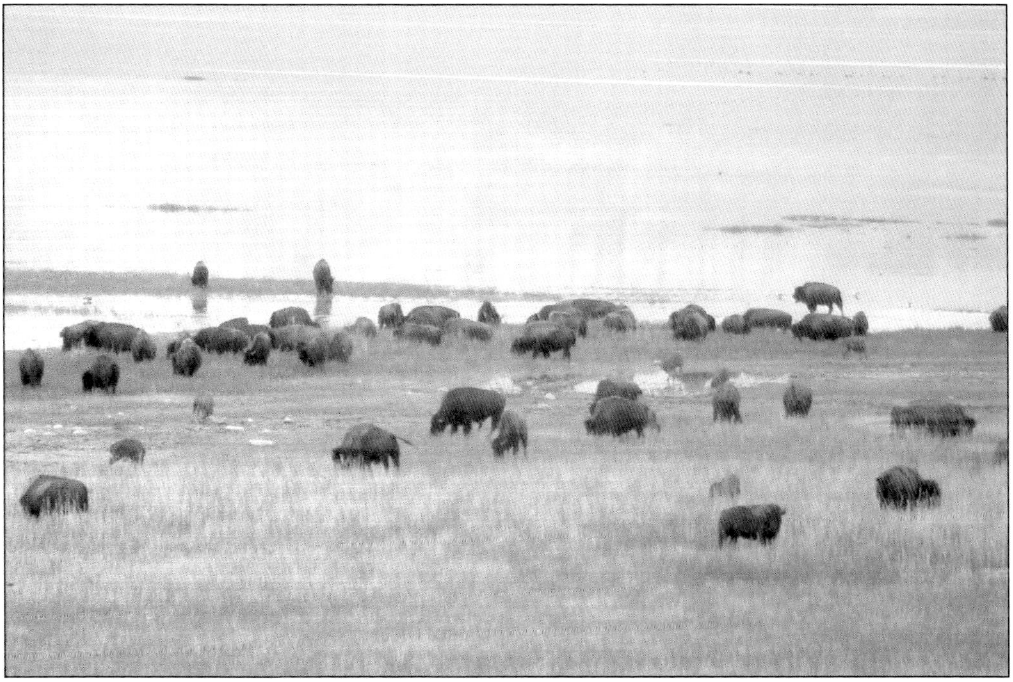

On February 15, 1893, island rancher John E. Dooly bought 12 head of buffalo and moved them to his ranch. (Other accounts record that John White purchased 17 head of buffalo.) This was a hunting venture meant to attract Easterners and their money. The buffalo flourished, having few natural predators, but the planned buffalo hunts never got under way.

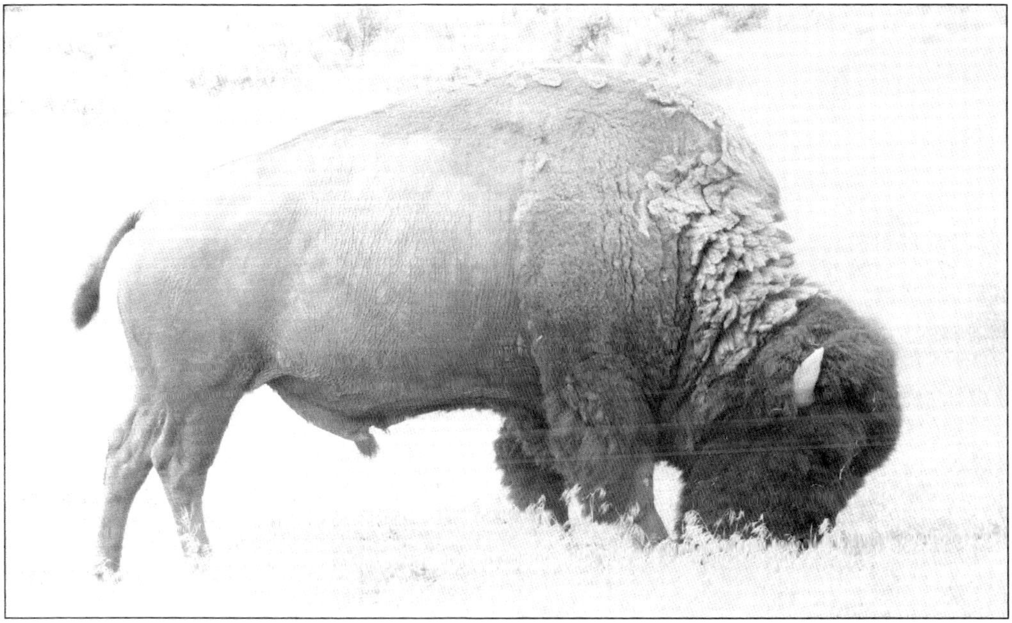

The large bull is a testament to the vitality of these huge beasts of the plains. The island is an excellent habitat for them, with lush grass and easy access to freshwater springs. Now, large calf crops are seen each spring (see previous photograph). The buffalo are now the major attraction for visitors to the island.

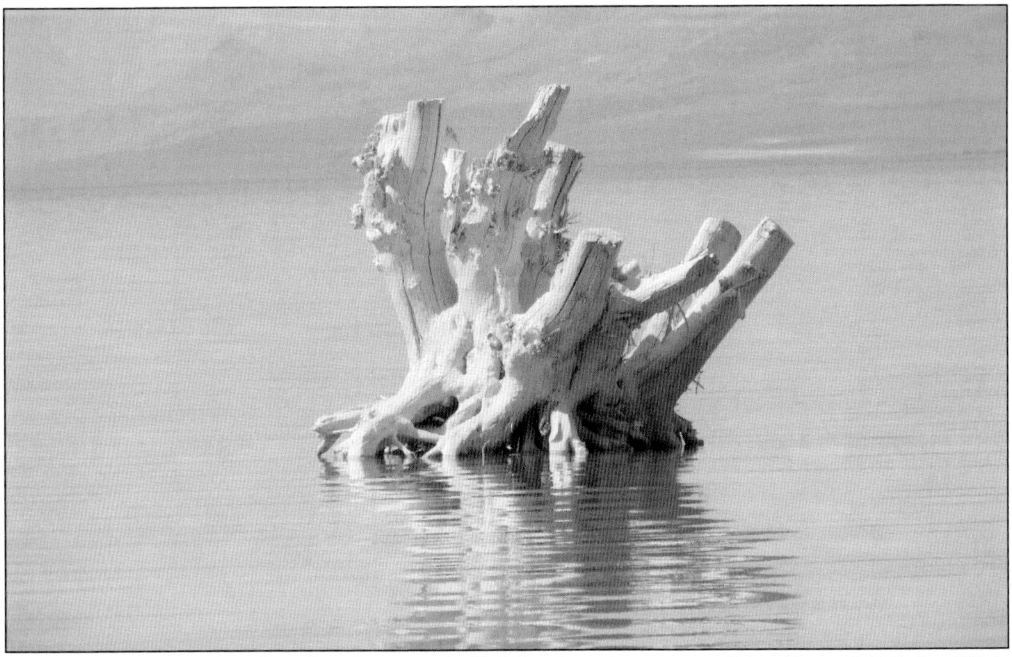

This old stump sits abandoned and stripped of life by the salty waters of the Great Salt Lake. With time, it will decay and disappear. The strong salt content of the lake prohibits fish from living in the waters. Tiny brine shrimp are the only creatures in the lake. They produce profusely, and their decaying bodies wash onto the beach areas, resulting in a rather foul seasonal odor.

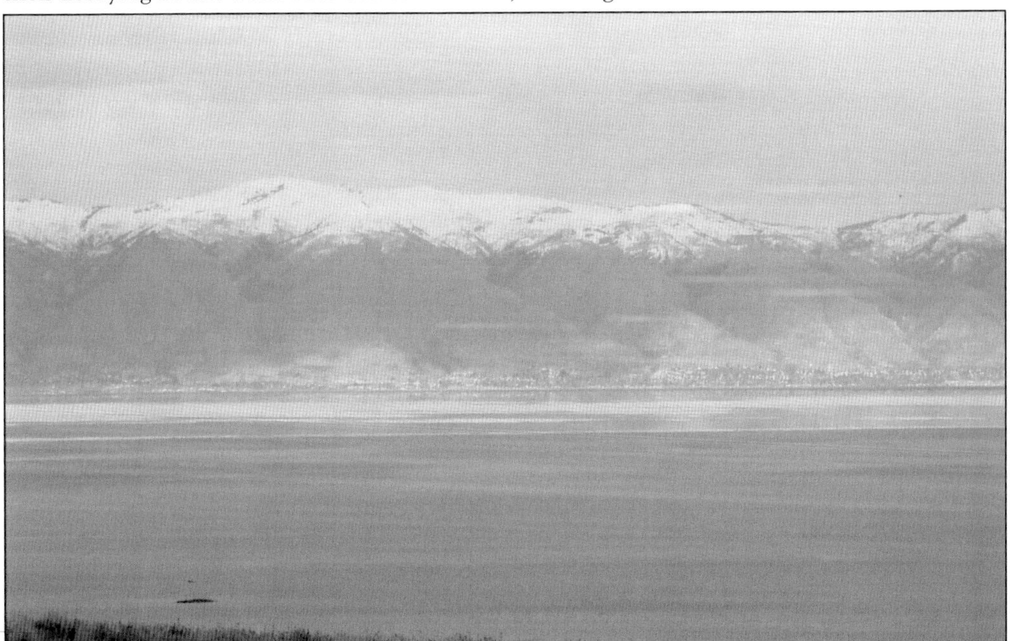

This is a winter scene of South Davis County as seen from Antelope Island. The small communities are built along the narrow strip of land on the lakeshore area. The mountains above are snowcapped in the winter. Each of the main canyons extending down from the summit carry freshwater streams, which are commonly named after the early pioneers that settled on them.

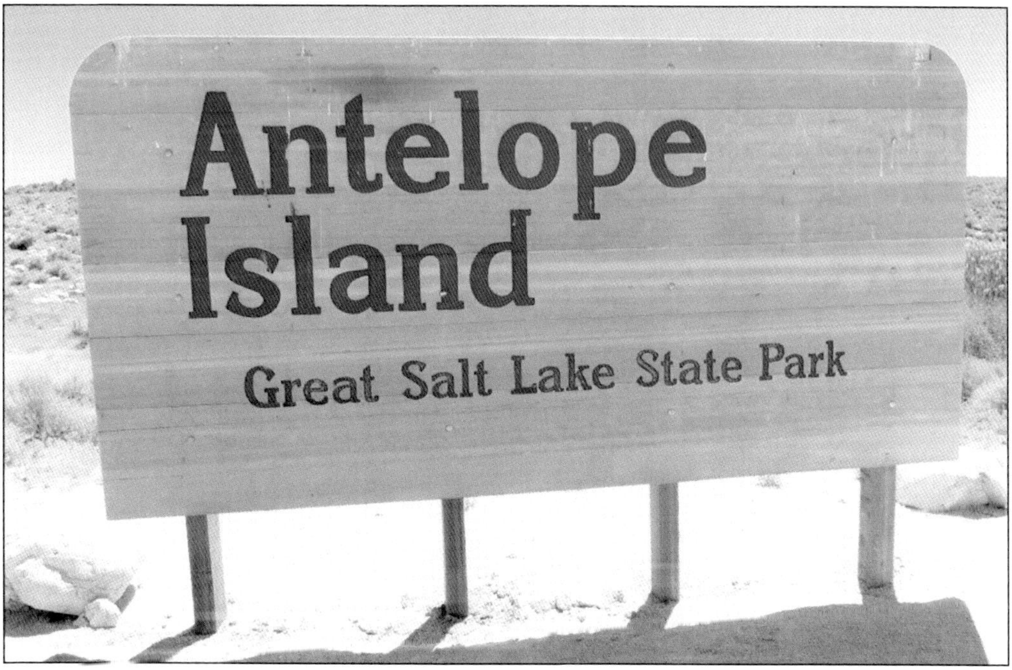

Antelope Island, accessed at 4528 West 1700 South in Syracuse, was declared a state park in 1969, but the state owned only the north portion. It was not until 1981 that it acquired the Garr ranch on the south, making the entire island a state park. Now, a small boat marina and beach with a gift shop are organized in the north, but the remainder of the island remains natural—a high desert environment totally surrounded by water. Over 300,000 visitors a year come to hike or just drive the roads and watch the buffalo and wildlife. But, there is a deterrent to human visitation. Small biting gnats, also known as no-see-ums, are plentiful from April to June, and most repellents will not stop them.

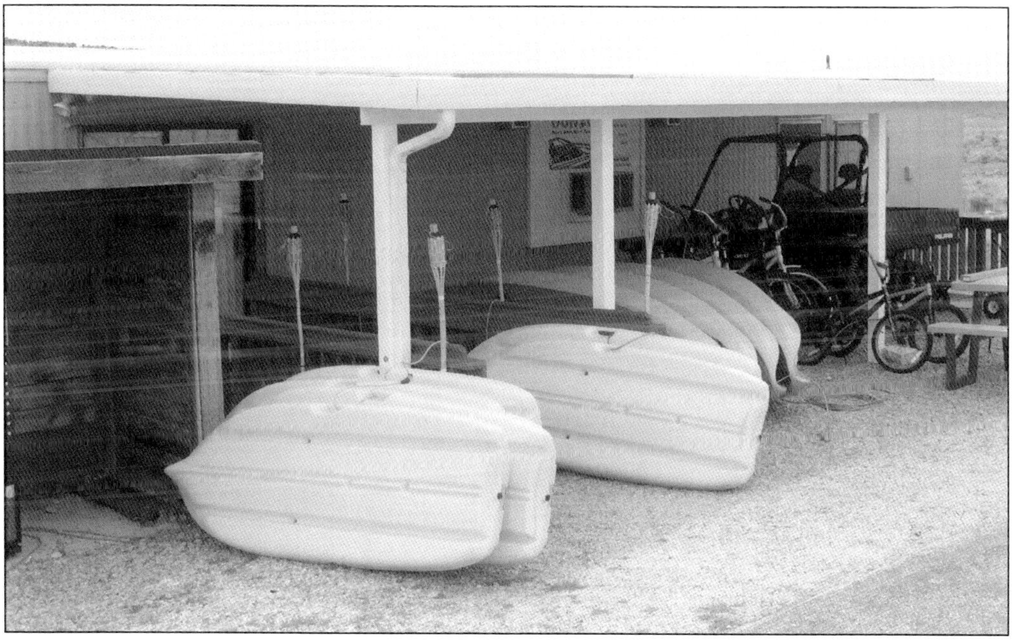

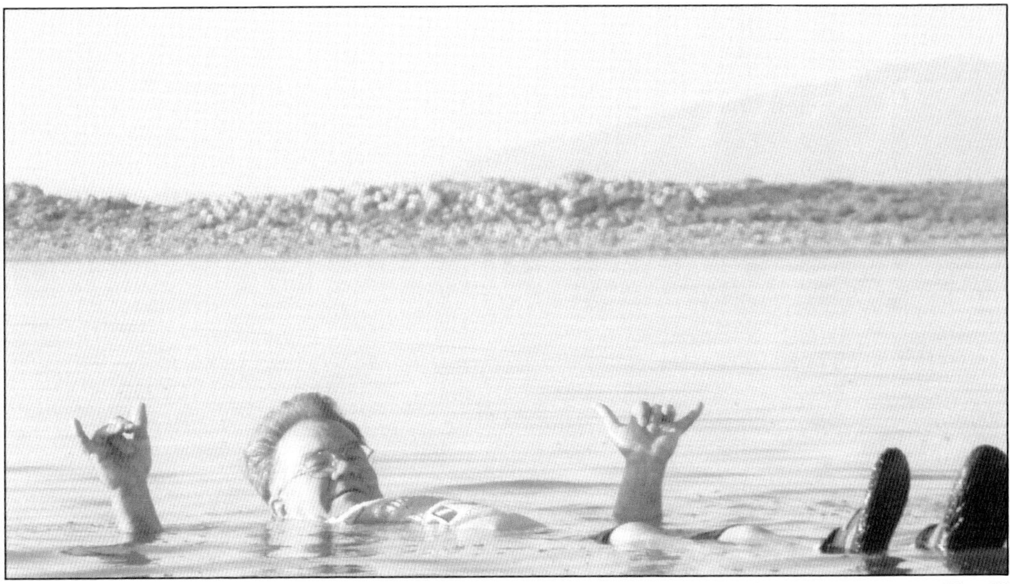

An unusual feature of the Great Salt Lake is the strong salt content of the water. Being a "dead" lake with no outlet, the salt content increases, diluted only by rain and snow. Bathers in the lake, such as Gary Willden (shown here), float and bob in the water, unable to sink. (Courtesy Joan Willden.)

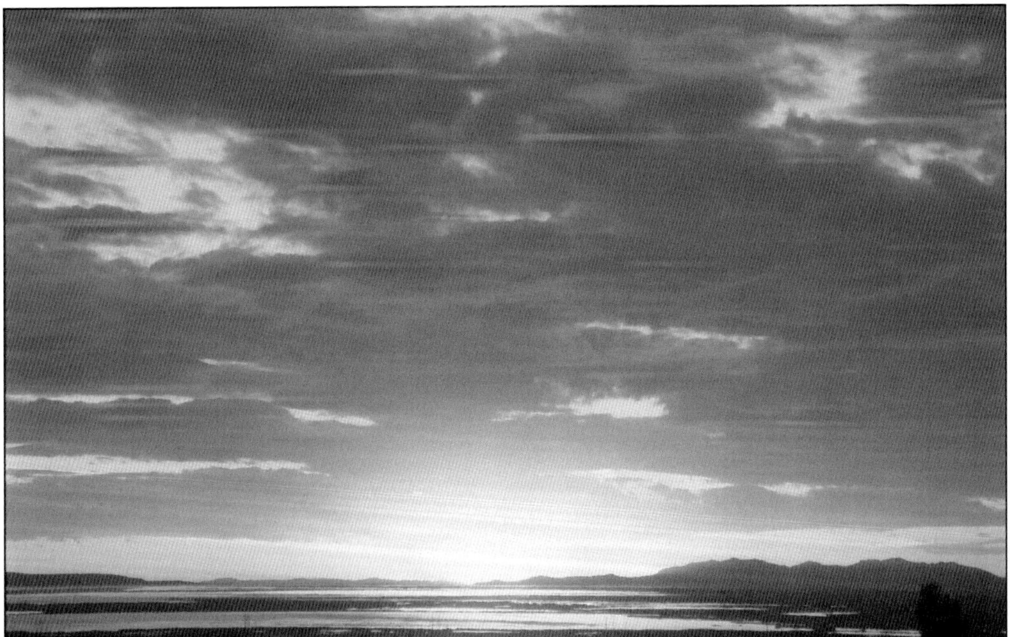

The beautiful sunsets over the Great Salt Lake, with the silhouette of Antelope Island on the horizon, are amazing. Throughout the year, the skies are painted with intense hues of pink and orange. The water in the lake shimmers in patches of gold. In addition, a sunrise from behind the eastern range of mountains will light the morning sky, causing the surrounding clouds to burn bright pink.

Ten

Hang on to Your Hats

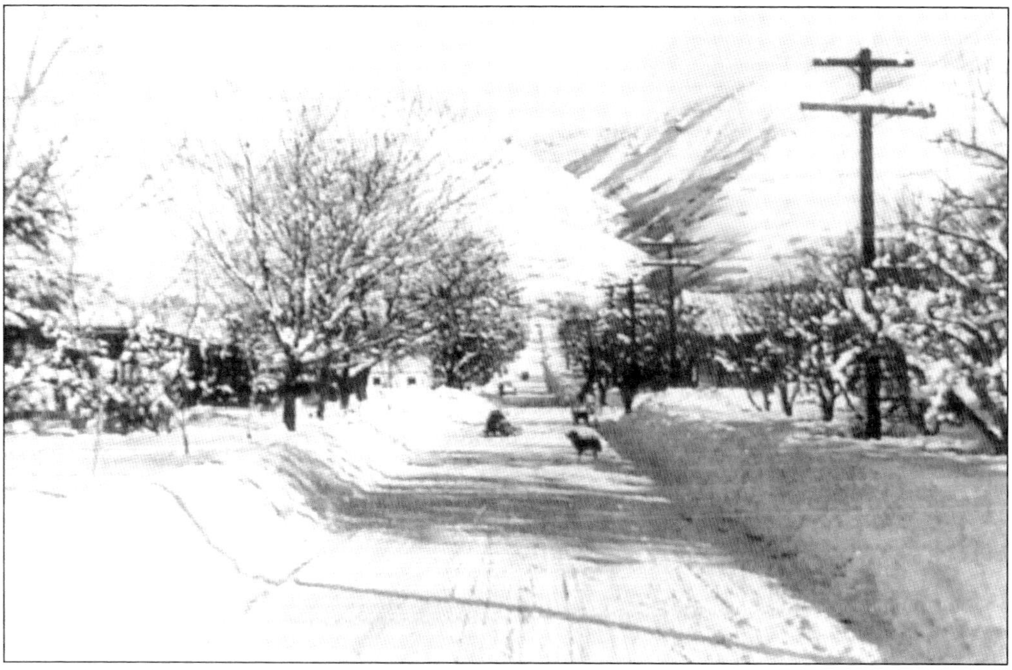

South Davis County receives varying amounts of snow from year to year. The average rainfall and moisture is 50 inches at the top of the mountains and 21 inches on the valley floor. This 1948 photograph, looking east on Center Street in Centerville, shows an unusually deep snowfall. Although such conditions make feeding livestock and getting around difficult, children delight in it. (Courtesy Nola Tingey Hatch.)

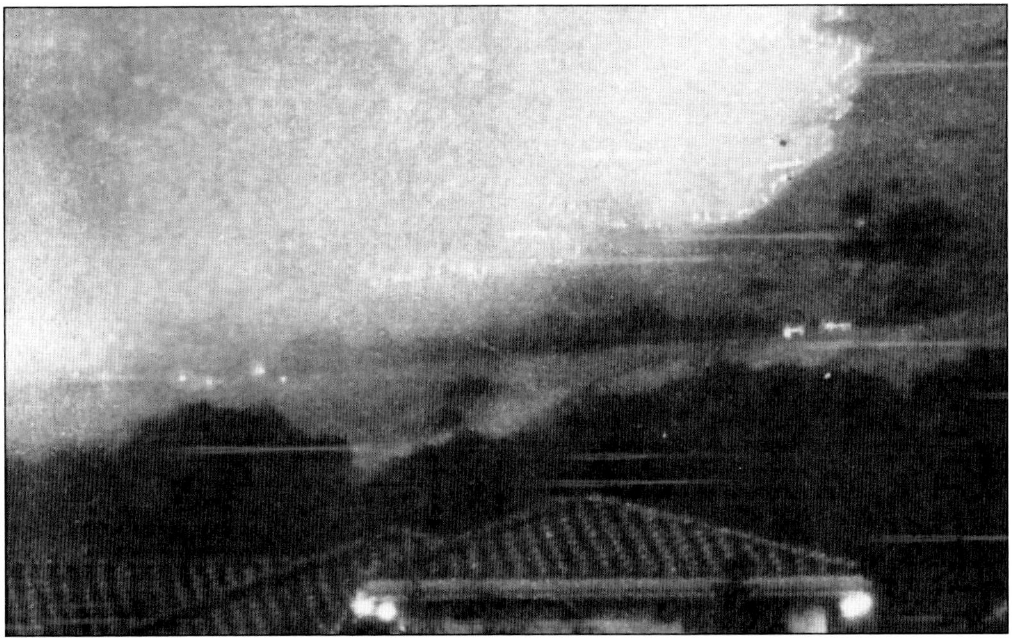

A familiar sight along the foothills and on Antelope Island are the wildfires caused by lightning or careless hikers. Dry grass in the late summer is the tinder, and all that is needed is a spark. Lightning, a stray bullet, or the careless use of fireworks can set off a blaze, and a fire line, like the one seen here, glows red across the mountain as the blaze consumes everything in its path.

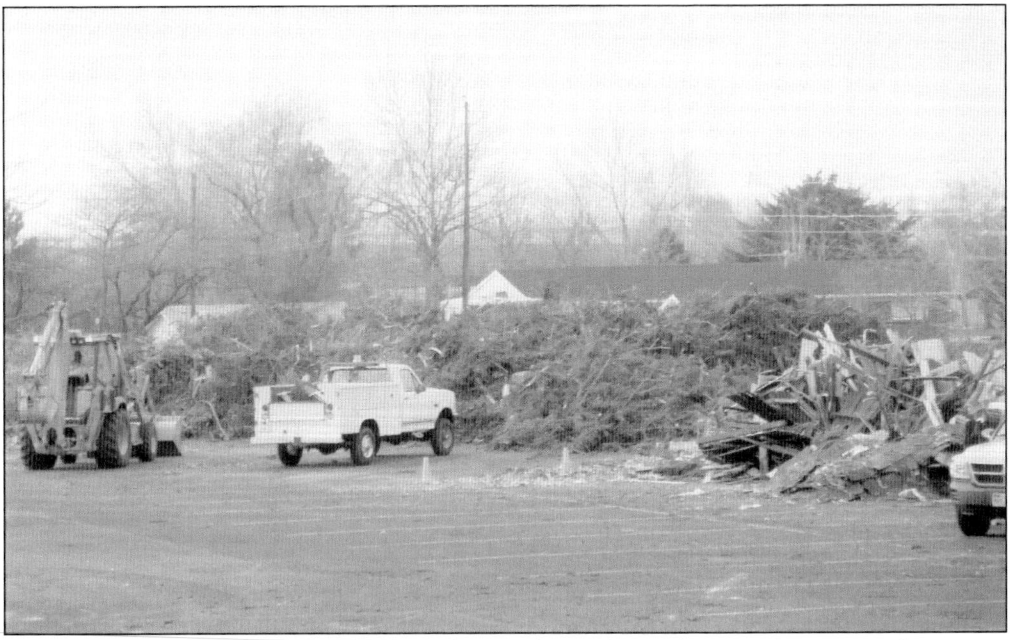

In this 2011 storm, mountain winds reached 110 miles per hour, throwing fencing, roofing, signs, and old spruce trees onto houses and sprawling into yards. High-profile trucks and railcars were tossed on their sides. Police and emergency teams responded, but it was the local citizens—neighbors helping neighbors—that put thousands of workers on the streets for a cleanup within 72 hours. Here, debris is piled up at a church parking lot following the storm.

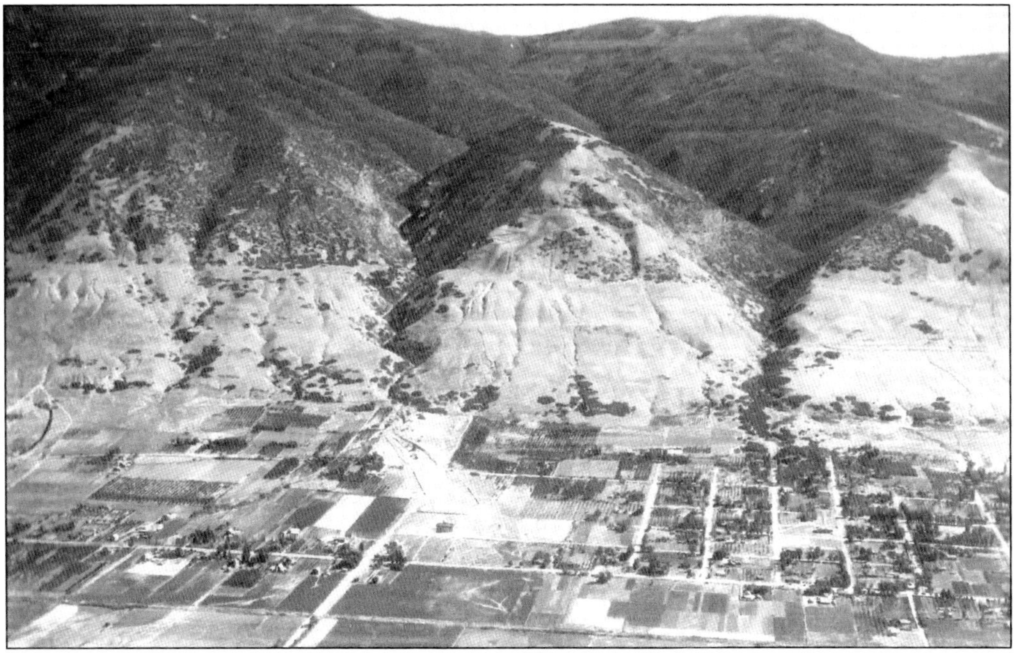

As the land in the valley was turned into farms and homesites, the early ranchers grazed their cattle and sheep farther up the mountains, clear to the Wasatch Ridge. Sheep ranchers had burned off acres of underbrush to protect the wool of their sheep from snagging on it. With the vegetation depleted and the soil compacted, the winter snow and spring rains could no longer be absorbed. The result was a flood of water and debris rushing down the canyons and onto the valley floor. Parrish Creek, shown below, flooded into the town of Centerville, wiping out farms, homes, and buildings in its path. (Both courtesy Centerville City Historical Records.)

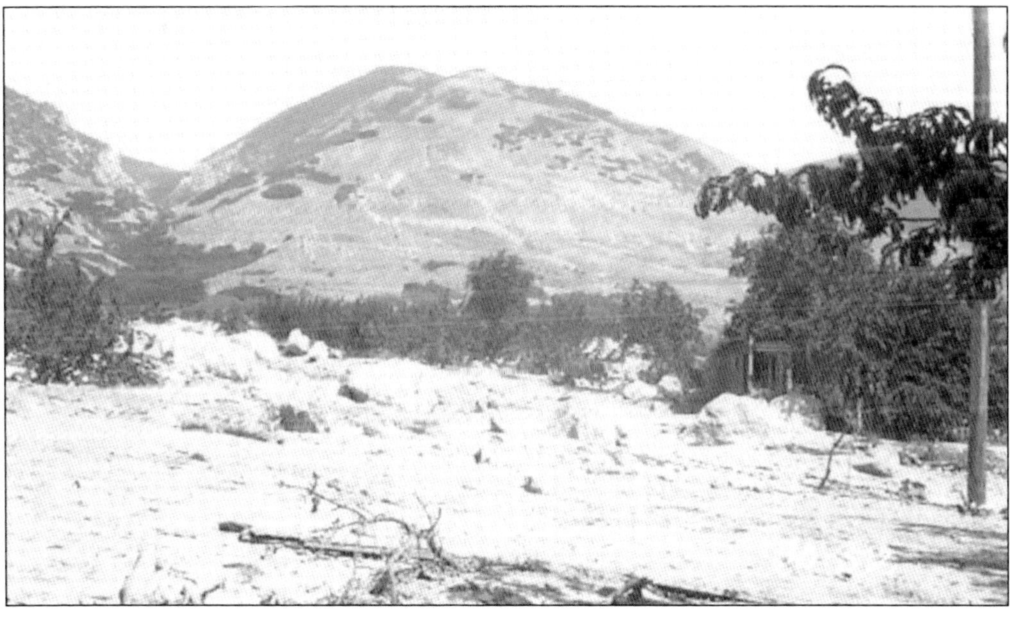

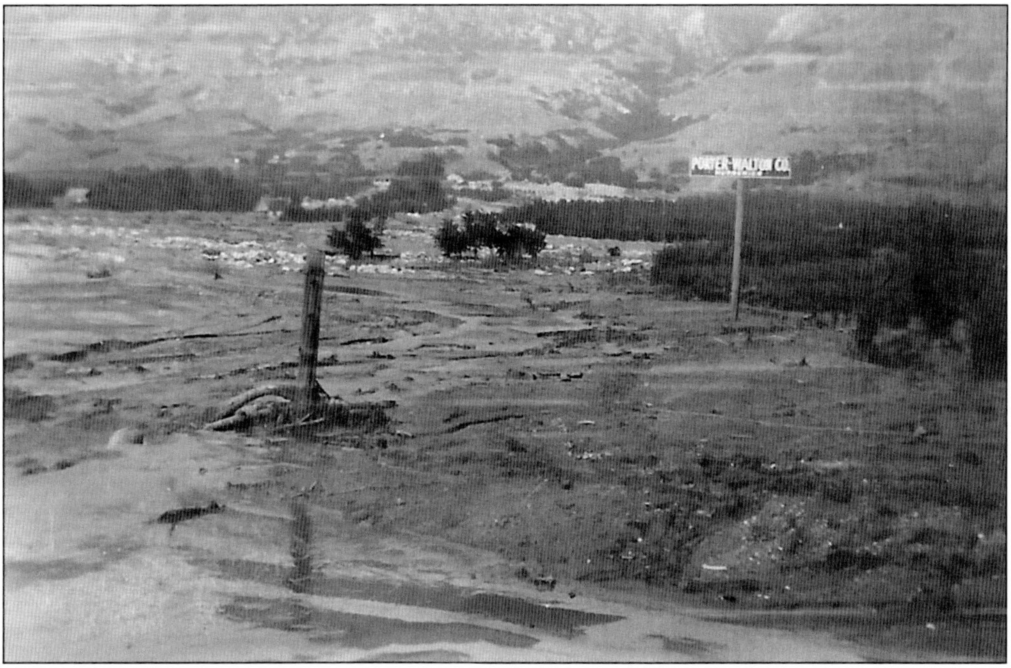

In 1930, the Porter-Walton Company had over 1,000 young trees growing on the side hill above. Water and debris washed them away, tumbling the containers and pots into pieces. The sign seen at the upper right is the only remaining evidence that there was ever a tree farm there. The photograph below shows the water rushing down the hill, wiping out homes and outbuildings. When the Wynn home was hit, Grandfather Hughes refused to leave when the rescuers came to help. But, as water flooded into the house and out the other side, he tried to float to safety on an overturned table. It quickly washed from under him, but, luckily, he was able to grab a guy wire on a utility pole, where Fred Petersen and others worked their way out to him. (Above, courtesy Kathleen Dalrymple; below, courtesy Centerville City Historical Records.)

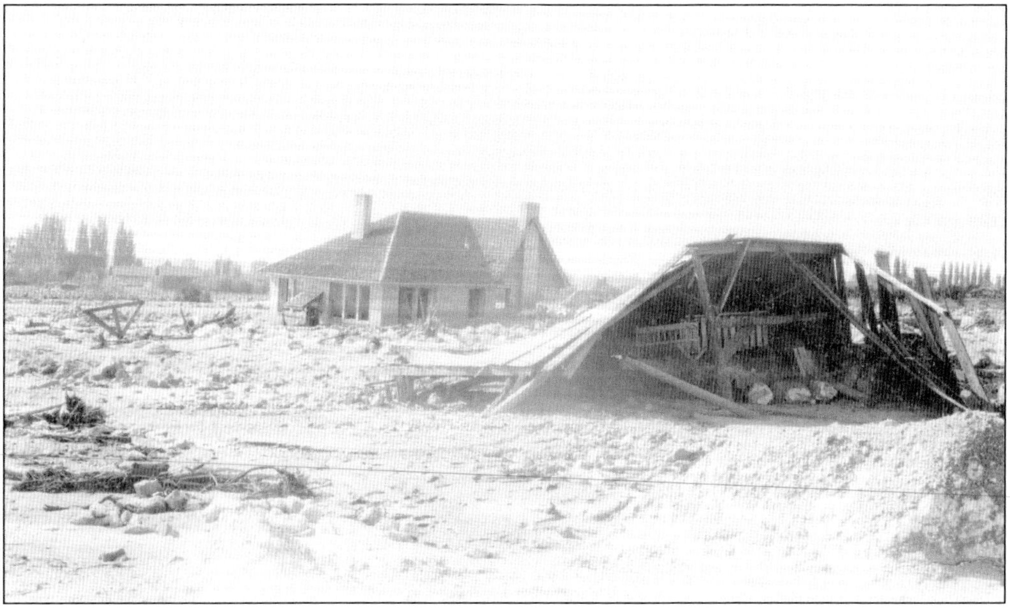

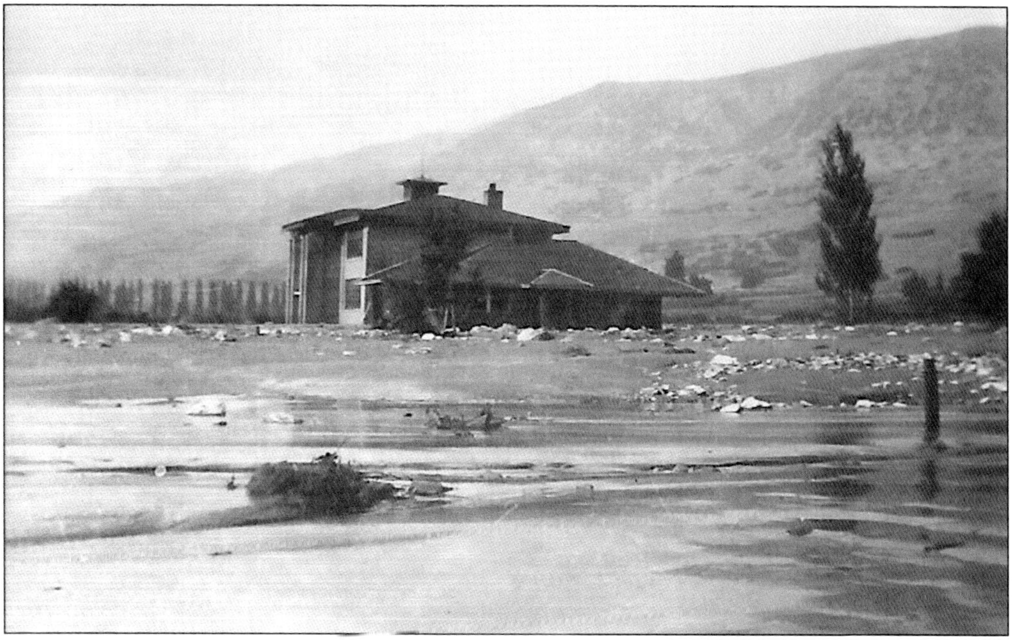

The floodwaters rushed past the elementary school (above), filling it with mud and rocks. When the water subsided, the mud stood several feet high against the east wall. The school was barely 15 years old, and the grounds and building were buried in mud and rocks. A community effort involving teams of horses and tractors was required to haul the mud away. The remaining raised bank on the east side of the school attests to the mountain of soil that was moved. The schoolchildren were released from class one day per week to pick up and move the rocks. The photograph below shows the water as it continued through the community and crossed Main Street. The debris finally dissipated near Sheep Road, and the water drained into the lake. (Both courtesy Centerville City Historical Records.)

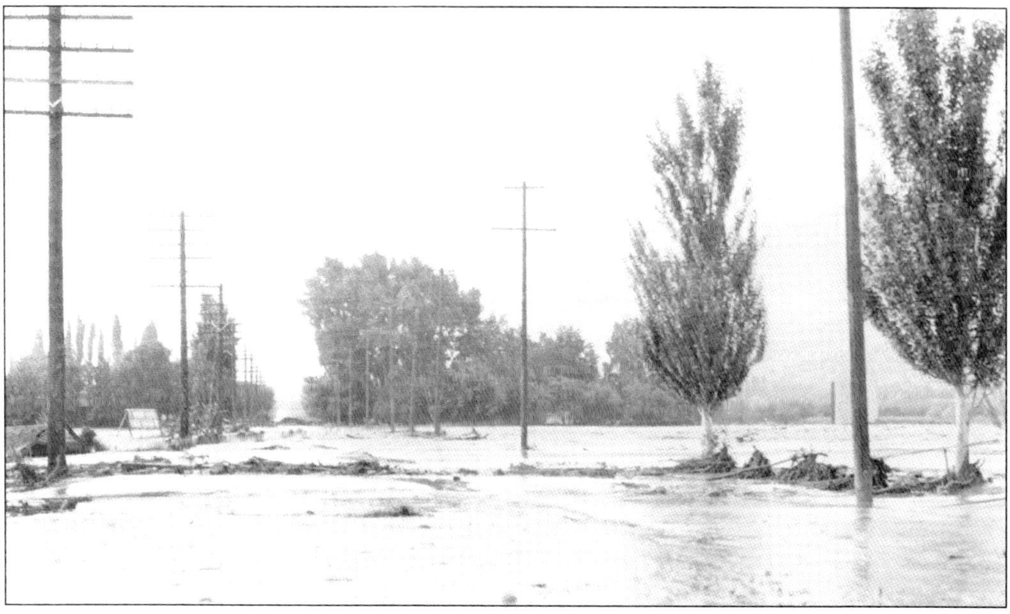

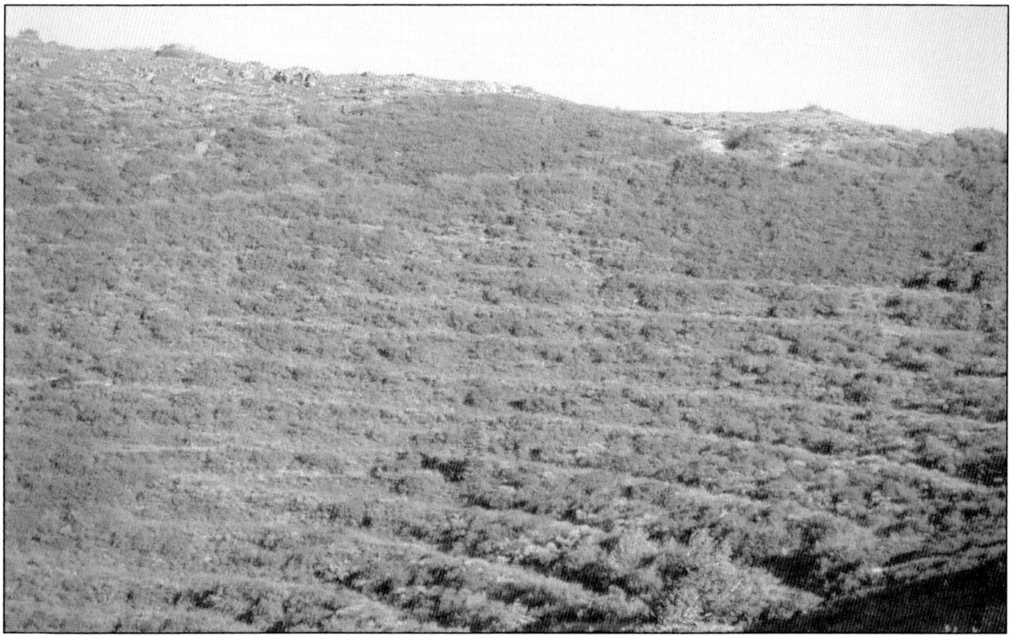

To prevent future flooding, the Civilian Conservation Corps (CCC) terraced the upper canyons from 1933 to 1936. This photograph shows the parallel contoured trenches, 25 feet apart and 10 feet deep. At the base of each trench was a ditch with intermittent small dams to hold rainwater or snowmelt, preventing the water from running directly down the gullies. The trenches and barren side hills were replanted with vegetation.

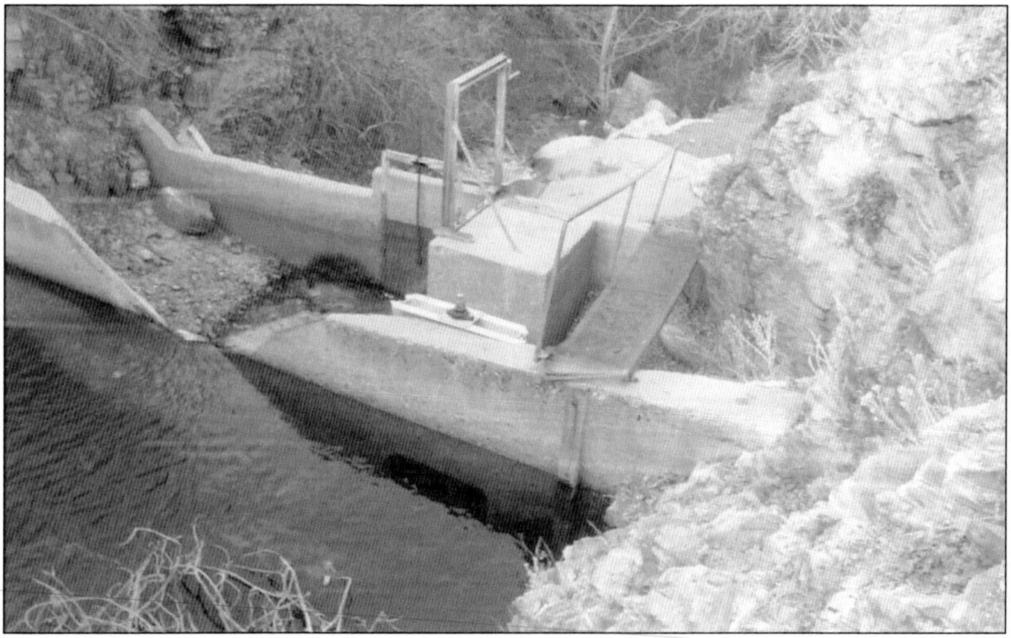

Stream monitors, like the one shown here, were constructed in the mouth of the canyons to measure the rate of runoff in real time. A small solar-powered radio transmitter is now mounted on the hillside above it to constantly send the reports back to the state water management offices. This data is also shared with the local communities and emergency response organizations.

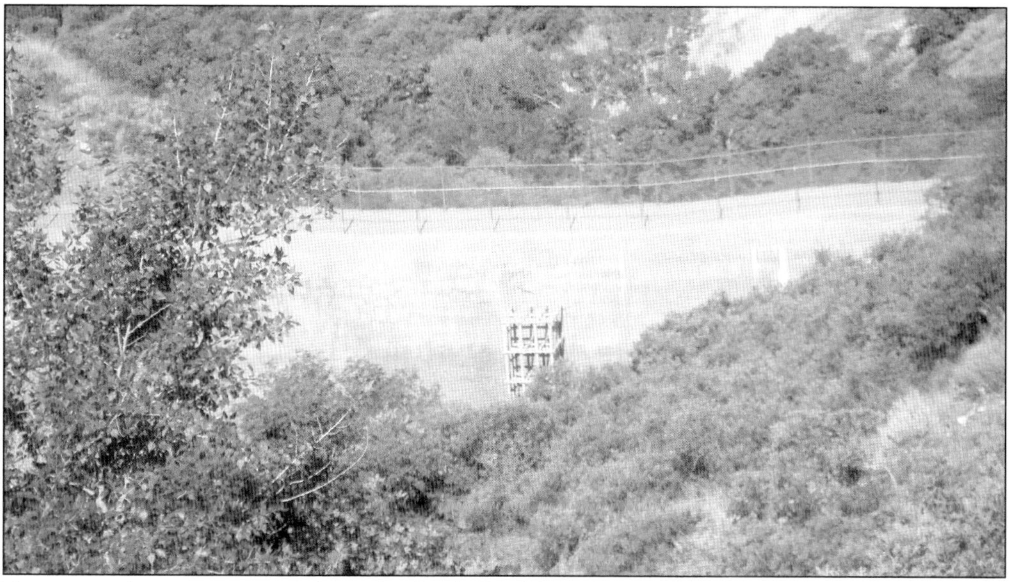

To protect the communities along the foothills, debris dams, such as the one shown here, have been constructed across the canyons. Future flooding of water, mud, and debris from the canyons will be captured by these catchments, delaying the onslaught long enough for the residents below to escape.

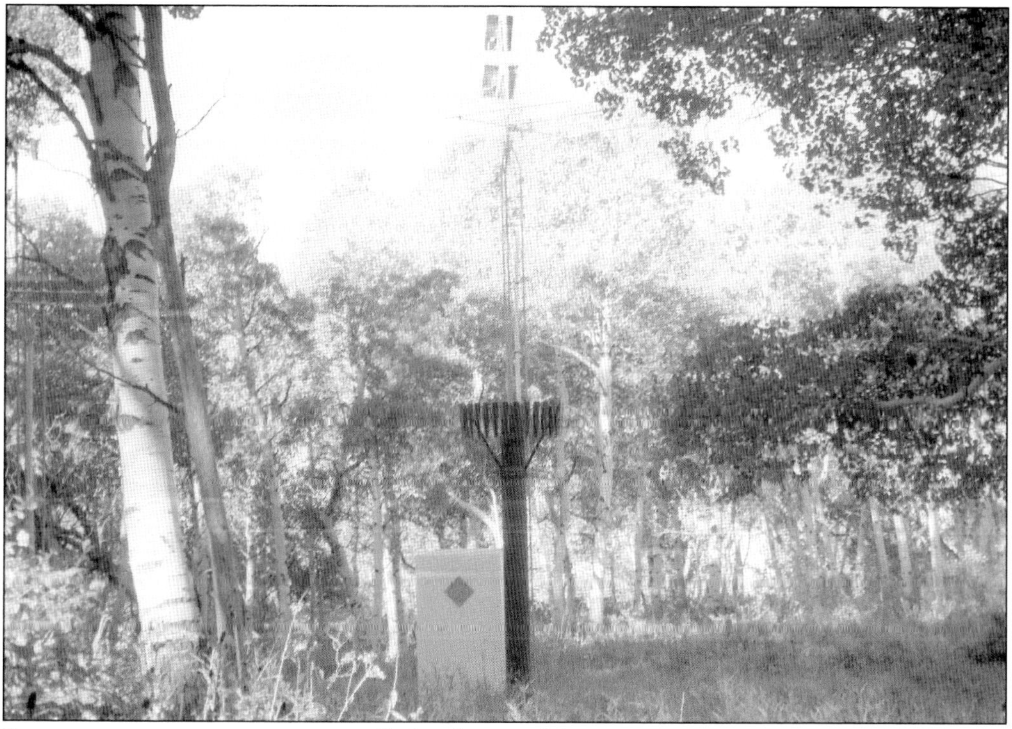

Snow monitoring systems were installed at the top of the mountains to measure the water content in the snow. A circular rubber mat is spread across an open pit, and a transducer assembly is mounted below the mat to measure the amount of distention occurring—the heavier the snow on top of the mat, the greater the distention. The data is then radioed to a central agency.

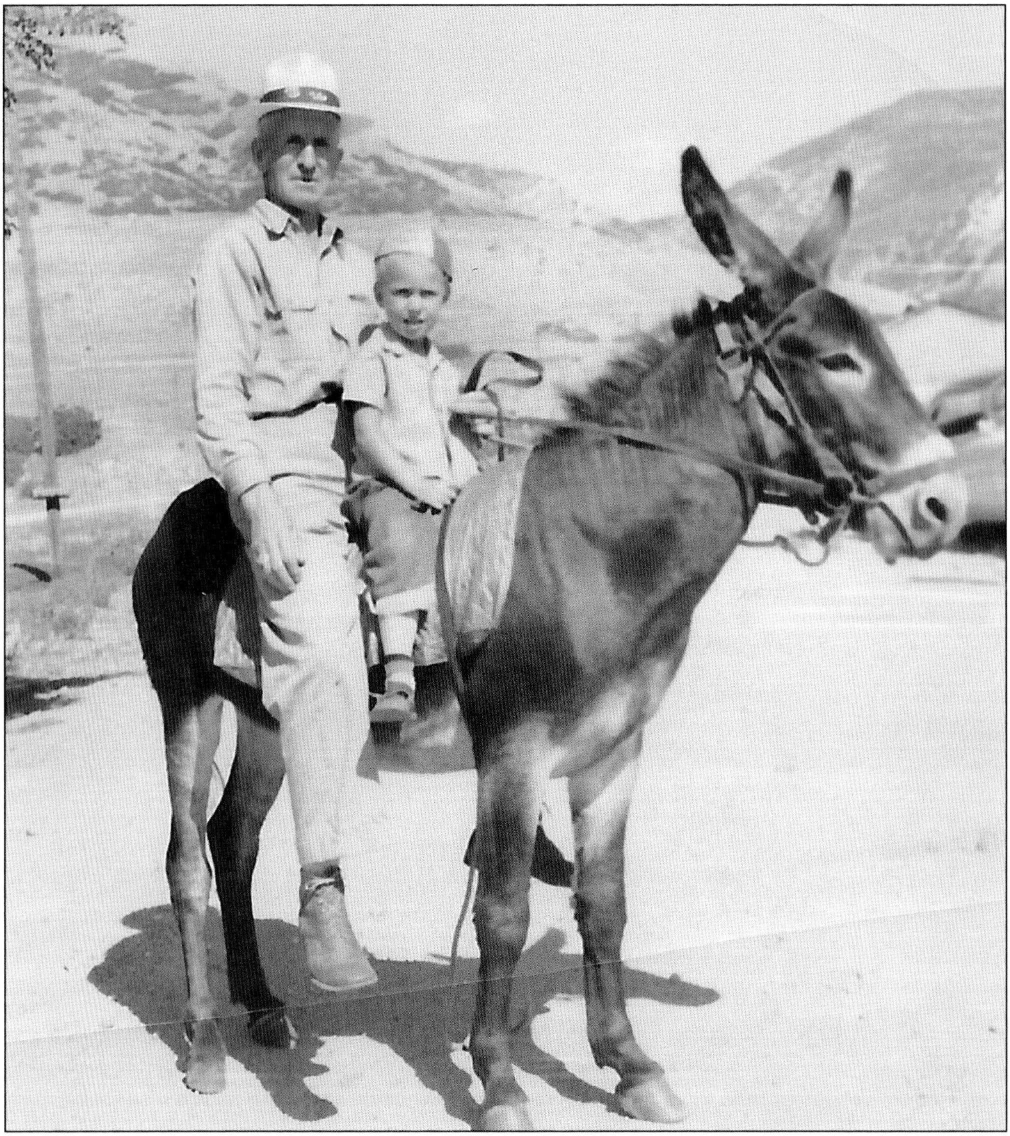

Everyone in Centerville knew Ned, John Brown's donkey. En route to Salt Lake City in 1933 with a load of cherries for the market, Brown encountered a disgruntled fellow along the roadside selling his "worthless donkey" for $3. Brown took the donkey back home, where it became a community pet, often borrowed for small jobs, to pull sleds, or to carry hikers up the mountain. But Ned was best known for his very loud braying. When the CCC workforce was building reservoirs and such along the foothills, it was customary for the foreman to ring a bell at the end of the workday. Because of the large area over which the workers were spread, it was difficult for all of them to hear the bell. But, surprisingly, Ned would bray every afternoon at precisely 5:00 p.m. The CCC workers soon learned that when Ned brayed, they could lay down their tools and head back to camp. John Brown and his grandson Mark Giles are seen here on Ned. (Both courtesy Mark Giles.)

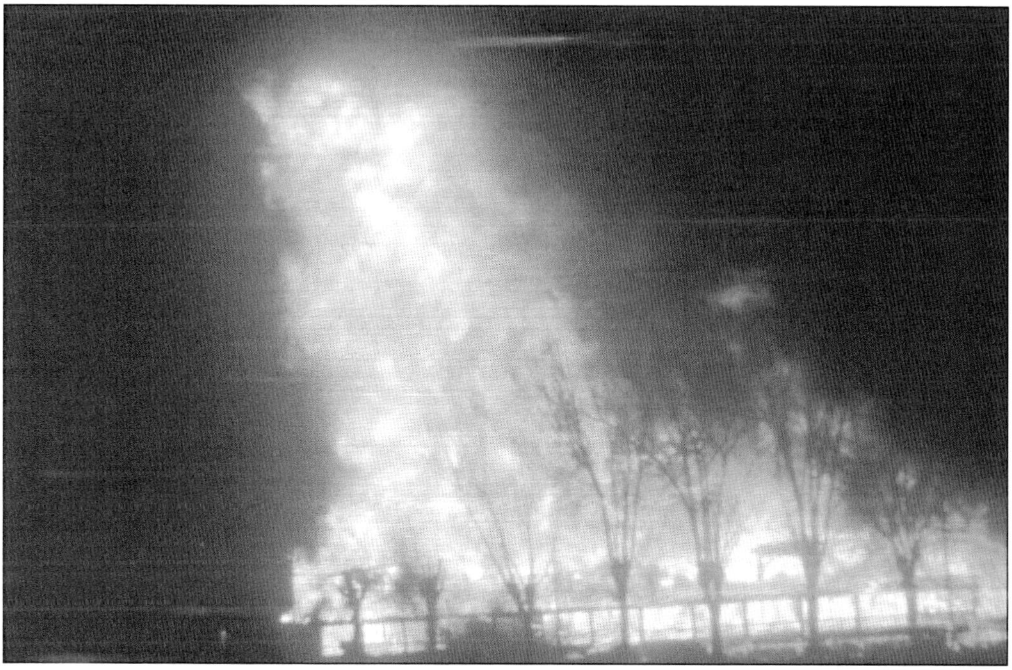

In 1953, a destructive fire broke out at the Lagoon Resort, destroying the loading and lift section of the old wooden roller coaster. Luckily, the main structure was undamaged. The loading section was rebuilt and updated with steel supports and a modern design. The photograph above shows the blazing fires reaching into the night sky. The photograph at right shows the damaged structure the next morning. Firefighting equipment was available at the resort, but the blaze was too hot, and it spread over too large an area to be stopped. Note the steel tracks at the bottom of the photograph, warped and bent by the blaze. (Both courtesy Lagoon Corporation.)

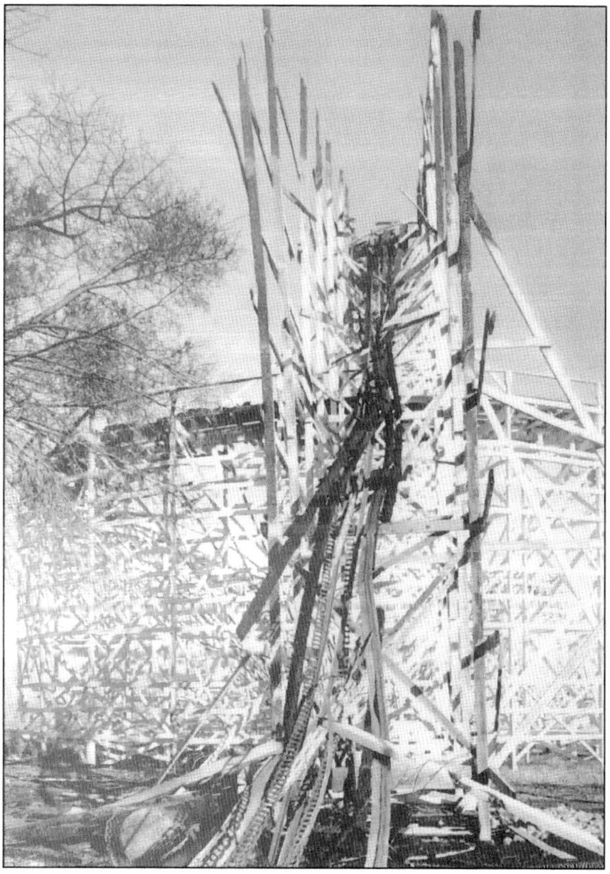